Israelites in Erin

Irish Studies
James MacKillop, *Series Editor*

Other titles from Irish Studies

All Dressed Up: Modern Irish Historical Pageantry
Joan FitzPatrick Dean

Compassionate Stranger: Asenath Nicholson and the Great Irish Famine
Maureen O'Rourke Murphy

Irish Women Dramatists, 1908–2001
Eileen Kearney and Charlotte Headrick, eds.

Joyce/Shakespeare
Laura Pelaschiar, ed.

Memory Ireland: Volume 3: The Famine and the Troubles
Oona Frawley, ed.

Memory Ireland: Volume 4: James Joyce and Cultural Memory
Oona Frawley and Katherine O'Callaghan, eds.

Representing the National Landscape in Irish Romanticism
Julia M. Wright

The Urban Plays of the Early Abbey Theatre: Beyond O'Casey
Elizabeth Mannion

Israelites in Erin

Exodus, Revolution, and the Irish Revival

ABBY BENDER

Syracuse University Press

Syracuse, New York 13244-5290

First Edition 2015
15 16 17 18 19 20 6 5 4 3 2 1

∞ The paper used in this publication meets the minimum requirements of the American National Standard for Information Sciences—Permanence of Paper for Printed Library Materials, ANSI Z39.48-1992.

For a listing of books published and distributed by Syracuse University Press, visit www.SyracuseUniversityPress.syr.edu.

ISBN: 978-0-8156-3399-0 (cloth) 978-0-8156-5342-4 (e-book)

Library of Congress Cataloging-in-Publication Data

Bender, Abby Sara, 1974–
Israelites in Erin : Exodus, revolution, and the Irish revival / Abby Bender. — First edition.
pages cm
Includes bibliographical references and index.
ISBN 978-0-8156-3399-0 (cloth : alk. paper) — ISBN 978-0-8156-5342-4 (e-book) 1. English literature—Irish authors—History and criticism. 2. Jews—Ireland. 3. Exodus, The, in literature. 4. National characteristics, Irish. 5. Irish literature—History and criticism. I. Title.
PR8755.B46 2015
820.9'9415—dc23 2015028364

Manufactured in the United States of America

Contents

Acknowledgments

This book originated as a dissertation in the English Department at Princeton University, and I begin by gratefully acknowledging my dissertation advisors Maria DiBattista and Tim Watson (now at the University of Miami), and beyond Princeton, Lucy McDiarmid, for their inspiring wisdom, support, and friendship. I owe a debt of gratitude to Paul Muldoon for his generosity in introducing me to the world of Irish Studies and so many of the wonderful people in it. While writing the dissertation on which this book is based, I received fellowships or other support from the Woodrow Wilson National Fellowship Foundation, the Princeton University Center for Human Values, the Princeton Fund for Irish Studies, the International James Joyce Foundation, the Notre Dame Keough Centre for Irish Studies, and the Yeats International Summer School.

A thematic project such as this one relies on the knowledge and kindness of friends and acquaintances, and I am grateful to everyone who passed on references and insights (and since I began this project many years ago, inevitably, and regretfully, this list will be incomplete). For their conversations, emails, questions at conferences and seminars, and in some cases comments on early drafts, I am particularly grateful to Michael Cadden, Heesok Chang, Vincent Cheng, Hasia Diner, Anne Fogarty, Eamon Grennan, Marjorie Howes, Brendan Kane, Howard Keeley, Declan Kiely, Joseph Lennon, David Lloyd, Angus Mitchell, Paul Muldoon, Cormac Ó Gráda, Eileen Reilly, Marilyn Reizbaum, Nigel Smith, and Tom Truxes. I want to particularly thank Alex Neel, Mary Burke, Barry McCrea, and Renee Fox for both illuminating observations and friendship.

I am especially grateful to both Vincent Cheng and Joseph Valente for their generous mentoring. I was indebted to them as scholars before I met either of them, and the continued support I've received from each has been an invaluable source of motivation.

During the summers of 2003–6, the faculty of the Irish Seminar at the Notre Dame Keough Centre in Dublin provided an education in Irish Studies that opened up new ways of thinking about this work. My thanks are due especially to Kevin Whelan, who revealed a world of rich archival sources, and Luke Gibbons, for his interest in and support of this project. Also in Dublin, Paddy Hawe was an endless resource and a tireless discoverer of unknown materials; I thank him for the many items that he tracked down, copied, and sent to me over the years.

My colleagues at New York University's Glucksman Ireland House have been inspiring and generous intellectually and personally. In particular I thank Joe Lee, John Waters, Marion Casey, Miriam Nyhan, and Greg Londe (now at Cornell). I am grateful to Anne Solari for making everything run smoothly. The students in my classes at NYU, particularly the James Joyce Colloquium and the Graduate Seminar in Irish Literature, have helped sharpen and complicate readings of Pearse, Lady Gregory, and Joyce, especially.

Several generous people gave me the invaluable opportunity to present this material to lively audiences: Mary McGlynn at the Columbia University Irish Studies Seminar; Anne Fogarty at the James Joyce Summer School in Dublin; Jay Barksdale at the New York Public Library (whom I also thank for facilitating work space in the Wertheim and Allen Study Rooms at the NYPL); and Joseph Valente at the University of Buffalo, where my seminar with the Modernisms Graduate Group expanded my thinking about the chapters on Joyce, and my conversations with Joe suggested higher stakes for this project than I've been bold enough to argue for here (although perhaps someday I will be so bold). I would also like to express my appreciation to the Schoff Fund at the University Seminars at Columbia University for their help in publication. Material in this work was presented to the University Seminar on Irish Studies.

I thank Greta van Lith and Virginia Ferris for their help with research and preparing the text, and Felicity Cable for research assistance in the Trinity College Archives.

Sections of chapters 2 and 3 first appeared together in condensed form as "Lady Gregory's Bible Lessons: *The Deliverer* and *The Story Brought by Brigit*," in the *Princeton Library Chronicle* (special Irish Theater issue) 68, nos. 1–2 (Fall 2006–Winter 2007), 124–44. I'm grateful to Gretchen Oberfranc for her thoughtful editorial suggestions. An adapted version of chapter 5, "The Bloomsday Seder: Joyce and Jewish Memory," appeared in *Memory Ireland, Volume 4: Joyce and Cultural Memory*, edited by Oona Frawley and Katherine O'Callaghan (Syracuse, NY: Syracuse University Press, 2014), 62–78. Oona Frawley offered most welcome encouragement at every stage, for which I'm very grateful.

The excerpt from Thomas Kinsella's translation of "Exodus to Connacht," from *An Duanaire, 1600–1900: Poems of the Dispossessed*, edited by Seán Ó Tuama (Mountrath, Portlaoise, Ireland: Dolmen Press, 1981) appears with his permission. Lines from James Joyce's poem on W. K. Magee (John Eglinton), published in Richard Ellmann's *James Joyce* (1983), appear by permission of Oxford University Press, USA. Lines from "Easter 1916" are reprinted with the permission of Scribner, a Division of Simon & Schuster, Inc., from *The Collected Works of W. B. Yeats, Volume I: The Poems, Revised* by W. B. Yeats, edited by Richard J. Finneran. Copyright © 1924 by The Macmillan Company, renewed 1952 by Bertha Georgie Yeats. All rights reserved. Lines from "Parnell's Funeral" are reprinted with the permission of Scribner, a Division of Simon & Schuster, Inc., from *The Collected Works of W. B. Yeats, Volume I: The Poems, Revised* by W. B. Yeats, edited by Richard J. Finneran. Copyright © 1934 by The Macmillan Company, renewed 1962 by Bertha Georgie Yeats. All rights reserved. Lines from "The Man and the Echo" and "Come Gather Round Me, Parnellites" are reprinted with the permission of Scribner, a Division of Simon & Schuster, Inc., from *The Collected Works of W. B. Yeats, Volume I: The Poems, Revised* by W. B. Yeats, edited by Richard J. Finneran. Copyright © 1940 by Georgie Yeats, renewed

1968 by Bertha Georgie Yeats, Michael Butler Yeats, and Anne Yeats.

For kind permission to reprint the engraving featured on the cover, I thank Steve Bartrick at antiqueprints.com.

At Syracuse University Press Glenn Wright first expressed interest in this book, and I'm thankful for his support during the very early stages of the project. The two anonymous readers for the press offered many valuable suggestions that I've tried to take into account here. I am indebted to all the staff at SUP, to Jill Root for her thoughtful editing, and most especially to Deb Mannion. For all of her work in the past year and the many encouraging and entertaining emails, I am immensely grateful.

Two reading groups, many years apart, improved drafts of these chapters immeasurably, whatever their current deficits. In the first instance, I thank with all my heart Elizabeth Brewer Redwine and Natasha Tessone, without whom I cannot imagine having completed the dissertation on which this book is based, and in the second, Mary McGlynn and Claire Bracken, who truly shepherded *Israelites in Erin* into its present form, not only as astute readers but as stimulating writers themselves. The intelligence and support of these four women—through all manner of crises—has meant everything to me.

Natasha Tessone is in almost every case my first reader, and her rigorous critical sensibility always leads to moments of clarification. I am honored to have her in my life as literary critic and dear friend.

Lucy McDiarmid has been there from the start of this project—as dissertation director, mentor, model scholar and writer, and general inspiration. Beginning with our first conversation at Lissadell House in Sligo, she has been a source of good advice; above all, she is a good friend.

Without the support and dedication of Ann Raftery, this book would not have been completed. I will truly never be able to thank her enough for all she has done for my family and for me.

Ambrose, Bram, and Ziva Raftery have suffered this book for a very long time, and they will certainly be the happiest to see it (at last) in print. I will always be grateful for their much-tried patience and their sustaining love. My sister Rebecca Bender has, throughout, been an extraordinary source of support. Finally, my wonderful parents, Barbara and Carl Bender, have followed this project for many years now; they know how much it means to me to have their love and their unfailing support, and it is to them, with infinite gratitude, that I dedicate this book.

Israelites in Erin

Introduction

The Ideologies of Exodus

From the seventeenth century through the twentieth, a common strain of Irish lament involved the analogy with the Jews. Ireland's preeminent bard of the nineteenth century, Thomas Moore, followed the Irish-language poets of the 1600s when he wrote in his ballad "The Parallel" of the two nations similarly "conquer'd and broken."[1] The publisher of D'Arcy McGee's *A Popular History of Ireland* (1864) aired the widespread belief that both the Irish and the Jews had suffered more than other people.[2] In the first decade of the twentieth century George Bernard Shaw suggested, somewhat less morosely, "Jews . . . just like Irishmen . . . languish in their own country, and flourish in every other."[3] But beyond the gloomy note of comparative affliction, the Irish compared themselves to Jews (or their biblical predecessors, Israelites) not only to mourn the past, but to look forward and imagine how Ireland might become a modern, independent nation. The fact that no modern Jewish nation existed was just the first of many paradoxes.

These now-exhausted habits of analogy were, indeed, often paradoxical; first, in their mutual insistence on exceptionalism (two chosen peoples, alike in their uniqueness) and second, in the contradictoriness of the comparisons: the Irish, like the Jews, were a territorial nation; the Irish, like the Jews, were a diasporic nation; the Irish language, like Hebrew, kept the nation together; the Irish language, like Hebrew, was not needed to keep the nation together; the Irish, like the Israelites, resisted the temptations of culturally assimilating, of eating from "the fleshpots of Egypt"; the Irish, like the Israelites, could not resist the temptations of the fleshpots. The twentieth-century playwright Brendan Behan characterized the instabilities bluntly: "Other people have a nationality. The Irish and the Jews have a psychosis."[4]

Both groups understood their nationality in complex, even incongruous ways. For Irish cultural and political nationalists in the late nineteenth and early twentieth centuries, the paradoxical analogies above all represented debates about how Ireland should define itself as a nation. And the biblical story of Exodus—of Israelite liberation from Egyptian bondage—dramatically called to mind the complexities of their own experience, particularly during the anticolonial movements of the last century. The fraught birth of the Hebrew nation at the foot of Mount Sinai became a way of imagining Irish struggles, and a key analogue for resisting English colonialism. *Israelites in Erin* investigates the central place of the Exodus narrative in cultural and political rhetoric in Ireland, and the ways that rhetoric was assimilated and transformed in literary texts. From the metaphoric identification of the Irish with enslaved Israelites in seventeenth-century bardic poetry, to the imagining of Home Rule leader Charles Stewart Parnell as Moses, to James Joyce's envisioning of the promised land as the "new Bloomusalem in the Nova Hibernia of the future," Exodus provided a narrative of liberation that had potency, religious authority, and—most importantly—the sense of ambivalence about independence that also characterized the Irish experience. Between 1890 and 1922, a period of intense political and cultural activity beginning with the fall of Parnell and the literary revival and concluding with the achievement of the Free State and the publication of Joyce's *Ulysses*, Exodus served as a central narrative for the birth of the nation. *Israelites in Erin* analyzes the uses of that narrative, and also witnesses the Israelite analogy being slowly but certainly replaced with a New Testament rhetoric of freedom, as the Christ story replaced Exodus as an archetype for revolution and liberation.

While scholars of seventeenth- and eighteenth-century Ireland (Breandán Ó Buachalla, Marc Caball, Niall MacKenzie) have written about the centrality of Exodus in those periods, the ways in which

Exodus circulated through nineteenth- and early twentieth-century writing and culture have rarely been seriously considered. Even as the Irish-Israelite analogy has been frequently remarked on, and examples of it often quoted, there is no existing analysis of where the analogy originated, how it spread through Irish culture, or why it could represent a variety of ideological positions. Nevertheless it was, in Joep Leerssen's phrase, one of the "ideas . . . doing the rounds at the time,"[5] and one that allows us to get at what was most desired, most troubling, and most unstable in the pursuit of Irish independence. Exodus played a role in debates about politics, land, Anglo-Irish versus Gaelic culture, the language issue, the Irish diaspora, immigration, and economic independence from England. When Joyce took Exodus as a central theme for *Ulysses*, he was engaging not only a rich and complicated biblical text, but a ubiquitous analogy that the Irish had fully appropriated. And Joyce was only one of many writers who found in Exodus a viable, if challenging, model for nationhood. Lady Gregory, W. B. Yeats, George Moore, and others were also drawn to the story of Exodus for the very reason that it complicated contemporary thinking about cultural and political nationalism.

Yet if Israelite liberation was one of the central metaphors for Irish anticolonial struggle in the early twentieth century—such an important and well-documented period in Irish history—then why has it not received more critical attention? Other tropes that were vital to imagining the nation—Ireland embodied as a woman, for example—have continued to inspire (and infuriate) Irish writers and critics in our own time, and there is a vast body of scholarship on figures like Kathleen ni Houlihan and the Shan van Vocht.[6] Why, then, have we failed to consider what it means that the Irish imagined themselves as Israelites? Perhaps with Exodus no longer circulating in contemporary culture we fail to see it in the past, for Exodus had all but disappeared from the Irish imaginative landscape even before the founding of the Free State. Indeed, it is my argument that the aura of the Easter Rising (1916), and more importantly the rhetoric that led up to it with its powerful figuration of freedom through blood sacrifice, is responsible for eclipsing Exodus and for pushing it out of both the political and the literary imagination. *Israelites in Erin*, then, recuperates the history of a liberation narrative that was once fundamental to anticolonialism in Ireland and testifies to the complexity of Irish nationalisms in the period. There are religious, political, and cultural reasons for the shift whereby Exodus was effectively occluded by the aesthetic of 1916, replaced, following the traditional Christian typology, by the story of Christ's sacrifice and resurrection. This book traces and tries to understand that process and the literary texts that engaged it, and also, I hope, provides balance to current critical preoccupations with the Rising in the years surrounding its centenary.

If today Exodus tends to fall under the radar in Ireland, that is not the case everywhere; it remains a powerful political idea, and many scholars have continued to examine its affinity for analogy.[7] The past decade in particular has seen a fairly astonishing number of books, both scholarly and popular, on the use of Exodus in American, and specifically African American, literature and history; Moses, the leader of the Israelites, is a figure who "has reverberated through the American story," as Bruce Feiler writes in *America's Prophet* (2009).[8] Most recently, John Coffey's impressive study *Exodus and Liberation: Exodus Politics from John Calvin to Martin Luther King Jr.* (2014) demonstrates both the historical scope and the contemporary relevance of the narrative.[9] *Israelites in Erin* is both like and unlike the work in American Studies; if occasionally we cover similar ground (explaining the way typology works, for example), the American and Irish uses of Exodus are necessarily different in their politics, their primary denominational affiliations, their physical force applications, and their literary and cultural preoccupations. My attention, therefore, most often turns not to the biblical source but to the texts of Irish cultural history: major narratives of cultural production, political power, and religious sectarianism, and smaller controversies produced by singing competitions, opening-night gossip, and outraged letters to the editor. The remaining chapters of this book will tell these big and little stories together: the stories that early twentieth-century Ireland told itself.

By the time *Ulysses* was published in 1922—the same year the Irish Free State was born—Exodus no longer seemed to be a meaningful way of articulating national struggles in Ireland; Pearse's writings and actions had replaced it with the New Testament narrative of Christ's death and sacrifice. I conclude with Joyce's novel, however, precisely because *Ulysses* asks us to reconsider Exodus as a meaningful analogy for Ireland at the very moment of the nation's devolution. In fact, it was Joyce's novel that initiated the present study: Joyce compels us to look closely at Exodus as a way of thinking about Ireland. But before we begin to look at the story of Ireland, I want to consider in some detail, and in a broader context, the biblical text itself and how it can be and has been read: its ideological flexibility, its unsettling ambivalence, and its paradoxical engagement with what seems to be the whole point of Exodus: the promised land of Canaan.

The Contentiousness of Exodus

The narrative is familiar. A powerful oppressor enslaves a people. One leader emerges from among them and with great difficulty succeeds in freeing the people. After forty years of wandering in the desert, a period of learning new laws and unlearning their former slavish subservience, the people—now a nation—reach their own, their promised land. (Of course, retellings of Exodus are strategic in what they leave out. In the lines above, absent are Moses's helpers, Aaron and Miriam; Moses's resistance to God's call and the people's resistance and hostility to Moses; and finally, the destruction of the Canaanites who live in the promised land. Many nationalist appropriations of Exodus are evasive of such elements that complicate the narrative, as we will see.)

To many nationalists, Exodus has looked like a story of national origin. But contemporary theorists of nationalism have not generally admitted ancient Israel into their canon. Elie Kedourie writes dismissively, for example, of the idea that premodern peoples "are suddenly seen to have been really acting in order that the genius of a particular nationality should be manifested and fostered."[10] He goes on, sarcastically, to write that "Moses was not a man inspired by God in order to fulfill and reaffirm His covenant with Israel, he was really a national leader rising against colonial oppression."[11] Yet Kedourie's rejection of this possibility discounts the ways in which nationalist movements have seen Moses as an anticolonial figure and have deemed the Exodus story central to their own political, cultural, and literary traditions. Given the power of nationalist mythologies, we cannot afford to ignore the ways in which nations have explained their histories to themselves; and not infrequently, it has been through analogies to other peoples. In *Imagined Communities*, Benedict Anderson offers a note to the effect that Zionism "marks the reimagining of an ancient religious community as a nation, down there among the other nations."[12] But this imagining had also taken place years before the Zionist movement, when the seventeenth-century Gaelic Irish compared themselves to the people of Israel, struggling against Egyptian (and for Egyptian, read English) power.

More recent studies have suggested that Kedourie, Anderson, and others are overly assertive in their insistence on the modernity of nationalism.[13] Indeed, Tony Claydon and Ian McBride claim that historians have finally revealed the truth about nationalism (a truth that perhaps the biblical analogizers have known all along): that it is not, after all, a modern phenomenon.[14] Anderson, as the most influential theorist of nationalism for the field of literary studies, has more or less convinced us that nations began in the eighteenth century. But what about, as Irish political scientist Tom Garvin proposes, "continuities between modern nationalisms and older traditions of collective identity?"[15] In particular, Garvin notes the "much copied" example of Jewish nationalism in the Old Testament.[16] While it is certainly not the purpose of this book to claim that the modern nation emerged at Sinai, we should recognize that in many modern versions of nationalism the model of the Israelites was and is meaningful. When I use the term "nation" to refer to ancient Israel, it is not to suggest the equivalent of a modern nation-state. It is, however, an imagined community (to use Anderson's term) held together, if not by print capitalism, then by a text (the Torah), an ethnicity, a religion, and a land (sometimes territorial, sometimes imagined). It has communal memories and, what Ernest Renan cites as equally important, communal forgetfulness.[17]

The hesitation to read the Israelite story through the lens of colonial and nationalist discourse is no doubt related to the fact that interpreting the Bible as a political analogue is inevitably fraught. Interpretation is informed by religious background, by political ideology, by the sections of the text one chooses to read. The author of the 1853 pamphlet "Ireland the Restorer of Israel, under the Protection of Louis Napoleon," for example, offers the following reading of scripture, giving page upon page of exegesis to support his assiduously argued thesis: that the Bible explicitly describes how the Irish should build "a railway over Judea"[18] in order that the Jews should more easily return to their homeland and hasten the second coming. What follows is one of his many proofs that it is the Irish who should lay the railway tracks: "If any one can doubt that Ireland is the island selected *above all other nations* for such immortal ends, to what other nation do these words in the 7th verse apply? They say, —'Thus saith the Lord, the redeemer of Israel, *his holy one, to the soul that is despised*, to the nation *that is abhorred*, to *the servant of rulers*.' How forcibly and graphically do these few words denote poor Ireland, *and Ireland only? It can be no other!*"[19] If this exegetical mode appears outlandish, we can witness a more subtle example in the realm of contemporary academia, one that similarly shows how reading the Bible, and the Exodus narrative in particular, continues to produce various ways of understanding the story, depending on who is doing the reading, and when, and where.

In 1986 Edward Said reviewed Michael Walzer's book *Exodus and Revolution* for the journal *Grand Street*, initiating a bitter exchange about the meaning and uses of the Exodus story. The original review and the letters that followed—a response by Walzer, another by Said—are fascinating, not least because they reveal the participants' entrenched ideas about the biblical text. The liberal position that each writer claims to occupy is overwhelmed by his inflexibility, and subsequently a debate over the embattled status of Israel/Palestine and a series of personal attacks all but edge out the purported topic of the discussion: the politics of Exodus. The central argument of Walzer's book is that Exodus is a useful archetype of radical revolution, a story of liberation from bondage that offers a politics of freedom and independence, a narrative appropriated by people struggling for civil, religious, and national rights. Said, however, counters with an exposition of "the irreducibly sectarian premises of Exodus,"[20] declaring that it is a narrative of divinely sanctioned settler colonialism and even genocide. The title of Said's review, "A Canaanite Reading," immediately reveals his position: he criticizes Walzer for ignoring the problematic and dangerous conclusion of Exodus, when the Israelites arrive in their promised land and exterminate or displace the Canaanites who live there. Moreover, he accuses Walzer of writing the book as a justification for Israel's treatment of Palestinians—a double-reading that Said in turn uses to analogically critique the treatment of Palestinians in present-day Israel/Palestine. For Said, the Canaanites—and by analogy, the Palestinians—are the group who most need and deserve liberation. At the heart of this argument (which is transparently inflected by the ethnic identifications of both scholars) is the question of who can claim the position of the oppressed—in other words, is the narrative of Exodus for or against the kind of inclusive liberation one would champion today? To bring the discussion into current literary critical/historical terms, we might rephrase the opposition: is Exodus a narrative for the forces of settler colonialism or a narrative for anticolonial liberation?[21] And to add another question: can it be both?

The Said-Walzer debate serves to highlight the continuing cultural, political, and literary relevance of an ancient biblical story that has been used throughout Western history to justify a range of ideologies. More specifically, the exchange illustrates the impossibility of talking about Exodus as a transcendent myth or archetype: both Said and Walzer read Exodus through history, specifically through the polarized lens of the current Israeli-Palestinian conflict. Said points out that much of the language Walzer uses to talk about Exodus ("*progressive, moral, radical politics, national liberation, oppression*") entered the political vocabulary in the context of anticolonial wars in the twentieth century, and Said insists that "the provenance of these is not Exodus."[22] And yet the language of anticolonial struggle often did emerge through a discursive framework invested in the

Exodus narrative. For Latin American liberation theologians, African Americans, and Irish nationalists, their political vocabulary was (and in some cases still is) suggested by the rhetoric of Exodus.[23] In this sense it is irrelevant if the experience of Israelite slavery in Egypt was, as Said writes, "hardly comparable with that of American Blacks or contemporary Latin Americans,"[24] for African Americans and Latin Americans were nonetheless deeply invested in using the Exodus narrative to describe their own struggles. To them, the question was not of comparing suffering or oppression, but of using the analogy to imagine a way out of it.[25] This book argues the case that such analogical thinking deserves attention on its own terms.

In *The Great Code* Northrop Frye acknowledges African American identifications with the Exodus story, and elaborates on the way such analogical identifications function: "The point is that when any group of people feels as strongly about anything as slaves feel about slavery, history as such is dust and ashes: only myth . . . can provide any hope or support at all."[26] But Frye's view is also incomplete, for "history as such" is never dust in the wind; the myths we choose have everything to do with history, not only our own but also everyone else's. It is history—not only in the sense of the past, but also as the historical present—that determines the ways in which a community appropriates Exodus. Thus an event like the founding of the State of Israel in 1948, when the Jews of post-Holocaust Europe reached their promised land, affected not only Zionist and Israeli uses of the Exodus trope, but other cultures' approaches as well. I will not dwell on Zionism's use of Exodus—a topic that has obviously been treated elsewhere—except to note that it contains both Walzer's and Said's versions of the narrative: ambivalent departure and triumphant arrival, freedom from oppression and freedom to oppress. Perhaps as Jacqueline Rose argues in her book on Zionism and messianism, the second element is a sort of pathological response to the traumas of the first.[27] Invariably the perception of the Jewish nation—as diasporic or territorial, oppressed or oppressing—inflects the ways in which other cultures articulate their own relationship to Exodus.[28] Ireland had already discarded the Israelite analogy by the time that modern Jewish history altered the meaning of Exodus-as-struggle, but the existence of the State of Israel was surely a factor in the changing use of the analogy in African American culture, and it is worth briefly considering this example. Paul Gilroy writes of the way modern African American leaders, including Martin Luther King Jr, "drew on the power of Old Testament patriarchy [and, as he writes, the figure of Moses in particular] to cement their own political authority. Yet this identification with the Exodus narrative and with the history of the chosen people and their departure from Egypt seems to be waning. Blacks today appear to identify far more readily with the glamourous pharaohs than with the abject plight of those they held in bondage."[29] In the Irish case too, as Elizabeth Cullingford notes, during the second half of the twentieth century the Israelite analogy disappears, as "contemporary Israel is no longer an appropriate model of 'the outlaw.'"[30]

Exodus as liberation is one side of the story; the other is Exodus as Manifest Destiny—another term for promised land—that is perhaps most explicit in the case of the pilgrims to America, that new Israel in which Native Americans were rendered obstacles to divinely justified territorial expansion. As Said points out, this was also the "essential" aspect of Exodus to Boers who expropriated land from blacks in South Africa. (Or witness former Democratic Unionist Party [DUP] leader Ian Paisley's sermons on the "chosen" Loyalists of Ulster.[31]) Yet while Said's focus on the moment of arrival in the promised land is undoubtedly necessary, Walzer's analysis of the earlier part of the story, the Israelites' ambivalent departure from Egypt, is even more fruitful for postcolonial readings of Exodus. (And, as I argue in the coda, Said eventually embraces precisely this idea in his final book, *Freud and the Non-European.*) Just as the end of the Exodus story appeals to colonialists who use it to justify displacements of native peoples, it is the beginning and the middle of the narrative that have been most frequently appropriated by people struggling for religious, civil, and national rights. The departure from Egypt offers a far more complex, ambiguous, and productive moment in the national drama than the triumphant scene of arrival. Said is correct to argue that Walzer fails to offer an adequate critique of the Israelites' violent arrival in Canaan, and even Walzer admits, in his response to Said's review, "perhaps I am not sufficiently alert to the dangers of Exodus politics."[32] However, we must not ignore Walzer's valuable critique of the essentialist ideologies that, inevitably, national cultures construct during nation-building. And we must recognize that the two poles of the Exodus story are connected. The ambiguities and anxieties that accompany the journey to the promised land are, then, the catalyst for its disturbing resolution: Israelite extermination of the unchosen, the other who already inhabits Canaan.

As the Said-Walzer debate reveals, it seems virtually impossible to think about the ideologies of Exodus outside history. With this in mind, I propose that instead of going around this history, we go through it, to see how Exodus was used in the particular context of anticolonial Ireland. The texts examined in this book do precisely what Said and Walzer do: they use Exodus to tell their own stories, sometimes in narrow ways, closing off parts of the story; sometimes in expansive ways, which illuminate not only particular cultural moments, but also the biblical text itself. In her 2002 book *Moses in America: The Cultural Uses of Biblical Narrative*, Melanie Wright bemoans the fact that biblical study "has tended to neglect questions of reception and the history of the Bible's influence as a source of both elite and cultural expression."[33] It is precisely the reception, subversion, and transformation of Exodus that are compelling in the Irish case, and the chapters that follow show how Irish redeployment of Exodus illuminates what was at stake in the key period of both cultural and political Irish nation-formation.

The Ambivalence of Exodus

In his 2005 book *Inventing Ireland*, Declan Kiberd suggests that "if many—perhaps a majority of—Irish writers and nationalists were slow to identify with movements elsewhere, this was because their minds were unresponsive to the comparative method, having been attuned to the revivalist idea that the Irish were unique, 'like no other race on earth.'"[34] In the years since that claim, much new comparative work in Irish Studies has brought to light significant evidence of Irish nationalist interest in and solidarity with other cultures and peoples, showing that the minds of Irish thinkers were perhaps not so unresponsive after all.[35] Yet Kiberd's point is nevertheless an important one, and it is in fact this very idea, "that the Irish were unique," that makes the comparison with the Israelites most appealing. The Exodus narrative was invoked strategically throughout the revival period—as it had been for centuries in Ireland and elsewhere—as a marker of chosenness: the people are specially marked by God, and their land is uniquely God-given and holy.

Poet Alicia Ostriker describes this dangerous—and finally, darkly ironic—element of the Exodus story in her book *The Nakedness of the Fathers: Biblical Visions and Revisions*:

> Sinai feeds the tenacious pride of those who consider themselves chosen, who will rejoice at the death of the unbeliever, the death of the apostate. It is a pride that will precipitate oppression, suffering, and martyrdom, the spilled blood of century after century, in religion after religion. It is a pride that will encourage the narrowness of the narrow in spirit, let there be no mistake. And as for the flower of intellectual evil that has most gorgeously blossomed in our own century, the doctrine of racial purity: this too, with its rhetoric, its simple appeal, is rooted in Sinai. For what is a Master Race if not the distorted mirror image of a Chosen People, at which all the devils in Gehenna laugh until their sides split?[36]

Like Said, Ostriker reveals the terrifying exclusions that allow the idea of a chosen people to transform into an ideology of Nazism. We must remember, though, that if the biblical Israelites are chosen, they are also beholden to a contract with God—and one that they continually fall short of fulfilling. Even the God of the Hebrew scriptures warns of the tenuousness of the Israelites' election and the constant threats to their unique identity.[37] There is, moreover, a paradox at the Exodus narrative's core, whereby the Israelites' moment of origin is entangled with the culture of the Egyptians, their hosts and then enslavers, for hundreds of years. Egyptologist Donald Redford offers an ironic rehistoricizing of Exodus as the very site of hybridity, as "part and parcel of an array of 'origin' stories to which the Hebrews fell heir upon their settlement of the land, and which, lacking traditions of their own, they appropriated from the earlier cultures they were copying."[38] Freud's reading of Exodus in his 1939 book *Moses and Monotheism* proposes a similar idea: that Moses was in fact an Egyptian king, whom the Israelites adopted and then murdered. In positing Moses as an Egyptian, Freud similarly imagines an Exodus that not only allows for, but is defined by its multiplicity and hybridity. Michel Foucault's suggestion that "historical beginnings are lowly . . . derisive and ironic, capable of undoing every infatuation"[39] is apt here, and the derision and irony inevitably complicate the use of the Exodus story as an archetype for a romantic national history. After all, who wants to remember that the Israelites, as they wait for Moses to bring the Law down from Mount Sinai, get tired of waiting and build an Egyptian-style golden calf to worship? For the desert is, as Jean-Christophe Attias and Esther Benbassa write in *Israel, the Impossible Land*, not only a site of "initiation," but also "adolescence" and "rebellion."[40]

The narratives, biblical and midrashic, of forty years in the wilderness reveal a people ambivalent about their liberation. As Avivah Gottlieb Zornberg writes, "The narratives and counter-narratives that will divide the people until they enter the Holy Land forty years later will be attempts to make meaning of the tension of the night of the Exodus; to compose a response to the imperatives of freedom. These narratives will play out all that is hidden, ambiguous, and unresolved in the experience of redemption. Through these narratives, which constitute the very process of freedom, fathers and sons will confront the unspeakable kernel of desire and shame."[41] Joyce's Jewish Leopold Bloom anticipates one version of this less-than-ideal journey to the promised land in what has been called his Freudian slip, when he remembers the Passover Haggadah and thinks "out of the land of Egypt and into the house of bondage" (*U* 118).[42] Not out of bondage, but *into* it. For Bloom, nationality has its own set of limitations: as a not-quite-really-Jewish Jew in Dublin, he constantly experiences the tension between his father's Jewish traditions and the Irish fleshpots—from pork kidneys to prostitutes—of city life. Emancipation is a complicated business, and as Andrew Gibson writes, *Ulysses* itself resembles "the unremitting and unendingly ironical work of liberation."[43] "The great paradox of Exodus," writes Walzer, "and of all subsequent liberation struggles, is the people's simultaneous willingness and unwillingness to put Egypt behind them. They yearn to be free, and they yearn to escape their new freedom. . . . The biblical narrative tells this paradoxical story with a frankness not often repeated in the literature of liberation."[44]

Walzer notes the failure to cover over the Exodus story's ambivalence and dissension, and it is Freud who perhaps offers the best explication of this in *Moses and Monotheism.* Rose suggests Freud's purpose here is "sowing dissension in the tribe. He does not want his people unified. Or if he does, he wants them unified differently. Not singular, created once in an act of divinely sanctioned recognition, which henceforth will brook no argument, but torn internally by the fragments of a complex, multiple past."[45] As Susan Handelman explains, Freud reads the biblical narrative as the result of a struggle between two opposing forces: "one sought to transform and falsify the text, turn it into its opposite; the other sought piously to maintain the story as it stood. Hence there are striking omissions, repetitions, and contradictions in the text."[46] Freud provides incisive commentary on the way a national epic must purge itself of ambiguities, writing that "the distortion of a text is not unlike a murder. The difficulty lies not in the execution of the deed but in the doing away with the traces."[47] The psychoanalyst sensed that the writing of the biblical account, as well as the Exodus journey itself, was occupied with the struggles within the Israelite community, and even within each Israelite himself or herself. However, not all of the "traces" of conflict and struggle that Freud locates in Exodus require subtle detection. Yosef Hayim Yerushalmi, in his book *Freud's Moses*, gently chides Freud for suggesting that all trauma must be relegated to the unconscious (or the subtextual), for in fact much of the ambivalence is made plain on the surface. Addressing Freud directly, Yerushalmi writes, "what eluded you was the most singular aspect of Jewish tradition from the Bible onward, to wit—its almost maddening refusal to conceal the misdeeds of the Jews."[48]

Yet Freud was right to see that something was being repressed, and there would be continued efforts to describe a more unequivocal version of the Exodus, to cover over some of the ambiguity. In the text of one midrash, "Israel deserved the exodus from Egypt because they did not change their names, did not change their language, did not engage in evil talk, and preserved the purity of their families. They did not change their names: They came to Egypt as Reuben and Simeon, and as Reuben and Simeon they left Egypt; Reuben did not become Rufus, Judah did not become Julian, Joseph did not become Justus, and Benjamin did not become Alexander."[49] While the passage apparently recounts the preservation of cultural identity (if anxiously, through the repetition of what Israel "did not" do), it also exposes a fear of assimilation in a telling slippage: the names that have been declined are not Egyptian, but rather Roman names, for in that period, the Romans ruled Judea. The anxiety about emerging from bondage as a unique nation is reinscribed in terms relevant to a later crisis of national identity. Gaelic League founder Douglas Hyde would reveal a similar concern in his 1892 address to the Irish National Literary Society in Dublin, "The Necessity for De-Anglicising Ireland." Hyde describes the struggle against assimilation and rails against "the decay of our language faithfully reflected in the decay of our surnames";[50] he explains that although some natives complied with the 1465 Act requiring Irishmen living inside the English Pale to take English names, "the greater [families]—the MacMurroghs, O'Tooles, O'Byrnes . . . &c.—refused, and never did change their names. . . . It was, however, only after Aughrim and the Boyne that Irish names began to be changed in great numbers, and O'Conors to become 'Conyers,' O'Reillys 'Ridleys,' O'Donnells 'Daniels,' O'Sullivans 'Silvans,' MacCarthys 'Carters,' and so on."[51] Hyde's text narrates both the refusal to assimilate by "the greater [families]" and the wish to reverse the current adulteration of Irish names. However, the desire to at once establish the purity of Irish identity, and to illustrate how English influence (and remember, Hyde himself is Anglo-Irish) has adulterated it, exposes the impossibility of a continuous, immaculate idea of "Irishness." Hyde would argue in the same speech that the tension was ultimately debilitating: "the Irish race is at present in a most anomalous position, imitating England and yet apparently hating it. How can it produce anything good in literature, art, or institutions as long as it is actuated by motives so contradictory?"[52]

Ambivalence and hybridity, not purity, are the realities of anticolonial struggle. To invoke Frantz Fanon, the "seething pot out of which the learning of the future will emerge"[53] is like the fleshpots of Egypt; it necessarily includes the simultaneously desired and despised culture of the colonizer. In Exodus 16:3, the Israelites say, "would to God we had died by the hand of the LORD in the land of Egypt, when we sat by the flesh pots, and when we did eat bread to the full; for ye have brought us forth into this wilderness, to kill this whole assembly with hunger." They yearn for what they had in Egypt. In the Irish case, this longing includes English money, English law, English policies, the English language, English literature. An article in the *Irish Review* in 1911, entitled "Fleshpots and Freedom," cast the Irish dilemma as the country's dependence on England, the attachment to the fleshpots: "Nationalist Ireland should make up its mind as to what it really wants, whether it is Fleshpots or Freedom."[54] The author, Arthur Burrowes, insists that "the Irish people . . . cannot have it both ways,"[55] that they must confront the reality of English influence in Irish life, since they seem "busier about the content of the Saxon stall than concerned with the milk and honey that may entail sacrifice to win."[56] Ultimately, Burrowes writes, the rhetoric of liberation reveals a chosen people heading right back to Egyptian slavery: "the Promised Land has been left to perorations, and we have been millions marching like one for the Fleshpots."[57] The people may be speechifying about their longing for the promised land, but ironically enough, they are marching in the wrong direction.

Exodus, Exile, and the Land

For Burrowes, as for many others, the promised land is a metaphor, a symbol of Ireland's cultural and political independence. To what extent, then, does Exodus insist upon the actual land as the physical site of the nation? It is true that, as Amardeep Singh suggests, "the metaphor of the 'promised land' continues to be important to a postcolonial mode of reading because of its emphasis on liberation and space, on the centrality of territorialization in the struggle against colonial authority."[58] And Exodus indeed seems to be about place, with its final goal of the land. In some ways, though, the very use of the metaphor itself seems to bracket the land's significance, for the Irish analogy depends on reading alienation from the promised land—where the people already live, after all—as psychological, political, cultural, and economic; the journey there would not entail literal travel, but social change.[59] More important, Exodus is focused on the wilderness, the absence of territory; even the eventual arrival in the land is countered with the exile from it that will follow. The Diaspora that would come to characterize the Jews as a people "without a land" began with a series of expulsions from Canaan that sent the Jews first to Babylon (around 586 BCE), and then, with the destruction of the Second Temple in 70 CE, to Europe. Harry Berger proposes that the Hebrew Scriptures offer a "message to all those who possess the promised land, or who long for it . . . to possess the land is to lose the promise. . . . The whole point of the conquest lies in the subsequent loss, and the significant wandering is not the migration to Canaan but the after-wandering, the wandering of exiles."[60] In other words, the fact of eventual dispossession—exile—also becomes part of the Exodus story; the Israelites' relation to their land is always fraught, and as Attias and Benbassa write, its "indirect, conditional, and fundamentally unstable character . . . will never totally disappear."[61] When modern Jews recall the story of the Exodus night at their annual Passover holiday, they admit that the liberation they celebrate is being recalled from a space of inevitable, perhaps existential, exile: the concluding aspiration, even for Israelis, is always the same: "next year in Jerusalem."

Through two spaces that are not, then, the promised land—desert and exile—Exodus can reveal modes of national identity that resist fixed notions of the territorial. To begin with, looking closely at the Exodus story we find that for the Israelites, the relationship with the promised land is not what primarily defines them. Rather the Torah, the text, replaces the physical space of Israel as the primary locus of national identity. As Attias and Benbassa write, "the Torah—the Land/book that was ritually read and untiringly interpreted, the primary material of liturgy—had replaced the lost land, while supplying everyone with the pretext and opportunity to evoke that land without cease."[62] Even as the land is continually evoked, Exodus resists a construction of national identity based on geography, favoring instead a textual identity. Thus the rabbis, accounting for the winding route the Israelites took from Egypt to Canaan, wrote, "Should not God have brought them in the quickest way? Rather God said, 'If I bring Israel into the Land of Israel now, they will immediately set to work in their fields and vineyards and neglect the Torah. Therefore I shall take them round about in the wilderness for forty years, eating manna and drinking from the miraculous well, so that the Torah will be absorbed into their very bodies!'"[63] The book of Exodus is also concerned with the Tabernacle—a moveable dwelling-place for God, constructed on His orders—whose description takes up nearly a third of the chapters. Everett Fox notes, "with the completion of this Dwelling, we find God resident neither of Sinai nor in the later Jerusalem, but rather accompanying the people 'upon all their marches'. . . . The sacred center here thus moves; it is a portable anchor that establishes stability wherever it goes."[64] Yet the notion of "stability" with the Tabernacle, or the text for that matter, is always undermined by the uncertainty of liberation; as Zornberg points out, "A dubious, unmarked route is chosen, for reasons that are related to a repressed desire,"[65] so that even as the people move toward the promised land, carrying both God and his text with them, they unconsciously wish to return to Egypt, to be free of the new land that will require them to follow a new law.

The privileging of text over place is what makes it possible (and necessary) for Joyce's Bloom to expand his definition of a nation from "the same people living in the same place" to the more inclusive "or also living in different places" (*U* 317). Bloom accepts the idea of a diasporic nation, one in which national identity does not inhere in a particular place. With the publication of Hardt and Negri's *Empire* in

2000, we seem to have the literary-critical culmination of the Joycean impulse toward diaspora—what, in another context, Maeera Schreiber has called "an active claim for a diasporic version of home and identity."[66] Even as work on nationalism continues to focus on the significance of place, theorists of globalization stress the emergent trend of movement. Hardt and Negri continually invoke a liberatory "exodus," although, for all of the theological fervor of *Empire*, they mean the word ostensibly emptied of its biblical/religious implications. National communities, like religious ones, are already obsolete in Hardt and Negri's empire, so that their exodus shares the structural feature of wilderness and hybridization with Exodus without simultaneously reconstructing a new, bounded sense of identity. They imagine "exodus" as a purely subversive force: the destruction of boundaries, a multiplication of ambiguities.[67] This investment in "the concrete invention of a first *new place in the non-place*"[68] is not unlike the constructive possibilities of "the wilderness of inhabitation," as Joyce describes it in *Ulysses*.[69]

As Benedict Anderson notes in his essay "Exodus," the "nationalizing" moment often comes in exile,[70] for exile inspires a powerfully imagined homeland, a stability-in-instability, or presence-in-absence. And very often Exodus, which is not a story about exile but about liberation, is misrepresented as a narrative of homecoming, as if the promised land was always already the defining element of the nation. It is true that Abraham, the Jewish patriarch, had been promised the land for his descendants. But Exodus is a movement *to* nationhood, not a return to it; as Martin Buber argues, the people only become a people, a nation, in the process of their departure from Egypt.[71] The Exodus is a forward-moving, not a circular, journey.[72] Nevertheless, since the start of the Israelite Diaspora in Babylonia, Exodus has been repeatedly reimagined as a return from exile, and going forth has paradoxically become a metonym for coming home. Since that first displacement, oppressed, colonized, and otherwise exiled peoples have repeatedly employed the narrative of Exodus to describe the return to a stable national origin, rather than the uncertain journey it was for the Israelites. For Ireland, the conflation of Exodus and exile produces something like an ideal anticolonial narrative: this nation that has never yet properly been a "nation" looks forward to becoming "a nation once again," in the words of Thomas Davis's famous ballad of the 1840s. Ireland could be born, and reborn, in the same metaphor of deliverance.

Yet the very word *exodus* also conjures a different use of the trope, and at times in Irish history a more pressing reality: the exodus of emigration, of exile. In nineteenth- and early twentieth-century Ireland, diaspora was imagined as an ideal form of nationhood by very few. The disturbing reality, in a country that saw a million and a half people emigrate during the years of the Great Famine, was a literal exodus, not a metaphoric one. Inevitably, this reality complicated the biblical rhetoric of Exodus by adding to the trope of nation-building another connotation, which included not only the nation's potential success, but also its failure. Although there was a certain amount of nationalist acceptance of emigration as part of Irish life, it existed only within a specific discourse of Catholicism; as Kerby Miller writes, "While the exodus was described, on the one hand, as 'divine destiny' and the emigrants as 'holy missionaries' for the Catholic faith. . . . [o]n the other hand, negative characterizations of emigration overwhelmingly predominated, and after the famine most clerics and nationalists united in condemning it. For Ireland as a whole emigration was seen as tragic because it deprived the island of its young men and women, its 'bone and sinew.'"[73] This bemoaned loss of "bone and sinew," like the "nerve and muscle, and heart and brain, / Lost to Ireland — lost in vain" of Lady Wilde's 1864 poem "The Exodus," reorganizes the biblical Exodus narrative to symbolize the negative associations of the literal and figurative loss of an Irish population in the nineteenth century. And as Luke Gibbons writes, didactic emigration stories popularized by *The Irish Homestead* similarly warned young men and women against "the fleshpots of foreign climes."[74] After the famine, exile became so widespread that it could be seen not as a temporary (if long-lasting) punishment, but as an element of national identity, and in this it mirrored the Jewish experience.

Jewish exile had, in fact, long been invoked in Ireland as a matter of comparative suffering, perhaps most famously in the nineteenth-century poetry of Thomas Moore.[75] Many, probably most, cultural nationalists of the revival period lamented exile, and insisted that Irish identity was critically related to the land, to being "racy of the soil," in the motto of the nationalist newspaper the *Nation*.[76] Yet for all of the tradition linking Irishness and soil, certain Irish writers questioned the association. "Irishmen were never made to be farmers," says George Bernard Shaw's Larry Doyle in *John Bull's Other Island*, as he observes with disappointment the mess his countrymen have made of their newly purchased farms. "We're like the Jews," Doyle explains: "the Almighty gave us brains, and bid us farm them, and leave the clay and the worms alone."[77] Shaw actively advocated an Irish diasporic nationalism modeled on that of the Jews, and he was particularly disturbed that Irishness should be defined by a fetishizing of place: "I am quite ready to help the saving work of reducing the sham Ireland of romance to a heap of unsightly ruins. When this is done, my countrymen can consider the relative merits of building something real in the old country, or taking a hint from that other clever people, the Jews, and abandoning their Palestine to put on all the rest of the world as a shepherd putteth on his garment."[78] Shaw was unimpressed by the new movement for a Jewish nation: "I don't know why the Jews should be looking for a land of their own. Their dispersion throughout Europe gives them so much power and influence. They get on wherever they settle, just like Irishmen, who languish in their own country, and flourish in every other."[79] If Shaw seemed blind to the problem of increasing anti-Semitism throughout Europe (from which he himself was hardly immune), the unavoidable Jewish Question highlighted the prospect of a more traditional nationalism embodied in the emergent Zionist movement.[80] The struggle for a Jewish nation-state was of interest to Irish nationalists of various political leanings, who had for so long looked to ancient Israelites as models of national identity. Yeats endorsed "a [Jewish] homeland in Palestine,"[81] even as he also echoed Shaw by remarking to William Rothenstein that "the Irish and the Jews are alike in that they are at their best and most fruitful as a ferment among men of other races."[82]

Shaw's approval of Jewish and Irish diasporas and his skepticism about Jewish and Irish territorial nationalisms were unusual but not unique. John Eglinton, another Anglo-Irish writer who was often in opposition to the mainstream cultural nationalists, wrote that "if a movement like Zionism were to originate among the members of the Irish race, the difficulty would arise that Ireland would not hold them all."[83] Eglinton was more interested in exploring Jewish modernity than Jewish antiquity as a model for Ireland, arguing, "Ireland must exchange the patriotism which looks back for the patriotism which looks forward. The Jews had this kind of patriotism, and it came to something."[84] Eglinton later noted that "the parallel with the Jews might be extended further: the principal achievements of the Irish, for instance, have not been in Ireland. . . . Again, the ancient Irish language is no more a bond of union among the Irish than Hebrew has been among the modern Jews."[85] But Eglinton was, like Shaw, in the minority in his politics as in his use of the analogy, and in 1902, in a lecture reprinted in the *Irish Catholic*, Gaelic League founder Douglas Hyde argued precisely the opposite point about language and nationality: "Do you know how the Jews, the most marvelous people in the world, keep alive their nationality? They would be as scattered as the mist were it not that the Jewish child is taught from his infancy his own language along with any other he may have to learn. In the future I hope the Irish child will have on one side of the book his own language and English on the other, and thus be treated as well as the child of the Jew."[86] The role of Hebrew in modern Jewish life was thus used to argue both sides of the Irish language question—a debate that Joyce incorporates into *Ulysses*, and that I will revisit in chapter 4.

Opposing uses of the Jewish parallel indicate the ways in which the presence of actual Jews, both in Ireland and as part of a broader European discourse about nationality, would complicate the Irish appropriation of biblical tropes. Ancient Israelites always had the same story; modern Jews had as various a sense of national identity as the Irish. Moreover, the Irish response to Jews was also mixed, with some nationalists rejecting them as foreign oppressors aligned with the English. As chapter 1 will show, the negative response to Jews unsurprisingly had the effect of undermining the Israelite analogy. In the *Jewish Chronicle* for 1906, "Halitvac," the Jewish Dublin correspondent E. R. Lipsett, wrote, "the Jews understand the Irish little; the Irish understand the Jews less."[87] For all of the imaginative connections that the Irish created in their literature, historiography, and political language, this was probably true. And while the Irish engaged with Jewish narratives and Jewish people (sometimes mythical, sometimes historical, occasionally real), it seems unlikely that the analogical rhetoric of the Israelite-Irish parallel often reached the Jewish communities of Ireland, which were, at least initially, extremely insular. Divisions of language and culture, as well as religious orthodoxy (including Kosher dietary restrictions), limited the Jewish community's sociability with their neighbors.[88]

Eventually, though, as Cormac Ó Gráda writes, "the [Jewish] community would integrate into the nationalist mainstream."[89] Perhaps the best evidence of this integration is the formation of the Judaeo-Irish Home Rule Association in 1908.[90] And in at least one case, we do find imaginative reciprocation in the Jewish community. Leslie Yodaiken sees the suffering of the Irish as approaching that of his own people: only "the bitter flood of Israel's tears, that in myriad cascades have ceaselessly swept down the steep decline of the ages, has ever exceeded the flow of [Ireland's] woes."[91] But Yodaiken goes further, and inhabiting the persona of a "foundling," he names "Erin my foster-mother." Yodaiken in fact describes Zion as a version not only of Erin, but more specifically as a kind of bewitching Kathleen ni Houlihan, who "croons a mystic song, sweet, triumphant, fascinating. And the power of music acts like a magic wand" upon the son of Zion.[92] With the return of the Jews, "her returning children," Zion "is no longer a widow, but a smiling bride"[93]—transformed, just as Kathleen is in the conclusion to Yeats and Gregory's famous play, where the old woman—Ireland herself—becomes "a young girl . . . [with] the walk of a queen"[94] as a result of an Irish man's sacrifice for his country's freedom. Yodaiken's imagery is evocative, but it is also an isolated example: a study of Jewish uses of Irish tropes of liberation would be a very short study indeed.

Chapter 1 of this book, "British Israelites, Irish Israelites, and Ireland's Jews," traces the political and literary uses of the Irish-Israelite analogy from its origins in medieval genealogy through its role in Irish-Jewish relations at the beginning of the last century. Moving through Irish history, I consider Israelite genealogies in early Christian Ireland, the emergence of a typological imagination in the seventeenth century, and the increasing nationalization of the Exodus trope in the eighteenth and nineteenth centuries. I begin this chapter at its chronological endpoint, however, by examining the remarkable incarnation of Exodus in 1902, when the imperialist British-Israelites attempted to excavate the Ark of the Covenant at Tara in County Meath. Through this example and others, I explore the irony by which, throughout Irish history, both colonial and anticolonial rhetoric enlists the same trope for opposite ends: by the twentieth century, the disenfranchised Irish had been sharing the Exodus trope with English settlers—who also saw themselves as Israelites looking for a promised land—for hundreds of years.

"Parnell, Lady Gregory, and the Fleshpots of Egypt," my second chapter, considers the problems of hybridity and adulteration in the context of an emerging national "Irish Ireland" identity. Home Rule leader Charles Stewart Parnell, like Moses, was a leader "apart"—a wealthy Protestant Anglo-Irishman leading a movement for Catholic Ireland. Parnell threatened national purity both through his infamous adultery with the English Katherine O'Shea and through his elite background. As Attias and Benbassa write of Moses, "brought up by Pharaoh's daughter, [he] incontestably bears within him the otherness from which it is his mission to free Israel," thus complicating the meaning of a national identity that would emerge from such "adulterating" leadership.[95] I argue that the production of and quizzical public response to Lady Gregory's 1911 play *The Deliverer*—an allegory of the Parnell story set amid the biblical Exodus—offers a complex picture of Irish cultural and political tensions in the period before the Easter Rising. This chapter traces not only the developing depiction of Parnell as Moses in the 1880s and '90s, but also the changing responses to the Protestant Ascendancy's appropriation of Exodus in an increasingly empowered Catholic Ireland. Additionally, this chapter reassesses the conventional view of Gregory as a conciliatory figure of the literary revival; in fact, her work explores precisely where possibilities for political and cultural compromise fail.

Chapter 3, "Anti-Exodus: Patrick Pearse and the New Liberation," examines the shift in the way Irish liberation was imagined and enacted in the years after Parnell's fall. I show how the Exodus paradigm underwent a radical reworking during the early decades of the twentieth century, and how the literary and political work of Patrick Pearse, a leader of the 1916 Rising, transformed the story of liberation in Ireland. Pearse's writings shift the narrative of Irish freedom from the Old Testament to the New Testament; from Moses to Christ; from the Anglo-Irish Ascendancy to the Catholic majority; from Parnell to Pearse himself. Pearse also purges from the story of revolution the complexity of Irish devolution and the ambivalence it engendered in the population, replacing these realities with a new narrative that insisted on purity. In turn, in the years after the Rising, Lady Gregory and other revivalist writers would contest Pearsian messianism by invoking the ghost of Parnell.

Joyce's encyclopedic critique and revision of earlier nationalist uses of Exodus are the focus of chapter 4, "A Pisgah Sight of Palestine from Dear Dirty Dublin." Joyce's "epic of two races (Israelite-Irish)"[96] is deeply invested in the respective births of these nations, but also in the relevance of Exodus to individuals, particularly, of course, Stephen and Bloom. While Joyce scholars (especially those working on Jewish elements) have long acknowledged the importance of Exodus in *Ulysses*, this chapter contextualizes that work through new archival, historical, and theoretical readings, including analyses of Joyce's reading on Jewish nationalism and the often remarkably analogous writings of his fellow Irishman John Eglinton; *Ulysses*' revision of John F. Taylor's speech on the Irish language, "The Language of the Outlaw"; and most importantly, Joyce's insistence on "the fleshpots of Egypt" as part of any imagining of the promised land. Exodus demands our attention in *Ulysses* in ways that have not been previously acknowledged, and here I aim to reposition Exodus as the central trope of the novel.

In chapter 5, "A Bloomsday Seder: Joyce and Jewish Memory," I show how Joyce engages the Haggadah, the text that recounts the Exodus story at the Passover holiday, as a way of reflecting on Irish national memory. Through its careful and critical attention to the biblical text and the traditions of the Seder, *Ulysses* ultimately reveals the paradox of Exodus as a narrative about the promised land that simultaneously insists on the wilderness, or non-place, as the site of the nation.

Writing Exodus in Ireland

In the essay "A Neglected Monument of Irish Prose," John Eglinton writes that the Bible is "the great national book of the Hebrews."[97] It is invoked not as a religious text, but as a template for an "original literature," as he terms it—one that might inspire some such national epic for the Irish.[98] But as a model of national literature, the Bible (and in particular, Exodus) hardly corresponds to the traditional programs of Irish nationalism. Someone like Hyde, who was similarly concerned with the idea of a national epic, would find the Bible, with its contradictory redaction of many voices and its alternately exposed and repressed failures of the chosen people, deeply problematic as a narrative of national identity. Yet the "anomalous position" Hyde had diagnosed in the Irish was not only inevitable, but fruitful for some writers; Joyce, of course, thrived on the motivations of the contradictory. *Israelites in Erin*, in its final chapters, explores *Ulysses* as an Irish version of Exodus—a story that contains voices of hesitation, refusal, and the desire for alterity as well as a code of national identity—that overcomes the narrow narrative of national purity and can in fact be read as a "heteroglossic epic" of the nation. David Lloyd has remarked on the fact of the national epic being necessarily monologic, that "the process of hybridization . . . [is] at every level recalcitrant to the aesthetic politics of nationalism."[99] Lloyd observes how narratives that chronicle national departure/revolution are compelled to obfuscate ambivalence or hybridity; yet Exodus is perhaps an exception. Exodus necessarily includes something like heresy—that is, the departing Israelites' resistance to the formation of a monolithic, inflexible, contained tradition. Exodus includes the Israelites' persistent wishes to return to the fleshpots of Egypt, the idols of polytheism, the possibilities of bicultural existence.

It is true that conservative, essentialist uses of the Exodus trope were widespread in the period of the Irish revival. But some Irish writers produced more nuanced and subversive explorations of the ambivalence at the heart of the trope; they used Exodus to imagine a nation that rejects (or at least admits to, exposes, and interrogates) land-obsessed, racialist, or otherwise limiting narratives of origin. Herbert Howarth, writing in the 1950s, suggested that the Irish "did not and do not want freedom any more than the English . . . want it. . . . Today they have the most oppressive censorship in the world."[100] But before the ideological narrowness of the Irish Free State and the Republic that followed—a state whose censorship and parochialism indeed sent many of its artists abroad—Gregory, Joyce, Yeats, and others employed Exodus to articulate a politically radical version of devolution, in which liberation was not an end, but a beginning. In the years before Exodus became lost to Irish history, it gave a view, not of the promised land, but of what the winding path itself might look like.

1

British Israelites, Irish Israelites, and Ireland's Jews

On June 24, 1902, a distinguished company of Dublin literati—W. B. Yeats, Douglas Hyde, George Moore, and Arthur Griffith—set out purposefully from the city to the "Royal County" of Ireland, County Meath. Their particular destination that day was an amateur excavation under way at the Hill of Tara, the site where Ireland's high kings had been crowned centuries earlier. Yeats and company were on a mission to protect both the hill itself and any Irish antiquities that lay within it, for indeed the English diggers were working to unearth a singularly momentous artifact (although not, in fact, an Irish one). These excavators, members of a British Israelite sect who believed themselves to be descendants of the lost tribes of Israel, were convinced that the biblical Ark of the Covenant was buried beneath that hill in the Irish countryside.

This unconventional theory of the Ark's secret resting place under Irish soil was authorized, as Mairéad Carew writes in her book on the bizarre episode, by a "strange mixture of early Irish history, genealogy and Old Testament rhetoric."[1] In a more immediate sense, the British Israelites were motivated by an understanding of themselves as God's chosen people, true inheritors of all that the Hebrew Bible had promised. The British Israelites would use their pseudoarcheological/biblical evidence to prove that this promised land—Ireland—truly belonged to them. According to the nationalist revolutionary Maud Gonne, who initiated the campaign to save Tara from the unsightly excavations, the diggers planned to present the Ark to Edward VII;[2]

in doing so, they would reconfirm the colonial relationship between England and Ireland, and the imperial power from which their project had sprung.

Meanwhile, Irish writers, politicians, and cultural nationalists, including those who journeyed to Tara on June 24, were already invested in the metaphor, if not the reality, that *they* were the chosen people, the Israelites of Old Testament enslavement and liberation. Although we might have expected Yeats and his colleagues to embrace any archeological evidence that would literalize their metaphor, in this case they rejected it, since it came entangled with the offensive imperialism of the British Israelites. (And needless to say, no evidence of the Ark was recovered.) Literary Anglo-Irish Protestants (and Yeats and Hyde especially) were particularly trying to disassociate themselves from the taint of their colonial past, as they faced Irish Ireland nationalists (including their Tara companion Griffith) who rejected them as non-Catholic and non-native. Yeats and his friends had traveled to Tara to condemn the excavation; at Gonne's urging, and rather astonishingly equipped with a shotgun, they meant to shut it down. Any association with English fundamentalists was to be sedulously avoided.

Upon their return from Tara, the writers composed an angry letter to the *London Times* protesting the excavation's desecration of their Irish national heritage. The letter, published on June 27 and signed by Yeats, Hyde, and Moore, exposes and attacks the ideological core of the British Israelite project: the Hill of Tara, "probably the most consecrated spot in Ireland,"[3] where Irish kings once ruled the autonomous Irish nation, was being ruthlessly torn up by the English in yet another act of cultural appropriation. Later that summer, in the poem "In the Seven Woods," Yeats would try to put the distressing event out of mind: "I have forgot awhile / Tara uprooted, and new commonness / Upon the throne and crying about the streets."[4] The British Israelite mythology, downgraded from ancient genealogy to "new commonness," is quickly dispensed with, but Yeats, like his poem, was clearly troubled by it. That the English should find the biblical Ark, that through their manipulation of Irish pseudohistories *they* should be the "chosen," and thus the rightful, people of Ireland, was an appalling notion for nationalists looking to prove exactly the opposite point. When Stephen Gwynn, also a Protestant nationalist, reflected on the incident in 1906, he was only slightly more inclined to find the episode comic. Gwynn describes the offenses of the "ridiculous" "vandals":

> A sect or persuasion which desires to establish that the Irish of today are the lost tribes of Israel (heaven knows, we in Ireland have few enough of the characteristic virtues or vices of the Jew!) convinced itself, or was convinced, that the prophet Jeremiah had reached Ireland, with the Ark of the Covenant among his baggage, and had finally interred this relic at Tara. Excavation undertaken in order to exhume it (and make Jews of us all in spite of our noses) resulted in the destruction of this little monument [the Rath of the Synods, a ringfort]. Everything in Ireland is something of a joke, but to demolish Tara in the search for any ark was past a joke. They might have looked for Noah's next time and dug more freely.[5]

Despite his wry tone here, it is worth noting that just pages later Gwynn forgoes Jewish jokes in favor of an earnest Israelite analogy. Describing the military success of Malachy over the Danes in the year 979, and the ensuing liberation of "2,000 captives," Gwynn repeats the saying of the Four Masters: "It was the end . . . of Ireland's Babylonian captivity."[6]

While trying to fend off someone else's arrival in their promised land, Yeats, Hyde, and Moore nevertheless retained Exodus as a narrative of Irish national liberation. Writing in the *United Irishman* in 1903, Yeats would reaffirm the value of the Ark, as if to clarify that in rejecting the excavations at Tara he was not rejecting the metaphoric potential of Exodus: "To me it seems that ideas, and beauty and knowledge are precisely those sacred things, an Ark of the Covenant as it were, that a nation must value even more than victory."[7] Refusing to abdicate the biblical trope to his opponents, Yeats held on to the centuries-long Irish investment in the Israelites as both literal and metaphoric ancestors. Indeed, Tara's association with Israelites was not a British invention but an Irish one, and it is just one example of the rhetorical power and persistence of the Israelite motif in Ireland. In 1900 Moses was perhaps as ubiquitous as Kathleen ni Houlihan.[8]

Still, the reverence with which certain revivalists viewed biblical genealogies was balanced by a heavy dose of suspicion from others. In 1903 as the Tara controversy continued to receive press in the Dublin papers, Yeats's frequent debating partner John Eglinton suggested that such "spurious Celto-Hebraic mythology" was highly questionable: "The bardic historiographers scanned Hebrew records of the origin of the human race, assuredly with more excuse than our modern 'Anglo-Israelites,' but with results far more perplexing to those who would now sift in these accounts the genuine from the fictitious."[9] If Eglinton cursorily dismisses the British Israelites, he also observes the convoluted way in which biblical elements appear in Irish history and pseudohistory; the accounts are many, various, and indeed perplexing. Yet biblical material provided powerful proto-national, and later nationalist, narratives for the Irish; and moreover it served to unify the various strands of Irish society in periods of anticolonial struggle. By the start of the twentieth century, negotiating the English appropriation of "their" Israelite story was something that Irish writers had been managing for years. Rather than teasing out every example, this chapter examines the most prominent biblical genealogies and analogies that were put to use on both sides of the colonial divide, from the beginning of English settlement in Ireland through the final push against English rule—the years in which Yeats, Gregory, Parnell, Pearse, and Joyce would try to save Tara in various, and often opposing, ways.

If for much of Irish history the Exodus story and other Israelite analogies circulated throughout the culture, by the close of the nineteenth century two factors combined to threaten the end of Exodus as a national analogy: the rise and fall of Parnell as a (Protestant) Irish Moses, and Jewish immigration. Someone like the Sinn Fein–founder Arthur Griffith, distressed by a new Jewish population and advocating an Irish Ireland agenda, would come to reject the idea that the Israelites were a parallel for the Irish. After so many centuries of identification, the biblical trope was eventually occluded because—as Griffith insisted—it was not Irish after all. This chapter looks back at the ways the Israelite analogy worked in Ireland up to the point when it became a site of such political and cultural contention.

Genealogies

The Bible was central to the way early Christian Ireland imagined itself, and the Hebrew Scriptures, in particular, were "thoroughly familiar" to monastic scholars; indeed, seventh- and eighth-century Irish historiography borrowed from Genesis and Exodus its narrative framework.[10] Kim McCone's book *Pagan Past and Christian Present in Early Irish Literature* (1990) argues boldly for the underacknowledged, fundamental influence of the Bible on early Christian Ireland, claiming that "the extent to which [Ireland's literati] modeled their assumed ancestors' status and actions on those of God's chosen people in the Old Testament is quite striking in its audacity."[11] These pseudohistories, myths of Irish origin, take us back to the patriarchs of Genesis: according to most legends, the Irish are understood to be descended from Noah's son Japhet.[12] In medieval Ireland, comparisons between St. Patrick and Moses, between Gaelic law and the Ten Commandments, between Irish and Hebrew, were common, and they implied a link of direct descent.[13] Hebrew artifacts, too, were thought to have made the journey—generally through Spain, it was claimed—to Ireland. Relics of a biblical past included part of the stone tablets inscribed with Mosaic law;[14] Moses's staff; and most famously, the stone, brought to Ireland by Scota, the daughter of Pharaoh, on which Jacob had lain his head when God promised him the land of Israel. This last became known as the Stone of Destiny (or Stone of Scone), thought by some to have resided in Westminster Abbey.[15] In *The Annals of Connaught* for the year 1537 we find a genealogy of "the Staff of Jesus, which was in Dublin, where it worked miracles and wonders renowned in Ireland from the time of Patrick to this time, which was in Christ's own hand when he was among men and in the hand of Moses, son of Amram at the drying up of the Red Sea before the children of Israel."[16] Moses's staff, a symbol of Israel's liberation, is traced forward to Jesus and, eventually, into Ireland. As an addendum to the object's history, we learn that the staff has now been "burnt by the English,"[17] and thus the story has been told not simply to signal Ireland's importance within Christian history, but to witness English attempts to destroy Irish ancestral/biblical memory.

Irish genealogies narrate early Gaelic participation in the world of the Hebrew Bible. As Joseph Lennon has shown, the eleventh-century *Lebor Gabála Érenn*, or Book of Invasions, synthesizes Irish history with biblical history, legitimating the former by connecting it to the latter.[18] Gaelic and biblical origins happen side by side in Egypt: the "Sons of Israel" and the father of the Gaelic people (Gaedil) "ratified a friendship"[19] at the Red Sea. So that Gaedil's people will not be enslaved as a result of this friendship, Moses suggests a joint escape and offers "an equal share of heritage in the land which god hath promised to the Sons of Israel."[20] Gaedil, however, declines the offer. The proto-Irish remain in Egypt and witness the destruction of Pharaoh's army in the sea. When the legacy of their friendship with the Israelites forces their expulsion,[21] they begin their eventual journey to Ireland, their own promised land.

Geoffrey Keating's seventeenth-century *Foras Feasa ar Éirinn*, or history of Ireland, relies on the *Lebor Gabála Érenn* and other early texts to make similar links with biblical history.[22] As in the *Lebor Gabála Érenn*, the point is not to make ancient Israelites the immediate ancestors of the Irish, but rather to place the Irish in the biblical story, which was still in this period the privileged way of understanding human history. The narrative Keating offers rehearses a similar encounter of reciprocal hospitality and true friendship between the two communities,[23] but it also focuses on the telling and retelling of the story of the Israelites: Aaron tells Niul, and on the same night when Niul in turn narrates "all that had befallen the children of Israel," the Gaelic patriarch's life is saved by Moses (incidentally offering an explanation for the lack of snakes in Ireland). The Israelite story becomes part of the Irish story, and thus the Irish have a particular claim on its meaning.

Well into the seventeenth century, as Colin Kidd has shown, "Mosaic history persisted"[24] in Ireland's Gaelic communities. It was central to national historiography and remained of more importance in Ireland than in other British ethnic discourses.[25] Yet the Gaelic literati had not forgotten their other, nonbiblical histories. If the ancient encounter with the Judeo-Christian God of the Israelites suggests a biblical origin, it is equally remembered that Saint Patrick brought Christianity across the sea to a pagan Ireland. McCone offers a compelling explanation for why such early texts can so easily accommodate the apparent dissonance: "We now have an obvious answer to the riddle of how early Christian Ireland's monastically oriented *literati*, working within a historical framework modeled upon the Bible, could conscientiously regard their pre-Christian past as an object worthy of earnest attention. In effect, narratives purporting to cover people and events prior to Patrick's mission and establishment of the true faith could be treated as a kind of 'Old Testament' of the Irish race, a socially, morally and aetiologically instructive God-given record perfected but by no means invalidated by the new dispensation of Christianity."[26] In other words, the early Christian writers used the principle of supersession, or typology, to organize their complicated relationship to their own history. Two cultures could thus be connected through a hierarchy that privileged one without invalidating the other: paganism, McCone suggests, could remain as a usable—if remote—part of Irish history.

Typology

Analogy is a familiar way of describing the relationship between two different things that are also alike, but typology tends to operate below our contemporary sightlines, and it requires some explanation. Typology—a word whose meaning has become diluted in some literary criticism—is more precise than analogy: a specific form for understanding the relationship between the Hebrew Bible and the New Testament. It expresses an "allegorical master narrative," as Frederic Jameson writes, that argues for the supersession of the Old Testament by the New: "The life of Christ, the text of the New Testament . . . comes as the fulfillment of the hidden prophecies and annunciatory signs of the Old."[27] As Northrop Frye summarizes it, the resurrection of Christ is the "antitype" (or fulfillment) of the Exodus: "Moses organizes the twelve tribes of Israel; Jesus gathers twelve disciples. Israel crosses the Red Sea and achieves its identity as a nation on the other side; Jesus is baptized in the Jordan and recognized as the Son of God. . . . Israel wanders forty years in the wilderness; Jesus, forty days."[28] Whether or not the early Christians consciously recognized, as McCone suggests, that a system of typology would allow them to accommodate their pagan history as an earlier version of the Christian present, it is clear that by the Elizabethan conquest, both the native Irish and the English settlers were thinking typologically when they invoked the Exodus story. That is, like most other Christians at the time, they thought of Exodus as a precedent, a story that would, as part of its core meaning, be repeated and fulfilled in another context.

In principle, typology is a purely religious way of understanding the relationship between Jewish and Christian scriptures. But its praxis works in two essentially opposite ways: as spiritual fulfillment, or as political fulfillment.[29] In the first sense, typological readings of the New Testament worked to filter out the nationalism so prominent in the Hebrew Bible; the chosen people's literal attachment to the land of Israel is rendered a metaphor for Christian salvation.[30] Early Christianity "turns away from this whole conception of any earthly Promised Land. . . . The Promised Land, which the Patriarchs took to be Canaan, turns out to be Heaven."[31] As Erich Auerbach writes, the typological reading of the Hebrew Bible renders it "lost as a book of national history": "In this form and in this context, from which Jewish history and national character had vanished, the Celtic and Germanic peoples, for example, could accept the Old Testament."[32] But early Irish history, to take the example at hand, teaches us that it is precisely the idea of the Bible *as* national history that makes it important in Ireland. And a longing for earthly political fulfillment would, in the national context, eventually become more powerful than the idea of universal fulfillment in Christ. During the course of the seventeenth century, we can notice increasing ambivalence about heavenly promised lands and a general trend in the direction of "applied" typology, in which a people's social, political, or religious struggles are not just analogous to, but typologically equivalent to, those of the chosen people. In this second application of typology, the struggle for the promised land is literal, as it was for the Israelites.

There seems to be a direct relationship between the way the Irish used typology and the emergence of an Irish national identity: the shift to political typology, unsurprisingly, signals an increasingly politicized people.[33] The transformation of the religious and rhetorical use of Exodus helps to illuminate Irish thinking about national identity, particularly as Exodus offers the same dual praxis as typology: on one hand, it is a story of religious fulfillment; on the other, one of worldly, political liberation. As Michael Walzer describes it, "Exodus is a model for messianic and millenarian thought, and it is also a standing alternative to it—a secular and historical account of 'redemption,' an account that does not require the miraculous transformation of the material world but sets God's people marching through the world toward a better place within it."[34] In Ireland, at various moments in the seventeenth century, the promise of a heavenly Canaan was inadequate comfort for a disenfranchised community, which required also an earthly deliverance. In "Exodus to Connacht," by Fear Dorcha Ó Mealláin, the forced migration west of the Shannon in 1652–54 must be accommodated as God's will; however, this exodus tests the faith of the people:

> Consider a parable of this:
> Israel's people, God's own,
> although they were in bonds in Egypt,
> found in time a prompt release.
>
> . . . .
>
> Likewise it shall be done to you:
> all good things shall first be yours.
> Heaven is your inheritance.
> Be not faint-hearted in your faith.
>
> People of my heart, stand steady,
> don't complain of your distress.
> Moses got what he requested,
> religious freedom—and from Pharaoh.[35]

Their journey west does not bring the Irish to a promised land; on the contrary, it banishes them from their homes to accommodate New English settlers. Redemption is imagined, then—ambivalently, it must be said—through "religious freedom" that has no territorial interest, for "here or Westward God is one." The poem offers a traditional typological imagining of the fulfillment of Exodus in Christian salvation: "Heaven [*not* Ireland] is your inheritance." But the poet seems to have a hard job of convincing the people: like the Israelites who have left Egypt for the uncertainty of the desert, they must be enjoined not to be "faint-hearted."

Whether their exile was seen as literal or figurative, the Irish were also contending with the idea that their suffering was a punishment of God's choosing: God punishes the Irish as he had punished the Israelites for their intransigence (a theme that emerges most pointedly in the period of the famine of the 1840s). God's wrath is imagined particularly after the "Flight of the Earls" in 1607, and can be seen in Eóghan Ruadh Mac an Bhaird's "Anocht is uaigneach Éire" [Ireland is lonely tonight], which repeats the providential idea in several stanzas:

> This is not the only time that after sin
> God has so sent torture great, and poverty,
> and slavery, famine, plague, and retribution.
>
> . . . .
>
> Moses' followers whom He loved, see what befell them:
> their war on the Creator was their ruin,
> and He refrained not from enkindling His anger.
>
> The people of Juda, His own tribe, who should have
> done God's will, got punishment more than any other
> for violating the High King's commands.[36]

The poem finally enacts a slippage between the Israelites' God and the Irish "High King"; yet here, the Israelite story is not a model for national liberation, but rather a warning, a prophesy. Rededicate yourselves to your faith, entreats the poet, and you will be redeemed.

While the God of the Israelites and the Irish was a punishing God, providentialism was ultimately optimistic, as Breandán Ó Buachalla notes, for it promised an eventual redemption.[37] If in "Ireland Is Lonely Tonight" Mac an Bhaird laments the absent liberator—"how shall the Captivity be ended for the fresh, fair race of Conn, for in Erin we have no Moses?"[38]—in naming the Israelite deliverer, he implies that Ireland's longed-for human liberator will eventually arrive in the flesh. Often it was the self-exiled aristocracy or the Stuart Pretenders who were imagined as the antitypes to Moses;[39] these men were specific political players whose envisioned return to Ireland would forecast earthly, not heavenly, freedom.[40] The biographer of Red Hugh O'Donnell, for example, writing in the 1620s, "consistently portrayed him as the one prophesied to come among his people 'for their relief and succour, to protect and free them from the merciless foreign tribe, as Moses, the son of Amram, came to the aid of the people of God to free them from bondage.'"[41] Providential punishment could also imply providential liberation, a move that Marc Caball enlists as evidence that bardic poets were beginning to evince a "militant" national consciousness.[42] In short, Irish writers began to harness the nationalism of the Hebrew Bible and, in opposition to English settlement, to deploy the full "potent political propaganda" of Exodus.[43] Increasingly, the fulfillment of biblical destiny was imagined as something that would happen through worldly actions and would have worldly results.[44]

It was the earthly Exodus story, then, that became most important to Gaelic Irish imaginings of national struggle, and provided what Ó Buachalla describes as "the central literary metaphor of the period"—one that was "invoked incessantly."[45] Indeed, the primacy of Exodus seems almost inevitable when we consider that the Gaelic literati were surrounded, as it were, with biblical material from all sides of Irish life.[46] There were the early Mosaic genealogies in the histories of Keating and his predecessors, and there was the Bible itself, circulated and read widely in Ireland in the 1600s—in Irish as well as English and Latin.[47] Also circulating through the culture were the Exodus themes ubiquitous in English and European discourse that the Gaelic Irish would have encountered both in exile abroad and at home.[48] These biblical stories irresistibly mirrored Irish oppression and exile.

Irish "Israelites" would have found their trope embattled, however, for in the English imagination the Irish were decidedly not the chosen people—the English were. Inevitably the presence of competing versions of the Exodus metaphor—all those embattled Israelites and Canaanites on both sides—looks ironic in hindsight, but as Niall MacKenzie notes, "apparently a kind of cultural undertow was pulling English, 'New English,' Catholic Irish, and Highland Scottish imaginations simultaneously towards the same mode of analysis."[49] The surplus of biblical analogies was by no means unusual; "scriptural politics" was the norm, as David S. Katz notes of the English case, and for good reason: "A partial biblical phrase, a sanctified word or two, served the dual purpose of conveying a synecdochic message . . . and ratifying it with the stamp of divine authority."[50] Thus Christians everywhere used narratives from the Hebrew Bible—and chiefly Exodus—as types for their own struggles.[51] New promised lands became particularly compelling during the epochs of imperial expansion and the rise of the European nation-state. From England to Ireland to South Africa to the Americas, biblical rhetoric circulated.[52] Tom Garvin has remarked that "a central feature of a good myth is how easy it is to transfer it to new soil and to new political purposes," and Exodus seemed always to take root.[53]

If we have seen the importance of typology in Irish discourse, it remains a commonplace that the Bible grew its deepest roots in Protestant countries, where national identity was most likely to be constructed on biblical frameworks; typically, "applied typology," in which the Israelite story finds its analogue in contemporary life, has been understood mainly as a Protestant undertaking.[54] In Ireland too English settlers employed Exodus rhetoric, figuring themselves as Israelites and the Catholic Irish as Canaanites or Egyptians. Cromwell claimed the Exodus as "the only parallel of God's dealing with us that I know in the world,"[55] and his new Israelites were "the godly of England."[56] As Alan Ford has shown, Protestant preachers in Ireland routinely used the trope to encourage "purity" in the midst of temptation for new colonists. One preacher in the Munster plantation noted that settlers would be consumed by God's wrath "if they do not speedily repent; neither covenant nor marriage must be made with idol worshippers."[57] Another reminded his congregation of how the Israelites "paid for their cruel mercy in not extirpating the idolatrous Canaanites."[58] The effect of this rhetoric may have been substantial on the colonial situation in Ireland: if previous approaches to the native community had not been overly friendly, Exodus rhetoric powerfully reinforced perceived differences between the conquering "chosen" and those who already occupied the land. It may explain, for example, the English disinterest in converting Irish Catholics, who were seen as irredeemably other: either "Egyptians" with a culture of "popery" and "paganism" or Canaanites defined by God as idolaters to be killed. Of course, the rhetoric of extermination could work the other way too: in 1645 the exiled Irish Jesuit Conor O'Mahony invoked Exodus 32, citing Moses's destruction of the faithless Israelites, to argue for the elimination of all non-Catholics from Ireland.[59]

Perhaps the most resonant English use of the Exodus trope appears in John Temple's *The Irish Rebellion* (1646), a book that Jarlath Killeen argues is the formative text of Irish Anglican discourse. Not only does Temple imagine the Protestants of Ireland—specifically in the context of their sufferings in 1641—as Israelites who have faced the "hardened hearts"[60] of the Irish people-as-Pharaoh, but he does so specifically as a way of inverting existing Irish Catholic rhetoric. Killeen notes how Temple, in his preface, "warns his readers that Catholics have begun to 'speak as if their oppressions might be paralleled with the Israelitish Envassalage in the land of Egypt.'"[61] Thus Temple goes on to describe the 1641 revolt in such a way as to convince generations of Protestant settlers not only of Irish barbarity, but of misuse of biblical analogy: "And, now, also did [the native Irish] take occasion to revive their inveterate hatred and ancient animosities against the English Nation, whom they represented to themselves as hard Masters; under whose government, how pleasant, comfortable and advantageous soever it was, they would have the world believe they had endured a most miserable captivity and vassalage."[62] Along similar lines, Sir William

Petty, chronicler of post-Cromwellian reform, dismisses Irish identifications with Israel in *The Political Anatomy of Ireland* (1691), noting that Catholic landlords and priests would—absurdly, he implies—"comfort their flocks partly by prophesies of their restoration to their ancient estates and liberties . . . by way of God's promise to restore the Jews to the kingdom of Israel."[63]

Sarcasm prevailed on the Irish side as well. It is not surprising to find that the English version of Cromwell-as-Moses was especially unacceptable, and his infamous biblical claims to chosenness particularly rankled. In 1653, the Independent minister John Rogers, recently back from his ministry in Ireland, described Cromwell as "the great deliverer of His people through God's grace out of the land of Egypt";[64] for this mode of rhetoric Irish nationalists had a long memory. Into the nineteenth century, Irish histories of Cromwell's incursion would rehearse, in tones both facetious and bitter, his purported biblical mandate. A. M. Sullivan, whose *Story of Ireland* (1867) has been called "the bible of popular nationalism,"[65] notes that Ireland was "an inviting field for what the Protector and his soldiery called 'the work of the Lord'":[66] "In Ireland there was an idolatrous people to be put to the sword, and their fertile country to be possessed. Glory, hallelujah! The bare prospect of a campaign there threw all the Puritan regiments into ecstasies. It was the summons of the Lord to His chosen people to cross the Jordan and enter the promised land! In this spirit Cromwell came to Ireland."[67] In 1837 the United Irishman William Sampson described "Cromwell's saints" as "false Israelites": "It was Englishmen of their own race and blood [Catholic 'Old English' settlers] that were then the '*Canaanites*' that they, for God's honour, were to 'kill and spare not,' and to root out as idolatrous, to make way for the chosen of the Lord."[68]

The seventeenth century had been, as Katz explains, the high point of "scriptural politics" in England, when the Bible was a "cultural common denominator."[69] English cultural approaches to sacred texts would change, however, along with Enlightenment critiques of the Hebrew Bible's literal truth and Mosaic authorship. But whereas scriptural politics waned demonstrably in England, the Israelite trope remained an important presence—if a changing one—in the Irish context. Genealogical links between the Irish and the Israelites, for example, experienced a renewal in the eighteenth century, in both Irish and English sources. Biblical/Gaelic genealogies were reintroduced in works like historian Charles O'Conor's popular *Dissertations on the History of Ireland* (1753), in which the Irish are described as "A kind of ethnic Hebrews."[70] But most influentially, the renowned antiquarian and philologist Charles Vallancey, co-founder of the Royal Irish Academy, established a new mode of connecting the Irish and the Israelites through his work on ancient linguistics. For Vallancey, as Joep Leerssen explains, the Hebrew Scriptures were "the central model of cultural antiquity," and thus, "in that biblical context, it makes perfect sense to see kinship between Gaelic and Hebrew . . . since all linguistic difference dates back only to the Tower of Babel."[71] Vallancey's scholarship would serve a range of political uses—including, eventually, the British Israelite theory about the Ark of the Covenant. But Vallancey was also influential in Ireland, where his work provided modern evidence for the biblical ancestry described in much earlier Irish texts. William Sampson was most likely drawing on Vallancey when he wrote of the Irish language that "it has been traced by its affinities to that in which the word of God was delivered by Moses and the prophets."[72]

By the nineteenth century an obsession with biblical genealogies was widespread in Europe and America. For the British Israelites who would eventually dig at Tara, typological thinking of the sort that had buoyed Cromwell, combined with a literal genealogy reaching from Queen Victoria back to the lost tribes, was deployed to indicate modern British imperialism's biblical mandate.[73] British Israelites read genealogies as racial histories; as Kidd points out, in their hands "the message of the Bible seemed to be reducible to a kind of ethnology."[74] This racialism was particularly clear as the group's beliefs related to Ireland. The American Rev. Thomas Rosling Howlett comments, in his book *Anglo-Israel* (1892), that "the difference between [the inhabitants of the north of Ireland and the Scots] and those of the south of Ireland lies, not in their religion, but in their origin.

They sprang from different races."[75] Howlett insists that if the native Irish—modern Canaanites—are not driven out of the land, then in Moses's words, "it shall come to pass that those which ye let remain of them shall be pricks in your eyes and thorns in your sides, and shall vex you in the land wherein ye dwell."[76] "This," writes Howlett, "is the 'Irish Question.'"[77]

Other British Israelites answered the Irish question with the same potentially genocidal proposal, and used the same biblical evidence from Exodus: that, as Canaanites, the (Catholic) Irish must be expropriated, if not eradicated. Edward Hine, author of *Forty-Seven Identifications of the Anglo Saxons with the Lost House of Israel* (1878), repeatedly decries "these Irish Canaanites"; they must, he insists, "come under the dying out process."[78] Hine's argument illustrates the profound danger of Exodus as a colonial narrative, particularly when he makes the startling claim that "we have literally fulfilled Israel's mission by pushing the aborigines of our colonies to the ends of what was once their own country."[79] Moreover, British Israelism was anti-Irish not only in racial, but in political terms: "Ireland is one of our many possessions fairly won by conquest and it is absolutely impossible for England to lose any of her rightful Possessions without doing violence to Scripture . . . Therefore the notion of repeal becomes nonsense agitation."[80] Irish nationalist interests, such as repeal of the Union, are rendered biblically forbidden by British Israelite belief. And while the British Israelites were not quite mainstream, their politics essentially gathered up genealogical evidence in support of already widely held views on the subject of Ireland.

Analogy

In contrast to the divisive racial categorizing of the British Israelites, in the nineteenth century Irish Catholics and Protestants used biblical analogies and genealogies as a way of overcoming perceived differences in ethnicity (and real differences of religion and class) across Irish society. While most nineteenth-century Irish would not have considered themselves literal descendants of the Israelites, or felt they were typologically fulfilling the Bible, they were generally amenable to the analogical link with the chosen people. The metaphor served, indeed, to designate *all* Irish people as chosen—making them a unified nation. By the close of the eighteenth century, after all, it was not only the Catholic Irish who were invested in Irish independence, and analogical forms of thinking helped to integrate the various groups of Irish nationalists who were struggling for political and religious freedoms. At the forefront of the United Irish movement were members of the Protestant Ascendancy, enlisted by Wolfe Tone "[t]o unite the whole people of Ireland, to abolish the memory of all past dissensions, and to substitute the common name of Irishman in place of the denominations of Protestant, Catholic and Dissenter."[81] In keeping with this inclusiveness, the Israelite analogy in this period became nonsectarian as it became explicitly nationalist; it allowed a diverse nation to (at least rhetorically) figure itself as cohesive. The imagined unity was critical, for as David Lloyd notes, "the principal task of nationalism" in the nineteenth and early twentieth century "was to overcome the sectarian, class, and ethnic divisions that split Ireland."[82] Helpfully, both the Israelite analogy and scriptural politics more generally were native to all three communities that made up the United Irishmen: Catholics, Protestants, and the Presbyterian Scots for whom political typologies were even more explicitly prescriptive.[83] Exodus, with such universal appeal, would for now retain its status as an important national—and increasingly anticolonial—trope. Not until the 1880s would various factors begin to contribute to a newly sectarian understanding of Exodus, one that would eventually become inextricably linked to Protestant, Parnellite constitutionalists and would finally be disowned by most Catholic nationalists.

Until the first decades of the twentieth century, then, Exodus would serve as shorthand for national aspirations, and serve equally Gaelic/Catholic and Protestant Ireland. James Clarence Mangan's iconic translation of William Heffernan's eighteenth-century poem "Kathleen Ni Houlahan," which was hugely popular across the spectrum of nationalist ideology in the decades following the Union, offers a fine example of the trope's potential for wide appeal. Its providential mode in which the people "wait the Young Deliverer" accommodates a passive longing for freedom, while the percussive rhythm and strong rhyme, along with the invocation of the Aisling figure, Kathleen, suggest more militant, human action:

He, who over sands and waves led Israel along—
He, who fed, with heavenly bread, that chosen tribe and throng—
He, who stood by Moses, when his foes were fierce and strong—
May He show forth His might in saving Kathleen-Ni-Houlahan.[84]

Three other poets—Thomas Moore, Lady Wilde, and Michael Moran—helped to solidify the imaginative place of the Exodus narrative in nineteenth-century Ireland. Lady Wilde (mother of Oscar), considered by contemporaries to be "one of Young Ireland's most violent, emotional and inflammatory writers,"[85] found that the earthly action of Exodus modeled a path to freedom from British rule. Wilde's poems, published under the name Speranza in the widely read journal the *Nation*, epitomize the turn toward more aggressively nationalist literature. Of the poems she collects in her 1871 volume, at least eight allude to Exodus, and the two that bookend the collection take the trope as their central theme. Opening the volume is the poem "Dedication: To Ireland," in which Wilde calls out to God,

To come in Sinai thunders down,
And, with His mystic radiance, crown
Some Prophet-Leader, with command
To break the strength of Egypt's band,
And set thee free,
Loved Ireland![86]

While God and some Moses-figure will do the liberating, Lady Wilde relishes the task of stirring her country into action. She invokes the figure of Moses's sister Miriam, who, after passing through the Red Sea, "flung her triumphs to the stars / In glorious chants for freedom won." Through Miriam, Wilde thus creates, as Antoinette Quinn writes, "a role for the woman poet."[87] Quinn suggests that the role is not an entirely satisfactory one, and that Speranza is "a frustrated Miriam, cheated of the opportunity to celebrate"[88] after the uprising of 1848, which did not result in freedom from bondage. Yet the vigor of Wilde's poems also suggests that she thrives by imagining the liberation yet to come.

Exodus offers a language both patriotic and ecumenically religious, and Wilde's poems move between the republican ideal of "Liberty's paean" and "our just rights" to the still deeply embedded typological use of the Israelite analogy, in which the Irish are "The chosen of God"[89] and their struggles echo biblical ones. Liberation from Egypt, in the imperial age of applied typology, was already a metonym for secular, political revolution, but the religious element of divine right and responsibility remains. To what extent the latter genuinely represents a kind of scriptural politics, though, is debatable. The invocation of God here seems less genuinely religious than rhetorical; in "The Year of Revolutions," even if the people have "faith," and even if Wilde calls on God to smite her enemies, freedom will still require action, and patriots and heroes must *stem*, *cross*, and *strike*, not wait for divine intervention:

> With faith like the Hebrew's we'll stem the Red Sea—
> God! smite down the Pharaohs—our trust is in Thee;
> Be it blood of the tyrant or blood of the slave,
> We'll cross it to Freedom, or find there a grave.
>
> . . . .
>
> For the will of a Nation what foe dare withstand?
> Then Patriots, Heroes, strike! God for our Land![90]

Throughout the collection, Wilde entreats her country to awaken from a slumber of servitude, and particularly to move beyond "the conflicts of slave with slave"[91]—an acknowledgment that, like the Israelites, this is a problematic population, not entirely ready for freedom. As Marjorie Howes points out, "Wilde's work is obsessed with leaders," and it is no surprise that Moses emerges as the archetype of the elite leader of a difficult population.[92] The disunity Wilde diagnoses is best treated, in her view, with the civic nationalism of the French Revolution, in which "the stern will of a nation" is unified, and all who oppose it will be swept away.[93] Claiming that both sectarianism and a slave mentality inhibit Irish freedom, Wilde implies that the people must have *more* than faith; they will only be freed through human work and human change. In acknowledging that the population is ambivalent about liberation, Wilde anticipates the work of twentieth-century writers—especially Lady Gregory and James Joyce—for whom this element was what made Exodus both truth-telling and productive as a literary, cultural, and political trope.

By now Exodus was an easily accessible, formulaic, even clichéd metonym for the Irish anticolonial struggle. We find it, for example, as the topic of one of the era's most famous street ballads, "The Finding of Moses in the Nile," by the blind Dublin poet Michael Moran, known popularly as Zozimus. One contemporary explained how the text was resolutely public in nature, performed for "the attentive crowd, which drank in every word as it was spoken."[94] While the ballad begins with a straightforward (if orientalist) retelling of Moses's early life set "on Egypt's plains, where flows the ancient Nile," Moran concludes with the sonorous and familiar language favored by Mangan and Wilde. The biblical story is put into context with what had become a typical patriotic conceit:

> A conquered nation, though down-trod, it still is never crushed,
> A Liberator always comes when Freedom's voice is hushed;
> And so our own dear land, in time we all shall see
> The Saxon rulers gone—Old Ireland shall be free![95]

"The Finding of Moses in the Nile" has fallen into obscurity, but along with the poems of Wilde (and Moore, as we will see), it helped to shore up—across all realms of Irish society—a rhetorical framework within which a future Irish leader (Parnell most especially) could take his place.

Moran's poem is better remembered, however, in its less patriotic form. A street ballad is necessarily fluid, and the fact that different printed versions exist is unsurprising. Yet the playful text that Yeats reprints in his essay on Moran ("The Last Gleeman") in *The Celtic Twilight* (1893), similarly entitled "The Finding of Moses," is radically different from the lines quoted above. As Yeats describes it, Moran "could ill brook solemnity, and before long parodied his own verses in the following ragamuffin fashion,"[96] and it is from this parody that Yeats quotes. If this poem claims in its first line to be, like its more earnest predecessor, set "In Egypt's land, contagious to the Nile,"[97] we know from geography ("I'll search every nook / From Phoenix Park down to Donnybrook"[98]) and dialect that we are in fact in Dublin. Pharaoh's daughter, upon finding the "smiling babby" on "the strand," "tuk it up, and said with accents mild, 'Tare-and-agers, girls, which av yez owns the child?'"[99] Exodus had become a familiar enough story of Ireland that it could be comically relocated to the heart of the Hibernian metropolis, recast as the story of a misplaced bastard child, and subsequently emptied of any religious or national sentiment.

Moran and Wilde, despite their different backgrounds, were both writing in a tradition established earlier in the nineteenth century by the "Bard of Erin," Thomas Moore, whose *Irish Melodies*, in particular, were read across the social and political spectrum in Ireland and Britain—by "poor Irish patriots as well as fashionable Londoners."[100] As Emer Nolan writes, Moore "did more than any other single figure in the nineteenth century to create an Irish nationalist sensibility,"[101] and his nationalism was frequently dressed in biblical narratives. Indeed, some of Moore's best-known works explore Old Testament moments of exodus, freedom, and exile. In his collection *Sacred Songs*, "Sound the Loud Timbrel," subtitled "Miriam's Song," celebrates the triumph of departure from Egypt. Among Moore's most enduring compositions, the song was taken up by African Americans and sung publicly to mark victories against slavery, and later, institutionalized racism.[102] Like Moore's other compositions that do not mark their similarity to the Irish case directly, this song nevertheless evokes it powerfully. In fact it is impossible not to read the Jewish nationalism that characterizes one grouping of the *Songs* (including "Sound the Loud Timbrel"; "Weep, Children of Israel"; "Fall'n is thy throne, O Israel!"; "Awake, Arise, Thy Light is Come"; "Go Forth to the Mount"; and "War Against Babylon!") as an extended metaphor of the Irish case. Moreover, if the Irish tradition of invoking the Israelites was Moore's birthright, his friendship and literary interchange with

Lord Byron would also have encouraged the poet to pursue biblical themes, for Byron was likewise deeply immersed in writing compositions of Jewish nationalism and exile in his *Hebrew Melodies.*[103] Yet Moore's relationship to this material is ambiguous, and a wider reading of his work will demonstrate the beginning of the breakdown of the Israelite analogy—a turning point in Irish discourse.

The connection between the Irish and the Jews was both explicit and unequivocally sympathetic in Moore's early poem "The Parallel," which appeared in the eighth volume of his *Irish Melodies* in 1821. In his journal, Moore called the composition his "Hebraico-Hibernian Melody," and noted that it was "founded upon the whimsical idea of a mad Irish scribbler of the name of Hamilton that we, Paddies, are descended from the Jews—upon which hypothesis I found a parallel between Erin & 'the sad one of Sion'—England of course, Babylon—."[104] Although the poem did not reach the iconic status of ballads like "Silent, O Moyle" or "The Harp that once through Tara's Halls," Stephen Gwynn would later describe it as characteristic of the poet's "extraordinary eloquence."[105] The parallel of the title evokes two nations, not only oppressed but in exile: the Irish, banished both literally and figuratively from their homeland, and the Israelites in their Babylonian captivity. A commensurate experience of misery, rather than a struggle for freedom, links the two peoples "in shame and in sorrow": the Jewish nation with its "wither'd-up heart," and the Irish nation "conquer'd and broken." The Irish, like the Jews, long for days of autonomy and kingship:

> Like thee doth our nation lie conquer'd and broken,
> And fall'n from her head is the once royal crown;
> In her streets, in her halls, Desolation hath spoken,
> And "while it is day yet, her sun hath gone down."[106]

The poem ostensibly concludes with victory for the Jews of the ancient past; yet while Babylon may now "lay low in the dust," the liberated Israelites (and the parallel Irish) seem to remain in melancholy exile. And for Moore, at least in "The Parallel," restoration seems less of a concern than revenge on the oppressor: the poem concludes not with the freedom and return of the Irish/Israelites, but with the utter destruction, and indeed historical annihilation, of England/Babylon, "a ruin at last for the earthworm to cover."

While the ruin of Babylon *implies* an end to exile, no liberated, or liberating, people appear here. The result is an overall sense not just of divine providence, but of human ineffectiveness. Moreover, the grammar of the poem occludes both the agency for liberation and any visibly liberated group. No human leader, no throng of people, no divine figure acts; instead, the oppressing nation metaphorically drinks from its own cup of bitterness—a self-destruction of sorts. But even Babylon itself does not "drink"; it is the *cup* that is made the subject of the stanza's sentence and has "drench'd her own lips." Passivity is reflected too in MacAlise's illustrations for the 1846 edition, in which a young man stares off into the nothing of a blank distance, not seeming to notice the round tower—a synecdoche for Ireland's ancient past—in the valley behind him. If the sons of Ireland do in fact "remember the bright things that bless'd them of old," those memories produce no action. The poem is ostensibly political, but in a way that abstracts what elsewhere is a concrete model for national emancipation. Moore forgoes the struggle and triumph of Exodus for the passive longing of Babylonian exile, and in doing so backs off from the more radical potential of Exodus.[107] National identity inheres not by looking forward to freedom, as it would in Wilde's poems, but by looking back; this is the familiar melancholy note that characterizes so many of Moore's *Melodies.*

But it is not only Moore's nostalgia that undermines his use of the Israelite trope—it is, rather, a more explicit dismantling of his earlier text. Moore footnotes "The Parallel" thoroughly to provide biblical chapter and verse, but it is his first note, in which he explains that "these verses were written after the perusal of a treatise by Mr. Hamilton, professing to prove that the Irish were originally Jews," that is most worthy of our attention. Such genealogies were, we have seen, not uncommon, and the reference does not seem particularly curious until Moore cites Hamilton a second time, in his satirical 1824 "novel" *The Memoirs of Captain Rock.*[108] In a discourse on Captain Rock's ancestry, the Jewish-Irish genealogy is presented not as the inspiration for nationalist nostalgia, but rather as satire, in which the name Rock may have "some connexion with the *Saxum Jacobi*, or Stone of Jacob, which (according to Mr. Hamilton, who has written to prove that the Irish are Jews) was brought from Egypt to Ireland, some time before the general Exod [*sic*] under Moses, by a portion of the tribe of Joseph, called Eranites, and is now under the coronation chair, in Westminster Abbey."[109] If this is familiar material, Moore then proceeds to facetiously rehearse Hamilton's additional "striking proofs" of Jewish ancestry for the Irish—nonsensical tautologies all. "The Irish being thus indisputably proved to be Jews," Moore concludes, "it is to be hoped that the Irish country gentlemen . . . will, when forced to take refuge in the arms of their brethren of Israel, find them considerate and compassionate, if it were for nothing but old consanguinity's sake."[110] Here Moore transforms the Jewish genealogy into a satire of scriptural politics, a newly ironical attitude that unsettles and perhaps even disowns his earlier analogy, and forecasts the way a long-established biblical trope would soon begin to fracture under the pressure of both increased sectarianism and anti-Semitism.[111]

From Israelites to Jews

From Moore to Moran, those who invoked "that chosen tribe" as a model for liberation could not have anticipated that their metaphoric Israelites would soon be arriving, literally, on Irish shores. The new Jewish population would complicate the ways in which both Exodus and the Israelite-Irish analogy more broadly were used in cultural and political discourse in Ireland. A land of extreme emigration from the nineteenth century until the end of the twentieth, Ireland's largest foreign-born population from outside of the United Kingdom and America (whose emigrants were mostly of Irish ancestry) was, until the Celtic Tiger of the 1990s, composed of Jews from Lithuania who arrived in the greatest numbers between the 1870s and 1910s.[112] Israelites had been in Ireland's imagination for centuries, but living Jews presented different challenges from ancient and metaphoric ones; as Elizabeth Cullingford notes, "when the Other with whom the Irish choose to identify is a long-dead civilization this practice of retro-empathy may bolster native pride, but it requires no exertion in the present."[113] "Exertion in the present" was precisely what was now at stake as the Irish confronted a once-rhetorical parallel face to face.

Andrew Gibson offers a useful summary of how the Irish-Jewish analogy becomes troubled in this period of immigration, when, as he writes, "in certain nationalist quarters, as Jews enter Ireland in greater numbers, the Irish-Jewish identification traditional within the culture breaks down."[114] First, Gibson notes that Jews—even the impoverished peddlers arriving from Lithuania—were seen by some Catholic nationalists as colonizers: "They threaten to 'plant their heels' on the people's necks and impose a worse 'slavery' than did Cromwell."[115] In making this link between Jewish and Protestant settlers, these nationalists ironically shore up the Unionist mythology of British chosenness.[116] Consequently, Gibson explains, amid this reanimation of Cromwellian (and British Israelite) rhetoric, nationalists become either anti-Semites or supporters of both literal Jews and the Israelite analogy.[117] The ideological function of the Israelite analogy, so recently used to promote unity within the nationalist movement, splits down sectarian lines.

The fracture that Gibson describes was catalyzed by the Limerick "pogrom" of 1904, in which a Redemptorist preacher initiated a hateful boycott against Jewish businesses, fueled by both racism and economic jealousy.[118] Members of Father Creagh's church badly beat several Jewish men, and Jewish families with businesses were eventually forced to move from the city. Arthur Griffith responded with his own anti-Semitic rant on the front page of the *United Irishman*, calling Jews "usurers and parasites."[119] Yet Griffith does not entirely disown the Irish-Jewish analogy, for he includes one caveat in his polemic, with praise for "those honest and patriotic Jews who desire the re-establishment of the Hebrew nation in Palestine": "For the small minority—the Zionist Jews—the patriotic men who desire to reconstruct the Hebrew nation, and who feel bitterly the humiliation of their race through the sordid pursuit of gold by the majority—we have the same esteem we have for all patriotic and lofty-minded men."[120] The Zionist

Jew, in Griffith's assessment, becomes a metonym for the exiled Israelite longing to return to an ancient homeland. But the non-Zionist Jew—the Jew who is not compelled by the idea of a physical return to the "nation"—is inscribed as the Israelite who stays by the fleshpots of Egypt, engaged in "the sordid pursuit of gold" in the land of the other. Griffith's rhetoric divides the Jew into two peoples, one continuous with its ancient (national) past, one shamefully disconnected from it: what Marilyn Reizbaum describes as Griffith's "bifurcation of Jews into a historical, almost mythological people and a modern European body. . . . the two images, past people and present, are separated . . . allowing for the vilification of one part and the promotion of the other."[121] Jews who seemed to reject the trope of ancient Israelite nationalism threw centuries of Irish rhetoric into confusion.

Along with his increasing anti-Semitism, Griffith developed a resistance to the Israelite analogy, arguing for not only racial, but aesthetic national purity. In 1904, some months after the Limerick incident, he explicitly disavowed Exodus as an Irish narrative. At the national "Feis Ceoil" (Irish Musical Festival) of that year, the prize-winning cantata was "The Exodus: A Sacred Cantata," with words by the poet (and future Easter Rising martyr) Thomas MacDonagh and music by Benedetto Palmieri.[122] The libretto—which, as MacDonagh's biographer Johann Norstedt notes, has been ignored by musical and literary critics[123]—is a straightforward exposition of the biblical text, with solos for Moses, Aaron, Pharaoh, and Miriam. But set amid the cultural nationalism of the revival, the subject was hardly innocuous. Opening with a chorus of Hebrew women calling upon God, the libretto echoed the recent surfeit of Exodus-themed nationalist poetry that had only increased after the death of Parnell (more on this in chapter 2), and it sounds not unlike Wilde: "Long in bondage and chains we have suffered . . . We implore Thee in humble subjection, / The fair land of our fathers restore."[124] The one extended review of the performance was published in Griffith's *United Irishman*, and as Norstedt points out, the review "attacked the cantata on the grounds that neither . . . its music, lyrics, nor general subject had . . . anything to do with Ireland."[125] According to this review, "The Exodus," "despite its disingenuous claim on our reverence for things sacred, must . . . be called foreign."[126] As Norstedt suggests, MacDonagh "must have been considerably annoyed by such criticism; and it is incredible—whether or not MacDonagh had this in mind—that so strident a nationalist newspaper as the *United Irishman* could not see the similarity in the plight of the ancient people of Israel and that of the modern Irish."[127] Griffith, who almost certainly wrote the review himself, was as aware of the analogy as anyone—in fact he had used it himself in his comparative study of Irish and Hungarian nationalism, published in the same year.[128] Thus, rather than an oversight, this is a conscious snub, a pointed attempted to now reject Exodus as "foreign" in a way it had not been perceived before.

Although Griffith did not speak for the entire Catholic community, it was mostly Protestant writers (at least until Joyce) who continued to identify with both ancient and modern Jews.[129] Yeats, in 1901, imagined himself as Moses, and as the following chapter will show, Lady Gregory recycled the Exodus story as an Irish allegory throughout her life. Douglas Hyde repeatedly invoked the Jews—contemporary Jews—as models for national linguistic renewal, and Standish O'Grady would denounce the persecution of Jews, "brothers in a common struggle."[130] Most famously, however, it was the Catholic Michael Davitt who wrote a series of rebuttals to Griffith and the Limerick incident.[131] Upon his death Davitt was honored with a funeral wreath from the Jewish community of Dublin, "in grateful remembrance of Davitt's efforts on behalf of the one race which has suffered more than the Irish,"[132] as Francis Sheehy-Skeffington wrote in 1908. Sheehy-Skeffington described Davitt as "the prophet who had led [the people of Mayo] out of the wilderness,"[133] a trope possibly borrowed from those who had used it of Parnell, but also originating in Fanny Parnell's poem "Michael Davitt," published in the Boston *Pilot* in 1880:

Out of the slime and the squalor,
Out of the slough of despond,
Out of the yoke of Egypt,
Out of the gyve and bond[134]

Fanny Parnell was writing well before her brother Charles Stewart became, for the Irish people, the unequivocal Moses; yet the trope rings prophetic for Davitt as well, who would devote so much energy not only to Irish liberation, but also to Jewish rights and freedoms.

A decade before the events in Limerick, Davitt had made the following speech, published in the *Freeman's Journal*: "The Jews have never to my knowledge done any injury to Ireland. Like our own race, they have endured a persecution the records of which will for ever [*sic*] remain a reproach to the 'Christian' nations of Europe. Ireland has no share in this black record. Our country has this proud distinction—freely acknowledged by Jewish writers—of never having resorted to this un-Christian and barbarous treatment of an unfortunate people."[135] Davitt was echoing an Irish rabbi, Dr. S. Hermann Adler, who had made similar comments when he consecrated the headquarters of the Dublin Hebrew Congregation in 1892, telling his community, "you have come here, my foreign brethren, from a country like unto Egypt of old to a land which offers you hospitable shelter. It is said that Ireland is the only country in the world which cannot be charged with persecuting the Jews."[136] Adler, in turn, was echoing Daniel O'Connell, who had famously supported the Jewish emancipation bill in Britain, writing in 1828, "Ireland has claims on your ancient race, as it is the only Christian Country that I know of unsullied by any act of persecution against the Jews."[137] This transmission of transnational sympathy has been remarked upon, but perhaps even before O'Connell expressed it, the idea was already circulating in Ireland. In a letter written in 1820 and reprinted that year in the *Jewish Expositor and Friend of Israel*, we find much the same conceit expounded by the Rev. L. Way. He writes, "The Scotch have *heads*, the English *hands*, but the *Irish hearts*, and *their desire* is, that Israel may be saved:—this triple cord, bound with love, will not easily break. —The Irish *never persecuted* the Jews, and now they *are blessing them*."[138] The *Jewish Expositor*, it should be noted, proffered an ideology profoundly at odds with anything that could be acceptable to either Irish nationalists or Jews; it was published by the London Society for Promoting Christianity Amongst the Jews, and the "triple cord" was meant to bind Ireland into the British Empire, while the "blessing" of Jews meant their conversion. Irish non-persecution of Jews, then, was a theme apparently shared by British evangelical imperialists, Irish Jews, and Irish nationalists alike.[139] The trope circulates, finally, into Joyce's *Ulysses*, in which the headmaster Mr. Deasy jokes that Ireland never oppressed the Jews because she never let them in (*U* 36).[140] Deasy's anti-Semitism reverses the sympathetic rhetoric that had become part of the conventional wisdom about Jews in Ireland, and Joyce seems to ominously acknowledge that the Irish-Jewish connection central to *Ulysses* is easily reversible in the wrong hands.

The Lost Tribes in Ireland

In 1901, with the excavations at Tara under way, Griffith's paper found an opportunity to attack simultaneously both Jews and British Israelite Unionists: "instead of thanking Providence for the disappearance of ten of the twelve tribes of Jewry, a number of people in different ages had been striving to find them out and inflict them on a world suffering from the villainy of the remaining two."[141] Whether or not the remark originated with Griffith himself, it has the same repeatable quality as Deasy's wisecrack, and it is not surprising that we hear it again, a decade later, in a review of Irish novelist George Birmingham's *The Lost Tribes* (1914).[142] But by the time Birmingham's novel appeared, the British Israelites seem to have been forgotten in Ireland: no Irish reviews of the novel (or English ones, for that matter) make any mention of the group, whose name is evoked in the book's title.[143] And there was no shortage of reviews; Birmingham—the pen name of James Owen Hannay, a Church of Ireland minister and committed cultural nationalist—was hugely popular in his day, and the novel was both widely noticed and well received.[144] While the British Israelite excavation at Tara had been a real political controversy at the turn of the century, it had now passed into the realm of the farcical. Moreover, by 1914 the Israelite analogy had become—as the following chapters will show—increasingly irrelevant in Ireland. Parnell-Moses was long dead; Lady Gregory's 1911 Exodus allegory *The Deliverer* had proved either incomprehensible or unpalatable to Dublin audiences; and a new narrative of Irish liberation, based on Christian theology and shepherded by Patrick Pearse, was ascendant—and soon to be reified by the Easter Rising. Why, then, does Hannay choose to resurrect the Old Testament trope? Resurrect may be too strong a word: the novel is more like a coffin, a final, comic laying to rest of a narrative no longer relevant for Ireland. That Hannay, for whom biblical analogies were genuinely important in all of his writings—novels, sermons, articles, memoirs—should be the one to finally dismiss the presence of Israelites in Erin is perhaps a fitting irony.

There are not many references in Hannay's novel to the British Israelites, but a lost-tribes theory catalyzes the novel's plot. An Irish expatriate, Nathan P. Dann, holds as his singular belief "a sort of modification of the 'British Israel' theory": "he clung to the faith that he and his fellow-countrymen were descended from Ephraim and Manasseh."[145] Dann dies before the story begins, but his lively American wife knows her husband's hobbyhorse; when she arrives in Ireland after his death, Mrs. Dann unwittingly manages, through much goodhearted meddling, to unsettle not only every piety of British Israelite belief, but to destroy any remaining reverence for an Irish biblical heritage. Upon surveying the Irish village of Druminawona, she is struck with the notion that the inhabitants have biblical faces, and she moves quickly to extrapolate from this resemblance. Mrs. Dann, however, is less than doctrinaire in her understanding of her husband's theory, and she perceives the villagers not as Israelites from the Hebrew Bible, but as first-century Jews—the Jews of the New Testament.[146] And they are not just any Jews, but the "worst" Jews, Judas Iscariot and the high priest Caiaphas (or Ananias, she is not sure which): those whose depiction in the gospels helped to instantiate Western anti-Semitism.

In her insistence that these are the forebears of the Irish, Mrs. Dann radically undermines the ostensible appeal of the genealogy. But she also undercuts the entire premise of British Israelite belief, which argues that the Jews of Jesus's time (and hence modern Jews) are ethnically different from the "true" Israelites who had become lost in making their way north to become the Anglo-Saxons of Britain.

If one critical element of British Israelite ideology is the ethnic/racial component that elevates the Anglo-Saxons (and Anglo-Irish) as "true" Israelites against the false Jews of modernity, another is casting the Gaelic Irish as Canaanites. Yet in the novel there is no hint that any one sector of Irish society is more or less a chosen people than any other—Dann (whose name suggests that he *is* descended from the Israelite tribe of Dan) shares his ancestral line with *all* "his fellow-countrymen." Instead of presenting the Israelite genealogy as unifying rhetoric that could overcome Irish cultural and religious divisions, Hannay casts it as the opposite: equally repellent to all.

Even worse than her discovery of "bad" Jews is the fact that Mrs. Dann wants to advertise them. She decides to "boost" the town socially and economically by constructing a tourist trap of religious, artistic, and antiquarian interest: "a Miracle Play, acted by the descendants of those vanished Israelites."[147] Mrs. Dann's miracle play would cast the villagers—both Catholic and Protestant—not merely as Jews, but specifically the most anti-Christian Jews of the Gospels. Any glamour surrounding the lost tribes, any value in biblical genealogy, is turned around: these Jews—Christ's killers, in the tradition of the miracle play—are surely not the ones the Irish would choose for their literal and metaphoric ancestors.[148] Hannay's two lethargic clergymen, the Protestant Mr. Mervyn and the Catholic Father Roche, are in agreement that "we can't have the people of the parish, either Catholic or Protestant, passed off as Jews,"[149] and they must find a way to curtail the scheme, faced with Mrs. Dann's forceful personality and their own stereotypical inefficacy.

Mrs. Dann believes that "there ought to be money in those Ten Lost Tribes."[150] Her plan for boosting the sleepy village seems reasonable enough to the local people, who appreciate her pragmatism and are hoping for a payoff; for the right price, they will adopt any Jews as ancestors. This materialism, which willingly trades on both the holy Bible and Irish antiquarian value, is ultimately one of Hannay's targets. Yet the cumulative effect of Mrs. Dann's mistaken biblical chronology—her casual approach to both scripture and demotic culture, her journalistic cynicism and savvy, and finally her economic pragmatism—is to suggest not so much the dangerous use to which such a genealogy might be put (as in the case of the imperialist British Israelites digging at Tara), but rather, its ultimate powerlessness. The various clergymen who become so involved in preventing the plot to Judaize Druminawona succeed, but only by virtue of Mrs. Dann's distractibility; the lost tribes are not so interesting after all. Hannay's most radical dismissal turns out to be structural: the entire idea of the lost tribes is swiftly banished from the novel once a romantic marriage plot intercedes, carrying the lovely Delia Mervyn and her American suitor, Bobby Sebright, through to their engagement. Mrs. Dann alone regrets that the objections of parish priest, Protestant clergyman, and Catholic bishop have prevented her from "making something out of the Ten Lost Tribes,"[151] but she, too, has moved on. Such unsatisfactory Israelites as those Hannay imagines could not possibly have any place in Irish cultural life.

Hannay takes a cynical measure of the declining value of the Israelite genealogy in Ireland, and perhaps also admits a defeat for biblical narrative in general. If Mrs. Dann is less than particular about the details for her pet project, Father Roche, the Catholic priest, is profoundly uninformed. And consequently (as Mr. Mervyn intuits), he will reject Mrs. Dann's scheme because "it might set people thinking on religious subjects, which is dangerous. It might, since the subject of it was likely to be more or less biblical, lead to an irreverent intimacy with matters better left to the Church."[152] This bit of satire is more or less canned—part of the familiar Protestant disdain for Catholic restriction on Bible-reading. Still, in parodying the "danger" of the Bible, Hannay registers the precarious place of biblical, or more particularly Old Testament, themes, in the years before the Easter Rising. If the Israelite analogy had so recently been worthy of bitter debate in the pages of a nationalist newspaper, a matter of years had rendered it something far more damaging to its rhetorical survival: inconsequential. The arc of the Israelite analogy in Ireland, which had reached its peak around the time of Parnell's death in 1891, was now in a rapid decline.

2

Lady Gregory, Parnell, and the Irish Deliverer

By the late 1880s, with Home Rule on the horizon, it seemed that Ireland had finally found its Moses in the Irish Party leader Charles Stewart Parnell. But in December 1889 Parnell was accused of committing adultery with Katherine O'Shea, and one year later he was unseated from party leadership. He died in October 1891 at the age of forty-five, succumbing, James Joyce wrote, to "a broken heart."[1] This was a more fitting description perhaps than the clinical version offered later—indeed, a heart attack—that could never sufficiently mythologize what was a truly momentous event in Irish political, cultural, and even literary history. This episode that, in other circumstances, might have been remembered as a banal controversy surrounding a fallen politician, was instead transformed into the "Parnell myth," in which the distant and mysterious "uncrowned king of Ireland" and "leader of the Irish race" became Ireland's betrayed messiah, the rebuking ghost of the literary revival. At the time when the controversy took hold, Parnell—and Ireland—had seemed to be approaching an Irish Canaan: "I should like," he had said, "and it is not an unfair thing for me to ask, that I should come within sight of the Promised Land."[2] While that was not to be, the Parnellite mythology that emerged in the early twentieth century nevertheless retained the biblical trope that had been narrating Ireland's struggles for more than two centuries. Exodus provided an especially apt analogy for the story of Parnell, and in turn, Parnell's story offered evidence that Exodus was a viable liberation narrative for Ireland. At least many writers of the revival, and particularly Anglo-Irish ones, saw it that way.

But Parnell's Protestant Ascendancy background, like his relationship with the English O'Shea, appeared to threaten national purity in an increasingly Catholic-identified country. Exodus, then, offered a way of spinning that difference as a necessary part of the liberation story. The Anglo-Irish Protestant deliverer was, paradoxically, the key to the nation's freedom from England; as in the biblical model, Moses's ability to lead the Israelites from Egypt was inseparable from his upbringing as an Egyptian prince in Pharaoh's palace. Parnell, as the leader who brought the Irish to the verge of the promised land, was the protagonist of a story of Irish liberation that depended on his Ascendancy background, his difference from those he led. It was a powerful way for Anglo-Irish writers (who knew that theirs was a socially and politically declining class) to figure their own importance, and even centrality, in a changing Ireland—not least because, as the previous chapter has shown, Exodus was a shared vocabulary, already part of Catholic Ireland's political and literary self-image.

Exodus was just one way for the Anglo-Irish to fit themselves into a narrative of Irish Home Rule and affirm their cultural relevance as their political and economic power waned.[3] Seamus Deane maps out a much wider range of Anglo-Irish appropriations in which the Ascendancy wrote their story as "the spiritual heroics of a fading class." As Deane writes, "Irish culture became the new property of those who were losing their grip on Irish land."[4] The process of Anglo-Irish self-authentication through the revival was not, however, unselfconscious. John Eglinton, with typical astuteness, diagrammed the ironies in 1918: "For the past quarter of a century we have taken over from the Mere Irishman all of his terms and traditions, and have been chanting the sorrows of Kathleen ni Houlahan in strains 'more Irish' than anything in the ancient language of the country. Theoretically, this literature ought to be in that language . . . just as the Agnostics and Protestants who have chiefly produced this literature ought in theory to be pious Catholics."[5] The "pious Catholics" Eglinton invokes would have much the same idea about their rights to the culture. Thus just as this chapter maps the emergence of an Ascendancy-centered Parnellite-Mosaic mythology, we will begin to see signs of its dismantling by an unconvinced and ever more empowered Catholic Ireland. A focus on the production and public response to Lady Gregory's 1911 play *The Deliverer*—as Yeats described it, a "symbolical play ostensibly about Moses but really about Parnell"[6]—illustrates these cultural and political shifts as they played out on the stage of the Abbey. What follows, then, is an investigation of the developing depiction of Parnell as Moses in the public sphere, but also a preview of Ireland's eventual rejection of the Exodus analogy.

The Uncrowned King of Ireland

It is not surprising that Parnell should have been described as Moses given the genealogy of the Exodus trope in the Irish political imagination. What was remarkable, as F. S. L. Lyons notes, was the extent to which "Parnell . . . embodied, to a degree no one had previously approached, the idea of the prophetic figure destined to lead Israel to the promised land."[7] Embodiment is key here; there was an uncanny fit to the Moses-Parnell parallel that exceeded the general longing for leadership that inspired it. Parnell was Moses not only because he would be a liberator of his people—Daniel O'Connell, the author of Catholic emancipation in 1829, is known as "The Liberator" in Irish tradition[8]—and not even simply for his Ascendancy background. Parnell's mystique, even during his lifetime, was rather more complicated: in some descriptions he seems not just ethnically or religiously, but even mystically, other. His political rival, William O'Brien, records a meeting in 1886 in which Parnell appears as almost supernatural: "The overpowering fascination lay in the unearthly half-extinguished eyes flickering mournfully out of their deep caverns, the complexion of dead clay. . . . It was the apparition of a poet plunged in some divine anguish or a mad scientist."[9] Much of the language here—unearthly, half-extinguished, flickering, mournfully, dead clay, apparition, divine anguish—suggests a man only liminally human, a man half-dead, or undead, a haunting presence: perhaps, as one scholar has suggested, Parnell as vampire.[10] Of Parnell's more human qualities, his often remarked-upon mediocrity as an orator (or in the admiring terms used by his contemporaries, his reserve and his silence[11]) was shared with Moses, who says to God, "I am not eloquent . . . but I am slow of speech, and of a slow tongue."[12] In fact Parnell, like Moses, was said to have a stutter.

Michael Davitt, for whom Parnell was, as for so many others, the "Moses of the Irish race,"[13] summed up the leader's seemingly paradoxical persona in his book *The Fall of Feudalism in Ireland* (1904): "He was a Protestant, leading a nation chiefly Catholic; a landlord, commanding tenants in a war against his own class; a cold, reserved man, at the head of one of the most warm-hearted and impulsive of races; a sober, unemotional speaker, who never quoted an Irish poet but once, and did it wrong, in a country remarkable for passion and ornate oratory; a public man and leader who treated his party with icy aloofness for years, who lived away from Ireland most of his time."[14] Davitt furthermore notes, "his immense popularity with the Irish people was not due to any Celtic qualities. Of these he had not even a trace. There was no racial affinity between him and them."[15] Joyce would echo the theme in his Trieste lecture of 1907, "Ireland, Island of Saints and Sages," describing Parnell as "the most formidable man that ever led the Irish, but in whose veins there was not even a drop of Celtic blood."[16] To add yet another complication, Joyce observes Parnell's "crowning disgrace": that "he spoke with a distinct English accent."[17]

After Parnell's death, the Irish imagining of him as an exceptional figure only increased. Standish O'Grady is recognized as one of Parnell's first mythologizers,[18] and in his seminal book *The Story of Ireland* (1894) he inscribes Parnell as heir to the legendary heroes of the Tuatha de Danaan and "the misty Milesius and his misty Milesians."[19] In the book's last pages O'Grady, whose politics were Unionist, describes with respect and awe the funeral that made a nation pause: "While his followers were committing Charles Parnell's remains to the earth, the sky was bright with strange lights and flames. . . . Truly the souls of men were widely and deeply troubled that night."[20] Years later in "Parnell's Funeral" (1935), Yeats likewise described the foreboding sky that so many had noted that evening: "A bundle of tempestuous cloud is blown / About the sky; where that is clear of cloud / Brightness remains; a brighter star shoots down."[21] The specter of Parnell would continue to trouble the souls of men and women "widely and deeply" for many years to come, the belief in his haunting ghost accompanied also by a legend that Parnell had not, in fact, ever really died. Lady Gregory, for example, had recorded her encounter in Galway with "an old man . . . speaking with many gestures, his voice rising, and a crowd gathering about him. 'Tha se beo, tha se beo'—'he is living, he is living,' I heard him say over and over again. I asked what he was saying and was told: 'He says that Parnell is alive yet.'"[22] Yet this mythologizing is not merely hagiography; it becomes a means of social action, an intervention in the intense debate about how "authentic" Irish culture could include (or not include) Anglo-Irish politicians and writers.

The Battle of Two Civilizations

At this moment so critical to the Ascendancy's survival within the narrative of Irish culture,[23] Protestant writers like Yeats and Gregory were often at odds with their Irish Ireland colleagues. Two leading nationalist papers, D. P. Moran's *Leader* and Arthur Griffith's *United Ireland*, widely disseminated the position that Ireland must disentangle itself from the colonial power in all aspects of life, effectively shunning Anglo-Irish culture. Susan Harris points out that the Irish Ireland version of nationalism, "the vision of a restored, purified, and idealized Irish culture," was the literary movement's fiercest opponent, characterizing the negative public responses to the Irish Literary Theatre's early productions.[24] Even as Gregory and Yeats invested their plays with Irish culture, history, and mythology, their Irish Ireland colleagues generally dismissed these efforts. While today's scholars no longer subscribe to the false binary of "ideological nationalists" (Griffith, Moran) versus "independent artists" (Yeats, Joyce), there was clearly a split in Ireland's cultural/literary community.[25]

Moran openly acknowledged the sectarianism that vexed Irish cultural nationalism; he described it as "the Battle of Two Civilizations," and for him it could only be resolved by a complete rejection of ambiguity or hybridity in Irish life. He diagnosed Ireland's problem as the failure to develop a "distinct civilization";[26] in other words, Irish culture had been adulterated by English influence. Unrelenting in his attacks on the literature of the revival, Moran fulminated against plays like Yeats's parable of aristocratic superiority *The Countess Cathleen* (1899) and Synge's sexually subversive *The Shadow of the Glen* (1903); he charged the playwrights with undermining Irish purity in a number of ways, from maligning the chastity of Irish womanhood to misrepresenting the piety and morality of Irish peasants. One such attack of this genre, among many by Moran, Griffith, and Frank Hugh O'Donnell,[27] was this comment on *The Countess Cathleen* by the Rev. George O'Neill: "When one thinks what the general history of the Irish peasant has been—a history of religious and political martyrdom, of saints and rebels, of starvation *with the blessing of the priest preferred to all the flesh-pots of the proselytizer*—then it does seem cruel that a theatre professing to be above all things sympathetically national should at its first performance show them forth as demoralised poltroons, starvelings in soul as well as body."[28] But the Irish, in spite of their supposed piety, still yearn for the fleshpots of Egypt; as Harris writes, plays by Yeats and Synge (she refers specifically to *On Baile's Strand* and *The Playboy of the Western World*) assume "that the purity Griffith and the nationalists are defending is an impossible and unrecoverable thing."[29] Some revivalists refused to sanitize the reality.

Lady Gregory's plays were never as controversial as Yeats's or Synge's, and they incited no riots, but as a director of the Abbey she was still continually embattled. Lyons describes her as "perhaps more interested in reconciling opposites than in defining differences,"[30] and this conventional wisdom is endorsed by Ben Levitas in the comment that Lady Gregory tended to mollify Abbey audiences, "build bridges rather than knock them down."[31] If this was true in her life—and her most recent biographer, Judith Hill, also stresses Gregory's peacemaking persona—in some of her plays Gregory explores precisely where reconciliation fails. *The Deliverer* (1911) is certainly a departure from conciliatory tendencies, and this is precisely what makes the play work as an Irish version of the biblical Exodus. For the Israelites, the time in the wilderness was one of contention and resistance to liberation; Gregory must have seen the narrative as both descriptive of and instructive for an Ireland also on the (perilous) verge of freedom. But before Gregory set her Parnellite allegory in Pharaoh's Egypt, the link between Exodus and Parnell had been steadily developing for two decades.

Ireland's Moses

Parnell gave the most important speech of his life in the British Parliament's Committee Room 15 in December 1890. Fighting to retain his leadership and closing his appeal with an echo of Exodus, Parnell entreated his colleagues that "I should come within sight of the Promised Land; that I should come with you, having come so far, if not to the end of this course, that I should at least come with you as far as you will allow and permit me to come with you, at least until it is absolutely sure that Ireland and I can go no further."[32] It was Tim Healy who had first provided the association between Parnell and Moses—remarkably, because Healy would in a matter of months transform from supporter into foremost "betrayer" of the Home Rule Party leader (not to mention special enemy of Lady Gregory, Yeats, and Joyce).[33] In December Healy would lead more than half of the Irish MPs out of Committee Room 15 to form a new party leadership, but initially he declaimed, in a vote of confidence for Parnell, that the Irish leader "should not be abandoned 'within sight of the Promised Land.'"[34] The Exodus trope was then rapidly appropriated and deployed not only by Parnell but by his entire (then still unified) party. At the same public meeting during which Healy voiced what would be short-lived support of Parnell, the "American delegation," led by other (soon to be) anti-Parnellites Dillon and O'Brien, offered a pledge of support echoing Healy's theme of Exodus. Their statement read, "We stand firmly by the leadership of the man who has brought the Irish people through unparalleled difficulties and dangers, from servitude and despair to the very threshold of emancipation."[35] Several days later a *Freeman's Journal* editorial reported that "Ireland has with one voice pronounced her wish that this man should continue to guide her progress from servitude to home rule."[36] Although the "one voice" was soon to fracture irreparably, the Exodus journey would continue, for many years, to serve as the formula that dominated the discourse around Parnell—a movement from bondage to freedom that always seemed to stop at the threshold. In an illustration in *United Ireland* a month after his death, a robed, beatific, Moses-like Parnell gestures to the distant, light-filled Promised Land of "INDEPENDENCE." He stares into the eyes of a female sword-bearing warrior wearing a sash denoting her as "REBEL CORK," his right arm clearly showing her the path that now must be taken in order to enter Canaan.[37]

Parnell had called up the Exodus trope as early as 1877 at a meeting in Manchester, describing the English as "taskmasters."[38] Yet the earliest notion of Parnell himself as Moses oddly opposes the liberating image that would eventually become standard. In 1881 when Gladstone had imprisoned Parnell for working with the radical Land League, the prime minister used a biblical scene to describe Irish subversion. Gladstone claimed, in a speech that was printed in the *Times* and much quoted afterward,[39] that Parnell's plan was "to stand as Moses stood between the living and the dead; to stand there, not as Moses stood, to arrest but to extend the plague."[40] Michael Valdez Moses characterizes the image of Parnell here as "an inverted or demonic Moses, a false prophet and tyrannical liberator who inhabits the tenebrous realm between life and death, an alien and malignant force with the necromantic power to hasten the plague even to the shores of England itself."[41] Valdez Moses further points out that Gladstone has confused, whether purposefully or not, Moses with Aaron, who is in fact the figure described in the Book of Numbers. For Gladstone, Parnell's intimacy with radical agrarian reformers highlights the indeterminacy of the Irish leader's racial and cultural identity—he is imagined as a figure of contagion between Anglo-Irish respectability and the outrages of the "Mountainy Men." There is also perhaps a suggestion that this plague-ridden Moses endangers England by reason of his Jewishness, which renders him not only dangerously hybrid but also, according to the period's racial theories, physically degenerated,

1. "Thou Wilt Vindicate his Memory!" *United Ireland*, November 7, 1891.

a trait also ascribed to the Irish.[42] Casting Parnell as a liminal and contagious Moses evokes prejudicial attitudes about both peoples.[43]

The demonic Moses had appeared before in the English press. As Michael Ragussis writes, "the story of Moses in Egypt was used in Victorian England, especially in the 1870s, to underscore the idea of the secret Jew who subverts and eventually destroys the dominant culture in which he lives. . . . *Punch* ominously suggests the way in which the Jewish premier [Disraeli] leads his adopted people into (rather than out of) captivity."[44] But Ireland hardly had reason to identify with the powerful empire of Egypt, as opposed to the enslaved Israelites. Neither was the anti-Semitism that underpins the demonic Moses as widespread in Ireland as it was in England.[45] Even Griffith, among the most vocal of Ireland's anti-Semites and one who would, ironically, specifically reject Exodus as a "foreign" narrative,[46] would use the Moses trope as a model for nationalism. In his 1904 book *The Resurrection of Hungary: A Parallel for Ireland*, he wrote that Hungarian Count István Széchenyi "led his country within sight of the promised Land."[47] For Ireland Moses was still, unambiguously, a figure of liberation.

There was, however, one other occasion on which the trope was inverted and Parnell was explicitly opposed to Moses. The *National Press* published an anonymously written (and libelous) charge that Parnell had embezzled money from the Land League, and it included the following commentary: "If Mr. Parnell debauched Mrs. O'Shea, one of the commandments delivered to us by Moses called this 'adultery.' If he appropriated the moneys left in trust with him—and we are prepared to prove that he did—the same old fashioned law-giver called that 'theft.'"[48] This passage functions to doubly undermine the rhetorical power that Healy had invested in Parnell by identifying him with Moses the year before—and in fact, Malcolm Brown speculates that the author of the charge may have been Healy himself—attempting, perhaps, to undo an already powerful mythology. While Parnell is made into a hypocrite, one who identifies with the leader while breaking his laws, Moses himself becomes an "old fashioned law-giver" deprived of his revolutionary associations. The "law-giver" is, moreover, connected to a tradition that has clearly been superseded, as the Old Testament is superseded by the New, and Jewish law obviated by Christian grace. Along very similar lines would Pearse eventually dismantle and replace Irish uses of Exodus.

Yet writers of the literary revival eagerly took up the story of Moses, in part because of the very qualities that allowed some politicians to repurpose it in the ways described above: Exodus was in-between, hybrid, and even its revolutionary impulses contained their own opposites. Exodus was, moreover, about being on the cusp of something momentous, so that even Parnell's failure to obtain Home Rule would not undermine his place in the story of Irish freedom. R. Barry O'Brien's best-selling 1898 biography *The Life of Charles Stewart Parnell*—the book so influential for both Joyce and Yeats[49]—concludes, "[Parnell] brought Ireland within sight of the Promised Land. The triumph of the national cause awaits other times, and another Man."[50] Joyce, in turn, echoes O'Brien in the close of his 1912 essay "The Shade of Parnell," similarly describing a leader who, "like another Moses, led a turbulent and unstable people from the house of shame to the verge of the Promised Land."[51] Both authors perhaps owe something to Yeats, whose elegy for Parnell, "Mourn—and then Onward," likewise concludes with the march toward freedom. Published in *United Ireland* upon the leader's death in 1891, the poem apparently made an impression on readers of the paper: in the next installment of the weekly, a letter took up Yeats's, previously Parnell's, imagery, speaking of the betrayal as the "fierce rending of a noble-hearted leader by men whom he had led so bravely and so patiently through the weary wilderness and to the very frontier of the Promised Land."[52]

"Mourn—and then Onward" is widely acknowledged as bad poetry—deemed "embarrassing"[53] by Lyons, and possibly even felt so by Yeats himself, who never reprinted it in any edition of his work. Scholars have given it little attention, but the poem is not so banal as some have suggested. Its description of life in the wilderness of post-Parnell Ireland is worth quoting in its entirety:

> Ye on the broad high mountains of old Eri,
> Mourn all the night and day,
> The man is gone who guided ye, unweary,
> Through the long bitter way.
> Ye by the waves that close in our sad nation
> Be full of sudden fears,
> The man is gone who from his lonely station

Has moulded the hard years.
Mourn ye on grass-green plains of Eri fated,
For closed in darkness now
Is he who laboured on, derided, hated,
And made the tyrant bow.
Mourn—and then onward, there is no returning,
He guides ye from the tomb;
His memory now is a tall pillar, burning
Before us in the gloom.[54]

Although the poem is described by Brown as "a doctrinaire statement of the Fenian line,"[55] its ambiguities override such a clear position. Rather, as Sam Alexander illustrates in his attentive close reading, "the dominant tone of the poem with regard to the future is one of radical uncertainty," and the repeated images of "closing in" render somewhat disingenuous the revolutionary energies of the final stanza.[56] Yeats's poem, then, inscribes an important tension within the Exodus narrative: on one hand, there is the triumphal, providential, "fated" element of Exodus—the divine pillar of fire leading the Israelite-Irish on through the wilderness, the impression that Parnell continues to guide his people after death. On the other hand, Yeats also articulates why, precisely, Exodus could narrate the story of Irish devolution: both are narratives of *earthly* struggle, a "long bitter way" fraught with sadness, "sudden fears," alienation, and loneliness. Even with Parnell as a Godlike pillar of fire, Yeats suggests that the Irish will have forty years of wandering before they will reach their promised land.

A decade after Parnell's death, Yeats pledged himself and the Irish Literary Theatre to the biblical paradigm, this time highlighting more precisely its social relevance for the Ascendancy: "Moses was little good to his people until he had killed an Egyptian; and for the most part a writer or public man of the upper classes is useless to this country till he has done something that separates him from his class."[57] Moses, of course, had killed the Egyptian after witnessing the man's cruel treatment of a Hebrew worker; Parnell had opposed his own financial interests by working for Land Act legislation that transferred ownership from landlords to tenants. In his own writing of this period, both imaginative and critical, Yeats aligned himself with the political grievances and literary culture of the Irish poor. When Trinity College Professor Robert Atkinson claimed in 1899 that "all folklore is essentially abominable," Yeats responded with a letter to the *Daily Express* asserting that members of Atkinson's obsolete academic class—whose cynicism he attributed to "the bitterness of agrarian revolution" and "political excitement"—must be pushed "from their stools."[58] Yeats advocated idealism and imagination, "a criticism of life which will weigh all Irish interests, and bind the rich and the poor in one brotherhood."[59] As for the rest of the Ascendancy, Yeats wrote that they would "wander forty years in the wilderness that all who have sinned a particular sin might die there."[60] Further proof of Yeats's and Gregory's commitment to nationalism, their own "killing of an Egyptian," would come in 1902, with the allegory of violent rebellion *Kathleen ni Houlihan*. The play, in which a young man of the country marches out to battle to die for Ireland's freedom, would famously cause Yeats at the end of his life to wonder if he (never "they," although the play was co-written) had inspired the events of 1916: "Did that play of mine send out / Certain men the English shot?"[61]

We now know much of *Kathleen* to be Gregory's work, despite Yeats's claim of authorship.[62] And it seems Yeats had also "borrowed" the Moses theme—both the killing of the Egyptian and the forty years of wandering—from Gregory, who had written to Wilfrid Blunt in 1900, "I am . . . trying . . . to help every movement that brings back dignity to the country . . . while politicians . . . do their forty years wandering in the wilderness."[63] In her note to *The Deliverer*, Gregory publically reclaimed the sayings as her own: "I used to say in defense of friends of mine, who were attacked for wild acts, and Mr. Yeats borrowed my saying, that Moses was of no use to his people until he had killed an Egyptian. Then I began to say in relation to a 'gran rifiuto' of later days that some who had turned upon their leader would have their forty years of walking the sand. More lately in Kiltartan, I was told by one who had been present at the last meeting held by that deserted leader, how those who had crowded to him before had left him by order, and how fiery his words were and how white was his face. And, it was said 'The ancient Jews turned against Moses in the same way'" (303). In *The Deliverer* Gregory examines the elite figure of Moses, and more radically she pushes the episodes of grumbling against him in the wilderness to their inadmissible conclusion. The Israelites not only complain to their deliverer; they murder him. Putting pressure on the story of the Exodus, Gregory exposes its more unpalatable meanings; she looks to moments of ambivalence about liberation and recasts them as the central drama of the play. This was not only a literary reimagining but a political one: to admit the fractures in Irish society was also to choose sides in the nascent debate about cultural purity.

Lady Gregory's Bible Lessons

In the 1950s Herbert Howarth offered a Freudian formula for life after Parnell: "The Irish committed the crucial act of killing their prophet, and the guilt, the desire to purify the guilt . . . the belief that sacrifice assures rebirth, gave them irresistible vigour in the next generation."[64] Although this is an oversimplification that elides the significance of class, religion, and politics, Howarth's psychological-anthropological reading pinpoints a narrative of the sacrificial leader that was part of the European zeitgeist in the early twentieth century. Frazer's *The Golden Bough* and the writings of Nietzsche were influential for Yeats, Moore, and other writers of the Irish revival,[65] but it is Freud's vision of Moses as a sacrificial leader that most uncannily captures the concerns of the Irish imagination in the aftermath of Parnell. Indeed, in *The Deliverer* Lady Gregory seems to anticipate the narrative Freud constructs in his 1939 book *Moses and Monotheism*, in which Freud provocatively argues that Moses was an Egyptian and not in fact Hebrew by birth; that he was murdered by the Hebrews after bringing them out of Egypt to a new land; and that after several generations the people repressed the act of his murder from their national memory, becoming, in the guilt-laden process, monotheistic.[66] For Freud, "it is easy to imagine that one of [the Israelite revolts against Moses] came to another end than the text admits,"[67] and this murder of Moses is precisely the climax of Gregory's play too. The oedipal foundation of Freud's narrative, "a hero is a man who stands up manfully against his father and in the end victoriously overcomes him,"[68] jars against the well-established Arnoldian gendering of Irish-English relations, in which a feminine Erin and a masculine England are figured in sexual, not filial, union or disunion.[69] (It is also at odds with the story of Cuchulain, who unknowingly murders his own son.) Yet the similarities between Gregory's and Freud's readings of Exodus are striking.

Perhaps it was Gregory's extensive biblical training, which I will come to shortly, that allowed her—like Freud—to appreciate Exodus as a national narrative intensely rooted in "misdeeds" and ambivalence rather than triumphalism, and in her play she brings these traces to the surface. For both Freud and Gregory (as for Joyce in *Ulysses*), the important question about Exodus seems to be the one that Cathy Caruth, in her book on trauma, isolates as framing *Moses and Monotheism*: "In what ways is the history of a culture, and its relation to a politics, inextricably bound up with the notion of departure?"[70] While earlier uses of Exodus may have looked to the future arrival in the promised land, it is departure that is central to *The Deliverer*, and in the play Gregory reminds her audience that this painful extrication is also the central issue for Irish liberation from colonial rule.

Nowhere was the anxiety about a national departure—cultural, economic, and political—represented more publicly or with more energized controversy than at the Abbey Theatre, where so many of the nation's conflicts played out amid jeering from the audience and lectures from the stage. Between the well-documented riots surrounding performances of Synge's *The Playboy of the Western World* (1907) and O'Casey's *The Plough and the Stars* (1926), the production of Gregory's 1911 play offers a more subtle, but equally compelling, narrative of revivalist tensions. Gregory's self-described "crystallising of the story, as the people tell it, of Parnell's betrayal,"[71] evinces an unmitigated disgust with the unaccountable, vacillating sympathies of the Irish-Israelites.[72] Rather than following the King's Nurseling—the

Moses figure—out of Egypt to their longed-for homeland, the slaves stone him and throw him to the King's vicious cats, who complete the murder and literally destroy its traces: "They'll have the face ate off him ere morning" (276). This allegory of the renunciation, by Ireland's Home Rule Party, of their leader was picked up by Joyce the following year in the famous conclusion to his essay "The Shade of Parnell" (1912): "They did not throw him to the English wolves; they tore him to pieces themselves."[73] But what has generally been read as a crystallization, to use Gregory's word, of her post-Parnell bitterness, is in fact far more complex than has been recognized (with the exception of Joseph Valente's excellent new treatment of the play).[74] Rather, the play itself and the ways in which Dublin audiences responded to it are part of a larger story about how the nationalist Anglo-Irish, and Lady Gregory in particular, imagined their participation in the birth of a new Ireland. "We are not working for Home Rule; we are preparing for it,"[75] Gregory had frequently told colleagues at the Abbey Theatre, and what she reveals in *The Deliverer* is a people unprepared for liberation—politically, culturally, and spiritually. Here Gregory offers her most sustained and penetrating responses to the challenges of Irish devolution, and the looking glass she held up to audiences was met with disgust and disavowal.

Of all the revivalists, Gregory was almost certainly the best schooled in the biblical themes and stories that so often informed nationalist rhetoric in Ireland. Her traditional Protestant upbringing meant that, as Gregory recalled, "the Bible was read through and through at family prayers from year's end to year's end. . . . A chapter of the Old Testament in the morning, at evening prayer a chapter of the New."[76] Initially, though, the Bible seemed at home in Ireland not for the political analogies that would eventually become so central to Gregory's work even beyond *The Deliverer*, but for its literary affinities with Irish speech and writing. Lucy McDiarmid and Maureen Waters note that Gregory later reflected on how her weekly Bible lessons "gave her an appreciation of poetic language and prepared her 'to understand and recognize the beauty of our Irish dialect.'"[77] As Ann Saddlemyer describes it, the dialect was indeed "reminiscent of the King James version of the Bible and the Anglican Book of Common Prayer."[78] "Ordinary living speech" in Ireland, Gregory explained, "had the art common to Hebrew poets of repeating in the second part of the sentence an idea embodied in the first."[79] She imagined that a peasant ballad might preserve the sorrows of the country in something akin to the Old Testament psalms, "as was done for the Hebrew people."[80] Perhaps such ideas were fostered as Gregory learned Irish with her son Robert; their text was a translation of the Scriptures.[81] Certainly John Eglinton must have pleased Gregory with his compliment on her translation of *Cuchulain of Muirthemne*, the great mythological cycle of Ulster: "The style which you adopt I think you more than justify, and I take leave to congratulate you on having produced what will no doubt be the 'authorized version' of the 'Irish Old Testament.'"[82]

The particular connection between biblical narratives and Irish literature was also enacted in the way Gregory first acquired and read popular Fenian ballads: only after "repeating on . . . Sunday evenings Bible verses learned during the week" did the young Gregory earn sixpence to purchase the coveted "paper covered collections of national ballads, *The Harp of Tara*, *The Irish Song Book*."[83] Perhaps the link between biblical verses and Irish nationalist literature was accidental for Gregory the child, but the relationship was clearly meaningful for Gregory the playwright. The Bible would become for her not only a means of encountering Irish patriotism, but a way of interrogating it. The Parnell-Moses analogy had become trite and predictable by the turn of the century, but Gregory reinstates its meaningfulness in *The Deliverer*, in which Exodus becomes a site for subversive and incisive critique of an Ireland fumbling toward independence. As a later Abbey dramatist would write, "the birth of a nation is no immaculate conception,"[84] and Gregory's play bears this out in both graphic and subtle ways.

The Deliverer

From the start, *The Deliverer* articulates a fundamental difficulty of national emancipation: the simultaneous attraction to and repulsion from alterity, embodied in the archetype of the elite—and perhaps racially different—liberator. The very name of the King's Nurseling suggests that he remains in some essential way linked to the royal household into which he was adopted by Pharaoh's daughter, as do the alternative titles that Gregory noted on a draft of the play: *The King of Egypt's Son*; *The King of Foreign's Son*; *The King's Nurseling*; *Pharaoh's Nurseling*.[85] All of the titles mark the significance of the deliverer's elite status as a very particular sort of outsider to the people, and one slave worries, "he might maybe get through all the dangers and into the good country. It is himself would take the credit then, and be maybe craving to make our laws" (272). The brickmaking "Israelites," although initially enchanted by the King's Nurseling—who, as in the biblical text, kills an Egyptian overseer, discovers his Israelite heritage, and begins the process of freeing his people from the colonial "over-government"—soon begin to turn against him. Here, clearly, is one of the ironies that Gregory means to expose: whereas Moses/Parnell's Ascendancy background is the very thing that makes him appealing to the people, it is also perceived as a threat to national unity.

The motif of the elite leader had been explored a decade before *The Deliverer* in *The Bending of the Bough*, written for the Irish Literary Theatre by George Moore and produced in 1900.[86] The play's Parnell figure, Jasper Dean, is beloved by the people of Northhaven, a small country at the mercy of the industrially advanced neighboring isle, Southhaven. Dean, with his Southhaven background, is told, "your appeal is stronger because you are not of the people; you are the romantic element outside them, the delight they follow always."[87] *The Bending of the Bough* acknowledges the allure of Dean's pedigree, but as in Gregory's play, the hero is incapable of producing a happy ending for the downtrodden nation that stands for Ireland. Dean faces the choice of marrying his beloved Millicent Fell, a woman from Southhaven (read England), or fighting for the rights of his country—a decision that represents a clear opposition, since Millicent's financial interests are directly opposed to Northhaven's success. He chooses love and retires from politics. Although Millicent compares herself to the biblical Ruth, she is in fact her opposite: instead of joining her husband's people, Miss Fell [the name itself implies her lover's downfall] threatens to assimilate Dean into (English) banality and materialism. As Dean's advisor Kirwan tells him, "Miss Fell is the temptation that Southhaven sent you, and she sends to each some insidious temptation. Southhaven is always beside us to tempt us in our moments of weakness. No sooner do we become united behind any man than she comes to him with her hands full of bribes."[88] Dean succumbs to the fleshpots of Egypt that are Southaven; he fails in circumstances similar to Parnell, but by choice, and so without the glamour of betrayal or martyrdom. Moore's Moses-like Dean is not destroyed by his own people; he simply prioritizes romantic love over love of the nation. In much of Moore's later work, discussed in chapter 3, the failure of the deliverer to liberate his people would be more dramatic—as it was in Gregory's version of the Parnell story, in which the stones cast were real ones. What appears in Moore's play as disappointment surfaces again in *The Deliverer* as murderous betrayal.

In 1900 Gregory had felt the instinct to moderate Yeats's promise to their audience of more "patriotic" plays,[89] as this was distinctly not in line with the Irish Literary Theatre's mission statement to be "outside all the political questions that divide us," as they had written in 1897.[90] By 1911, however, she clearly felt differently about producing political material, and if *The Deliverer* cloaks its politics in allegory, it nevertheless makes a far stronger statement than Moore's play had. Indeed, to suggest, as Malcolm Brown does, that the play registers merely desperation—"it seems plain that Lady Gregory's object in *The Deliverer* was to borrow Parnell's luster to refurbish the image of her social class,"[91] he writes—is to greatly oversimplify the play and the playwright. If the play indeed affirms Ascendancy importance, it is in a very particular way: not as a now-outmoded class of landowners, but as a group who might offer political leadership in a time of revolution. And while Parnell had introduced the possibility of Anglo-Irish inclusion, his failure to bring Home Rule and the people's failure to follow him—two disappointments already realized—complicate that story.

Gregory, moreover, hardly idealizes the Ascendancy in the play; their degeneration is outlined in the opening lines, as Malachi explains the disintegrating feudal contract: "The time I was rising we were treated fair enough. But the nice stock is all done away with now, and buried and gone to the grave" (257). He adds, "there is nothing left in it at this time but tyrants and schemers." The Ascendancy is revealed as cruel and irresponsible in a notably Anglo-Irish way—"following foxes with huntsmen and hounds, or fowling after snipe and teal" (261). Yet while the play criticizes the Ascendancy, neither can it be described as patriotic in a nationalist sense: the Israelite laborers who represent the Catholic Irish are revealed as even less satisfactory citizens. They are, for one thing, hypocritically attracted to the King's Nurseling because of, rather than in spite of, his elite culture. It seems to have been a prevailing theme at the time, at least among certain Ascendancy writers. Just a week after *The Deliverer* played at the Abbey, Lord Dunsany premiered his similarly symbolic play *King Argimenes and the Unknown Warrior* on the same stage, convinced that Lady Gregory had plagiarized his theme. Ben Levitas points out that "it was as likely a shared capacity to conjure the zeitgeist,"[92] and indeed, Dunsany's play has only a superficial (if notable) resemblance.[93] Assuredly both the King's Nurseling and Argimenes are Parnellite heroes, allegories of Anglo-Irish leadership, and what the plays do have profoundly in common is exemplified in this exchange from *Argimenes*:

> ARGIMENES. Why would they not follow me?
>
> ZARB. Because you look like a slave. They will never follow a slave, because they are slaves themselves, and know how mean a creature is a slave. If you looked like a king they would follow you.[94]

In *The Deliverer*, the people themselves explain how little they wish to have a leader who inhabits their miserable condition; when the Nurseling takes off his royal robes, the slaves grow suspicious: "He has put on poor clothes like our own for a mockery" (272). Insecure and oversensitive, Gregory's Israelite-Irish cannot see the socially constructed—and in fact, unstable—nature of identity. It is left to the King's Nurseling to articulate: "Yesterday I was son to the King's daughter, and to-day I do not know, east or west, to what tribe or family I belong" (265). While the deliverer's elite background is valuable, it is not biological, and the racial essentialism that energizes the play's misguided slaves mirrors what Gregory saw as Irish Ireland's dangerous pieties.

Under the guise of allegory, then, Gregory casts religious bigotry and sexual repression as responsible for the failures of the nationalist movement, and specifically for the downfall of Parnell. The King's Nurseling's apparent lack of religious observance offends the slaves, who object that he appears to have no religion at all, "on the one or the other side" (271). "It would be a pity surely if he would not be stiff in his religion," says Malachi's wife; Ard reports, "according to what I am told, he's a real regular Pagan" (272). This is parody with a bitter edge: Parnell's perceived lack of a religious disposition was, if not originally troubling to his constituents, fodder that prompted many to reject his leadership in the aftermath of the O'Shea scandal.[95] But whereas Gregory's slaves claim to reject the deliverer on the basis of a sort of ecumenical failure of religiosity—that "to have broke out of their creed, and not to have joined in our own, he would not be a fitting leader for ourselves" (272)—this is in fact a cover for the slaves' Catholic bigotry. "I would be sorry to think he would be ignorant and not able to say off the Catechism" (272), says Ard's wife. The play thus explicitly casts Catholicism, with its dedication to catechism, religious "stiffness," and superstition (one character fears the "evil eye"), as a danger to national liberation. If Gregory did not publically express this view, we have evidence of her private feelings on the point; in 1921 she had written to a friend of the "bondage of the mind imposed by the R. C. Church . . . especially in Ireland."[96]

When the King's Nurseling's true origins are revealed ("he is not far in blood from ourselves," belonging "to one of the twelve families" [261]), the slaves celebrate with a series of folksy blessings, such as "the laugh that is in his eye should be sunshine to ripen the barley, and bleach the flax in the field!" (267). Soon, though, the people begin to fear the challenges they will face, and the excitement about the promised land shifts into anxiety. When Malachi's wife suggests that she will get the key to her ancestral home—"I have but to turn it going in, and to sit down beside the hearth"—she is told, "it is likely it is a tribe of grabbers you will find on the hearth before you"

(269). As freedom is revealed to be less than straightforward, and as internal antagonisms erupt, the deliverer faces a volley of curses and threats: "his path may be as slippery as the ditch where he was born," says one; "a long trembling to you" (275), cries another. John Kelly proposes that the quarreling of the Irish Israelites here is "a significant swerve from Exodus,"[97] but as we have seen, the Israelites' resistance to liberation is a central part of the biblical narrative, and Gregory reveals how profoundly the tensions already inherent in the biblical text express the Irish case. As Dan puts it, articulating his fear of the journey through the wilderness, "we will have a queer long road to travel" (271). For a variety of reasons, then—a paralyzing Catholicism, fear of economic instability, anxiety about cultural and ethnic purity, dread of the unknown—Gregory's slaves fail to accept their own freedom.

Still, if much of the play dramatizes the difficulty of liberation, there are nevertheless moments when Gregory idealizes elements of cultural nationalism. When the King's Nurseling performs precisely the killing of an Egyptian that Yeats had prescribed for the Ascendancy class (using Gregory's idea), the weapon used stands for Irish cultural renewal in its most demotic form: the Egyptian is killed "with one blow of the hurl" (265). Hurling, a native game that figures in Ireland's early myths and legends, had been revived under the auspices of the Gaelic Athletic Association (GAA), inaugurated in 1884 by Michael Cusack. The GAA advocated a cultural chauvinism that would oppose any sort of hybrid or Anglo-Irish culture, and so it is perhaps surprising that Gregory would so uncritically invest the hurley stick with such agency in her play. And yet Gregory engages this brand of nationalism with ease. Reportedly, two thousand GAA hurlers marched at Parnell's funeral—as Lyons writes, "in tribute to his supposed extremism in the last months of his life."[98] In the play, Gregory inscribes this iconic moment of apparent political and cultural unity between the people and Parnell as his act of renunciating Ascendancy exploitation.[99] The scene serves to represent one of the overriding tensions in *The Deliverer*: that Gregory's project of dramatizing the profound difficulty of Exodus—and more pointedly, Irish devolution—is also invested with her sympathies for an Irish nationalism that typically wants not to expose difficulty, but occlude it.[100] And while there are other moments of pure patriotic gusto, such confidence is also undermined by a sense of naïveté among the slaves. When one ventures to imagine the "Land of Promise," she suggests, "it is estated people we will be. . . . Hay and oats in the haggards, a stack upon every small patch" (267). But the promised land will not be as the people hope, and their expectations are the typical (and long-debunked) daydreams of the America-bound famine émigré: "There is honey on the tops of the grass" and "the smiths do be forging gold the same as iron" (267). Such fantasies as these, reflecting the mythologies of emigration, are clearly meant to expose unrealistic expectations. Any certainties about the boons of freedom are undercut by anxieties about responsibility, which are consequently banished with rhetorical bravado: a cycle that produces the discourses of essentialist nationalism and ultimately proves useless for Gregory's characters.

Despite the overwhelmingly negative message of the play—that even with Ascendancy leadership, the Irish obstruct their own path to freedom—there are elements of positive critique, of lessons to be learned. *The Deliverer* investigates, for example, in a limited but important way, the dangerous ideology of female purity that had come to dominate nationalist discourse. In the most pared-down formulation, Irish nationalism responds to the British patriarchalism that genders the Celt as feminine by using the same discourses to insist upon a sort of Irish hypermasculinity—one that invests the role of the Irish woman with an impossible responsibility to represent the impenetrable purity of Irish identity.[101] As Valente writes, what happens is that "imperialist discourse has inscribed a vicious symbolic circle in which sexual and socio-economic dominance reflect and authorize one another."[102] An Irish attack on English impurity, for example, might reverse the imperial gendering of Ireland as female and England as male, but only by implicitly acknowledging that the female partner will necessarily be the adulterated (and adulterating) party. In the same year as *The Deliverer* was staged at the Abbey, an article in *Irish Freedom* insisted, "England is an unclean nation. She is one of the most diseased nations in the world—socially, physically, and mentally. It is to this leper among the nations that our country is wed. . . . It is the clean strong good part of Ireland goes out of Ireland to mix with the scraps and pairings of England in the British colonies."[103] England is clearly feminine here: "she" is "unclean" and "diseased," while Ireland is made of that which is "clean strong good"—and clearly male (those who go off to the colonies).

Susan Harris writes of the "growing sense" among nationalists "that the integrity and purity of the domestic sphere and the female body as its center is necessary for all forms of national security—whether cultural, economic, or demographic."[104] Gregory's slaves express this ideology through their fear of the King's Nurseling's adulterating identity; they focus not on his personal failures (he appears to have none—a wishful reincarnation of Parnell), but the threat of his very presence. The men are almost immediately concerned with the sexual appeal he holds for their wives, and in fact it is the women's praise of him that catalyzes their betrayal, eventually leading to infighting that will bring along the handcuffs of the "over-government" officers (an image that replays the conclusion to Gregory's popular 1904 comedy *Spreading the News* in a much darker register). As Dan says, "the women are that cracked after him. You would say they never got a sight of any man besides a cripple or a deformed person before this day" (270). The women indeed note the sexual (and upper-class) appeal of the King's Nurseling: "he so well-shaped, and curls on every side of his poll, the same as a ridge of peas"; "his head held up so lofty and so high, and he having a hurl in his hand, and a crown of posies on his brow" (260–61). But although they may find the deliverer initially appealing, the women are also bothered by his potentially adulterating presence. Fixating on the Nurseling's uncertain parentage, Dan's wife notes, "it was a queer story his mother to go cast him out of her hand, and leave him to be reared by strangers," to which Ard's wife replies, "ah, how do we know was she wed at all at that time?" (273). Charges of sexual impropriety around the King's Nurseling—even if they are not, strictly, his own—are revealed to be at the crux of his betrayal.

The scenario in Gregory's play reimagines the case of Parnell and his fall from power in 1890. His ten-year romance with Katherine O'Shea had been, apparently, an open secret, and the Irish party had supported Parnell until Gladstone made it clear that Home Rule legislation would not go through if Parnell remained their leader. The reaction of "the Irish people" to the moral failure of their Protestant leader polarized the Home Rule movement; or as the conventional wisdom goes, the Catholic Church turned the people against Parnell. Years later Yeats would rehearse the latter view and advocate a Parnellite version of the O'Shea affair, in which Katherine O'Shea's husband knew of the liaison between his wife and the party leader who had facilitated Captain O'Shea's own rise in politics.[105] Yeats's poem "Come Gather Round Me, Parnellites" is modeled after Henry Harrison's 1931 book *Parnell Vindicated*, whose title expresses its argument:[106]

> The Bishops and the Party
> That tragic story made,
> A husband that had sold his wife
> And after that betrayed;
> But stories that live longest
> Are sung above the glass,
> And Parnell loved his country,
> And Parnell loved his lass.[107]

As Lucy McDiarmid has pointed out, "the syntactic parallel [of 'his country' and 'his lass'] makes the two activities of equal value and deprives the hearty, ballad-like love for a 'lass' of its adulterous pollution."[108]

Gregory's method of unadulterating Parnell is even more radical than Yeats's, because the blame is placed, not on the expected "Bishops and the Party," but on ordinary citizens, and by extension, Abbey Theatre audiences. In *The Deliverer*, the slaves who effectively accuse Moses's mother of sexual impropriety are intended to be ridiculous; Gregory is satirizing the sort of purity-panic produced by Griffith and Moran in their newspapers. She was also perhaps exploring her own feelings about the guilt of the adulterer: in the 1880s, her own affair with the anti-imperialist Wilfred Scawen Blunt had been a source of both passion and anxiety.[109] In effect, Gregory now exonerates Parnell for his adultery by making it incidental—the play argues that anxiety about Parnell's leadership, as an outsider in Catholic Ireland, existed even *without* his literal adultery, which of course does not figure in the play. The betrayal of the King's Nurseling, then, is motivated not by impropriety, nor by politics, but by sexual anxiety on the part of the slaves, who see in the elite deliverer the threat of exogamy. When they murder him—with the biblical punishment for adulterers, stoning—it is needless death, and intended to shock. In Ireland's case, Gregory suggests, the people will ironically reject even a biblically authorized version of devolution if it compromises the Irish Ireland ethos of national purity. But even the slaves realize they have made a grave error: "I wish I didn't turn against him," one says, "I am thinking he might be an angel" (277).

Another Case of Parnell

When the slaves of Gregory's play betray their leader, the Healy-esque Ard says, "the ships are ready. We have the password. Anyone could do the job now" (273)—a reference to the anti-Parnellite position of twenty years earlier. Further rehearsing the history of the split, when Malachi, the play's voice of Parnellite reason, is told that "the King's priest" has spoken against the deliverer, he asks, "is it at the bidding of the Egyptians you will give up the man of your own race?" (275), referencing Gladstone's demand for Parnell's removal. But for all the apparent explicitness of her allegory, much of the audience refused to understand. It seems, in fact, that the initial noncomprehension of the play may well have been deliberate, a rejection not just of the allegorical correspondence, but of the meaning that the allegory implied: you have betrayed your liberator, Gregory was saying to the audience, and now you will never be free. It was an unwanted message, for in *The Deliverer* Gregory exposes Irish materialism, alcoholism, prurience, prudery, suspiciousness, narrow-mindedness, divisiveness in crisis. Indeed, to an extent that has not been recognized, the play is a deep and serious investigation and critique of all those involved with the botched opportunity for liberation. Many in Dublin claimed that Gregory's meaning was obscure, but as we will see, more than one person would stand up to accuse the supposedly perplexed of being disingenuous.

The reviewer in the *Irish Times* wrote that "detailed notice of the play itself must be deferred; suffice it now to say that its central figure is Moses."[110] Of the twist of Moses's murder, he writes, "the place of such a play in the Irish dramatic movement is not very clear, unless it is intended as a political parable for Irish consumption." What else could it have been? It is difficult not to read such a review as insincere; the parable of Parnell as Moses had already been consumed willingly by the Irish public, and even the Unionist *Irish Times* would have been familiar with it. As easily as this one review might be dismissed, however, it represents what seems to have been a widespread noncomprehension of the play. The *Freeman's Journal*, too, suggested that there was "an application wider than the actual historical one,"[111] but as Brown writes, the reviewer does not speculate as to what that application might be. In his personal diary Joseph Holloway, after addressing the failures of the play's scenery and costumes (designed by Gregory's son Robert), echoes the impression of general bewilderment in his usual lively tone: "The audience looked on in wonder during the progress of *The Deliverer*, all wondering what it was about, and, why all the Egyptians spoke Kiltartan, like the natives of the region of Lady Gregory's brain where people only speak so."[112] Holloway describes several other assertions of confusion after the play, meeting one Thomas Keohler who thought "the play was hopelessly bad," and in reporting his confusion, hazards tentatively, "What was it about . . . Was it another case of Parnell?"[113] Apparently there was far worse being said than even Holloway reports. He writes, "[Fred] Jeffs was rich on *The Deliverer*, and said many droll apt things about it,"[114] but we never hear what they are. Thus in return for her widely dispensed critique, Gregory's play was itself panned widely across the social and political spectrum.[115]

One theory to explain the public's uncertainty about the meaning of the play—and perhaps, therefore, their dislike—is that *The*

Deliverer was also the first production at the Abbey to use Gordon Craig's new set design, and apparently the novelty of the screens he created engaged more of the audience's imagination than her play.[116] This is not to deny that the play is, at times, confusing. One particularly opaque passage has to do with "the King's cats," the vile creatures who tear the King's Nurseling apart at the conclusion. Malachi, singularly loyal and wise among the slaves, describes these threatening animals: "Those cats are a class in themselves. To claw you they would, and bite you, and put poison in your veins the same as a serpent" (258–59). Another slave, Dan, tells of an encounter with one: "To meet with one of them in the moonlight I did a while ago. I am not the better of it yet. It went into some sort of a hump, and said it had to walk its seven acres" (259). If the first passage offers a link with the biblical serpent of Genesis as a seductive deceiver, the second is admittedly obscure. Gregory only provides the substantive clue five years later, in her book *Visions and Beliefs in the West of Ireland*, where we find the same story in a section on "Monsters and Sheoguey Beasts." The details were presumably lifted directly from Gregory's notebooks, recounting folklore gathered with Yeats from peasants in Galway.[117] The passage in *Visions* offers some clarification, explaining that "cats is faeries, and every night they're obliged to travel over seven acres."[118] If the King's cats in *The Deliverer* are in fact the fairies or changelings of rural Irish folklore, it is a powerful irony, for Gregory conjures them to represent the Liberal Party who betrayed Parnell and Home Rule.[119] Brown supposes the cats "arisen out of Lady Gregory's bitter Protestant imagination,"[120] but this misses the point: she uses local peasant folklore to indict not the peasants themselves, but the English whose supposedly rational politics had destroyed Ireland's hope for self-government.

If the play's meaning apparently eluded audiences, even the most perplexed viewers did seem to know that there was something about Moses and Parnell in it. After seeing the play a second time, Holloway acknowledged in his journal "The King's Nurseling as the Moses-Parnell of the play."[121] Still, he also insisted that "the 'hang' of the story was hard to grasp."[122] But why was it so hard to grasp? Some of the resistance to the play seems to have originated with the very form of analogizing itself. Whereas Gregory includes anachronisms to expose the scaffolding of her project, using Irish constructions, words, and phrases throughout—*curragh*, *inver*, *stirabout*—Holloway finds himself annoyed with Israelites who sound Irish: "If Lady Gregory can't write anything else but Kiltartan why doesn't she stick to an Irish environment and then it would not so much matter."[123] And yet she has never for a moment left the Irish environment that Holloway fails to recognize. Gregory writes in her notes for *The Wrens* (1914), among the most explicitly political of her plays, that "sometimes in making a plan for a play I set the scene in some other country that I may be sure the emotion displayed is not bounded by any neighborhood but is a universal one."[124] But the change of setting is rarely, if ever, as random as she suggests here; dramatizing the story of Parnell in biblical Israel, for example, encodes in the story particular as well as universal meanings. Moreover, that Gregory's text refers specifically to the Irish experience is undeniable. In the play, when one slave explains the exodus from an original homeland by recalling that "the time of the great hunger drove them away" (257), he is ostensibly referring to Joseph's sojourn into Egypt during famine in the Book of Genesis. But the phrase "great hunger" is nothing if not shorthand for Ireland's terrible famine of the 1840s.

At least one reviewer objected to his contemporaries' apparently perplexed responses to *The Deliverer*. "M. M. O'H"[125] of the *Evening Telegraph*, clearly reacting to the sort of talk about the play that Holloway records, and perhaps even having read the early papers before turning in his own piece, vehemently disagreed with the other reviewers:

> Now, "The Deliverer" had not been many moments in action until one found himself saying almost audibly: "The Parnell Split, or I'm a Dutchman." It is, of course, not for us to put—as it were—words into Lady Gregory's mouth, still less to put thoughts into her head; but if her Jews be not Irish, and if the King's Nurseling be not Parnell, and if Dan and Ard be not—but people must guess for themselves

> further—if these things be not so, then never hang another man on circumstantial evidence. No doubt Lady Gregory found her story in the Old Testament, but if her inspiration did not come from Ireland, and the life of Parnell, then let guessing be abolished.[126]

This rebuke implies not only the transparency of the biblical analogy, but also the patent obviousness of the Parnell connection. But M. M. O'H wasn't entirely pleased with Gregory's use of the trope, even if he thought it silly to deny what was evident ("it is quite unnecessary to go to the trouble of tracing the parallel"). Rather, he writes, "in this instance the play is spoiled by being too direct, and yet not direct enough: at once obvious and obscure, and in urgent need therefore of an explanatory prologue or historical essay on the programme." Weighing in (if somewhat belatedly) on the side of "too direct" was William Stanley Braithwaite of the *New York Times*, who reviewed Gregory's volume of *Irish Folk-History Plays* in 1912, writing that *The Deliverer* was a "too obvious analogy in allegorical guise for the repudiation of Parnell by his countrymen."[127] Can the play in fact be both too direct and not direct enough? As the directly contradictory evidence of reviews and audience responses would suggest, it is worth taking this question seriously. Those who thought the play insufficiently direct may have been bewildered by the new scenery, or more likely, unwilling to accept Gregory's rather ferocious characterizations of all levels of Irish society. The other side, too, may have found the lesson tedious and belated. But in Gregory's defense, the play's critique derives from its use of analogy and its historical allusions, and to overemphasize these could have undermined its effectiveness *as* critique, offsetting the making strange that might have allowed the audience to register the horror of the play's conclusion before realizing it was, in fact, the horror of their own reality. A historical essay in the program would have made the drama just that—history. And Gregory, through her presentation of ancient Israelites and a decades-old Irish controversy, was actually focusing on the present.

Audiences seemed split between those who "got" Gregory's play and those who did not, and in the week after the performance, an exchange of letters to the editor in the *Irish Times* debated, again, the meaning of *The Deliverer.* "An Irish Alien," in his letter provocatively entitled "Wanted—An Irish Ibsen," writes dismissively of Gregory's most recent attempt, also objecting to other Abbey productions, including Synge's *The Shadow of the Glen* and Yeats's *The Hour Glass*: "I have come away every time wanting more—something more substantial, with more grit and commonsense in it."[128] Two days later, "E. Q. E." responded on behalf of Gregory and the Abbey: "As regards his ['An Irish Alien's'] rather cheap suggestion that the 'caterwauling of Pharaoh's cats last week was beautifully symbolical of the ancient Irish harp,' and that Lady Gregory has taken up the theory that we are descended from the Children of Israel, I can only shrug my shoulders and submit that he has missed the point. The delightful part is that he then proceeds to clamour for someone to show up the weak points of the Irish. As if the revelation of the black treachery and ingratitude of the Jews (or Irish?) in the 'Deliverer' was not almost Swiftian in its venom."[129] As "E. Q. E." notes, *The Deliverer* indeed offers a persistent, and at times aggressive, attack on the behavior of Ireland's citizens. As Ben Levitas writes of the play, "ill-bred ingratitude . . . was threatening a violent recurrence: and with the lesson came a taste of the author's usually shaded capacity for imperious disdain."[130] When the King's Nurseling appears before the people on the eve of their departure, he berates them: "You are on the brink of your escape! Keep your uproar till you are out of this!" (275). These lines could be—and in a real sense are—directed at the audience. Those watching the play may have recalled Yeats's lecture from the stage amid the protests on the second night of *The Playboy.* After the audience had drowned out the players and in no uncertain terms voiced their displeasure, Yeats spoke out against their provincialism. He told them that the (Anglo-Irish) directors of the theatre, at least, "had not such pliant bones, and did not learn in the house that bred them a so suppliant knee."[131] At least if Lady Gregory was calling the Irish slaves, it was in a slightly less direct manner than Yeats had done. Moreover, by ostensibly retelling a biblical and not an Irish story, Gregory had the freedom to chastise her audience; those who didn't want to hear the lesson simply declined to understand it. But Gregory also uses the play to insist upon what she saw as a necessary Anglo-Irish presence in Irish politics and culture—presented allegorically, without the air of moral and cultural superiority that would make such claims repugnant to much of the audience.

Or perhaps the audience's resistance to the play was their unwillingness to tolerate a story of failure as failure, rather than the triumph of failure. After all, they may have recalled the more favorable sensations produced by another direct address from the stage of Ireland's national theatre. When the imposing radical nationalist Maud Gonne played the title role in Yeats and Gregory's *Kathleen ni Houlihan*, she directed her words, we learn from Standish O'Grady, not to the other players but to the audience. Stephen Gwynn wrote that her performance "had stirred the audience as I have never seen another audience stirred."[132] She did not ask them to sacrifice their prejudices, nor to commit to the difficult work of liberation. She required something else: their blood, their deaths. The Old Woman—"Ireland herself"—says, "they that have red cheeks will have pale cheeks for my sake, and for all that, they will think they are well paid."[133] The polemical play, with its narrative of liberation through blood sacrifice, was a favorite among Abbey audiences, unlike Gregory's later, darker vision of anticolonial struggle. Somehow it was more appealing to die with purity and clarity than to live amid struggle and confusion. Additionally, there is no onstage blood in *Kathleen*, while the graphic violence inflicted on the King's Nurseling appears to have unsettled viewers. Holloway writes that "the ghost of the done to death King's Nurseling . . . was very substantial and 'real flesh and blood' looking as he stalked across the stage after the cats had done with him."[134]

The end of *The Deliverer* hints at the way the Irish liberation narrative would change in the coming years. The King's Nurseling reappears before the stunned slaves who murdered him: "Look! He is living yet. He is passing!" (277). Another says, "it is but his ghost." Most critics read the final lines of the play as evidence that he *has* risen, for as Edward Kopper suggests, the Nurseling becomes associated with Christ when Dan's wife echoes the Roman soldier of the

Gospels: "I wish I didn't turn against him. I am thinking he might be an angel" (277). Yet the idea of a risen Parnell, in the play as in Irish life, reveals only a kind of nostalgic wishful thinking; bitterness and stasis overwhelm the possibility of salvation, and the ghost of the lost leader haunts rather than redeems. But there would be an imaginative transformation in the years leading up to and after the Easter Rising. The figure of the Irish liberator would no longer be envisioned as the Old Testament Moses of Exodus, but as the New Testament Christ. Thus in 1935, when writing "Parnell's Funeral," Yeats no longer envisioned a Mosaic Parnell, but a Christlike, Eucharistic one. The image of consuming the sacrificed martyr is presented in its negative sense, as de Valera fails to do it: "Had de Valera eaten Parnell's heart / No loose-lipped demagogue had won the day, / No civil rancour torn the land apart."[135] Parnell had been betrayed instead of deified, and now he would also be replaced in literary culture as in politics. The role of the new Irish deliverer would soon be embodied, literally, by Patrick Pearse.

3

Anti-Exodus

Patrick Pearse's "New Testament of Irish Nationality"

In his book *Inventing Ireland*, Declan Kiberd offers a wry understatement of the differences between English Puritans and militant Irish nationalists: "If there is any substantive difference between the English revolutionaries of 1640 and the Irish insurgents of 1916, it is merely this: the English relied mainly on the Old Testament for their language, and the Irish on the New."[1] This assessment notes both the centrality and, given the long-standing Irish uses of the Hebrew Bible, the shifting nature of biblical language in the rhetoric of revolution. And we need not cross sides of the colonial divide to see such a shift, for the "mere" difference can also be found in the seemingly less dramatic juxtaposition of two generations of Irish nationalists: the Parnellites of the 1880s and '90s and the separatists of the 1910s. In the years between Charles Stewart Parnell and Patrick Pearse, changing cultural and political conditions catalyzed this new way of imagining liberation for Ireland, one that can be most readily observed as the move from Old to New Testament forms. Exodus, the archetype of freedom for generations of Irish nationalists, gave way to a Christological narrative that not only superseded it, but practically erased it. In 1988 Alan Titley would suggest that "our own 1916 has given us a creation story as good as any we were ever likely to get,"[2] and in the many recent commemorations and reconsiderations of the Rising leading up to its centenary, there is new attention to the rhetoric of 1916 as foundational for modern Ireland.[3] Meanwhile, the Israelite analogy that held Ireland's imagination for so long fades ever more completely into the past, and the new scholarship around the Rising reiterates the preeminence of the sacrificial narrative. But Pearse's Christological creation story was neither inevitable nor sacrosanct; it was a strategic if unconscious deconstruction of the biblical rhetoric of Old Testament—and Ascendancy-associated—forms of Irish nationalism.

Patrick Pearse—newspaper editor, headmaster, poet, playwright, and propagandist—would lead the combined armies of the Irish Republican Brotherhood and the Irish Citizen Army during Easter Week of 1916. The provisional president of a new Irish Republic, he would also be among the first executed for the rebellion. Pearse was the Easter Rising's chief rhetorician, and his New Testament version of Irish liberation from British oppression is reflected in the event's very name, with its implication of resurrection through sacrifice.[4] The powerful religious symbolism of his vision has indeed dramatically influenced Irish political, cultural, and literary discourse, yet even as Pearse's prevailing story of blood sacrifice became standard, it would nevertheless get a skeptical rewriting in the decades after his death. This chapter details, then, not only the Christian trope that replaces Exodus in Pearse's typology, but the ways in which Exodus quietly appears again in the years following the Rising and Independence—up to the moment when Joyce gives us, in *Ulysses*, a more vigorous return to Exodus. When Lady Gregory writes a version of the Christ story in 1924, it is, as we might expect, at its core a meditation on Irish liberation that cannot help but echo the now-ubiquitous Pearsian symbolism. Yet within her Passion play we find the old story of Parnell, the story of Exodus. And Gregory was not alone in reflecting on the past: the return of the repressed Parnell and the rejection of Pearse's sacrificial narrative appeared in texts by many writers, and proliferated almost as rapidly as the first hagiographies of the 1916 martyrs.

A Call for Clarity

After the Rising Yeats commemorated Pearse and the other rebel leaders in his poem "Easter 1916," ambivalently celebrating their sacrifice while observing the troubling nature of their ideological fixedness:

"Hearts with one purpose alone / Through summer and winter seem / Enchanted to a stone / To trouble the living stream."[5] Pearse himself had used a similar image of stone—"bedrock"—to describe such singularity, but for him it was a positive image of clarity, something crucial in life and, as he writes here, in poetry: "the clear sheer detection and statement of some naked truth, the touching of some deep bedrock foundation, the swift sure stroke at the very heart of a thing."[6] The rhymed pair of "clear" and "sheer" reinforces transparency of vision—rather than the opaque plashing waves of Yeats's "living stream"—as an ideal. Pearse's monocular approach is a common observation among his biographers: Ruth Dudley Edwards describes how "throughout his career, where others saw a web of complications, Pearse saw a single thread, and he fought to avoid tangling his vision" both in literature and in politics.[7] Pearse, it seems, was given to singularities and binaries even before his political conversion from cultural nationalist to separatist leader. In 1899 Joseph Holloway commented on an early lecture about Irish sagas, noting that the young man "was indiscriminately eulogistic to absurdity over his subject . . . Mr. Pearse missed his mark in not being somewhat critical in his appreciation."[8] J. J. Lee likewise observes how Pearse's early writings demonstrate "the pronounced tendency to speak in absolutes and superlatives, the axiomatic certainty reflected in the use of words like 'undoubtedly.'"[9] This was not atypical, of course; as Arthur Aughey writes, the Irish revolutionary disposition "revealed, above all, a concern for purity of heart and mind and soul. . . . It was also a singular obsession, for this identity, this Irish-ness, was one and indivisible."[10] The profound tensions and instabilities, psychological and aesthetic if not political, that appear in Pearse's poems and plays are ever suppressed—or intended to be—in his political writings.[11]

The idea that there was a "romantic simplification of complexity" resounds throughout William Irwin Thompson's 1967 book on the Easter Rising, *The Imagination of an Insurrection*; Thompson suggests that a failure of imagination occurred with the shift to a politics of separatism, that "in the movement from national identity to political action . . . consciousness of tragic complexity was simply knocked aside as an obstruction to national ambition."[12] Thompson is both right and wrong here: while the new nationalism strategically invoked clarity and purity, the rhetorical achievement of those ideals in a culturally, economically, and politically hybrid Ireland required some very powerful imagining indeed. Amid Ireland's various and contested cultural and literary projects of the early twentieth century, Pearse would complain that "the nationalist movement in Ireland has degenerated into a debating society. . . . In all our national or quasi-national organs we argue as to what a nation is, what nationality, what a Nationalist. As if definitions mattered!"[13] Sweeping aside debate would not be simple, however, for definitions and debate certainly did matter to Ascendancy writers like Yeats and Gregory, Irish Ireland nationalists like Griffith and Moran, as well as to more idiosyncratic figures ranging from the humanitarian Michael Davitt to the cosmopolitan John Eglinton. Nevertheless, Pearse urged clarity in the face of such apparently willful complication, as in his recruiting pamphlet of 1915: "We want recruits because we are sure of the rightness of our cause. We have no misgivings, no self-questionings. While others have been doubting, timorous, ill at ease, we have been serenely at peace with our consciences. The recent time of soul searching had no terrors for us. We saw our path with absolute clearness; we took it with absolute deliberateness. . . . Whatever soul-searchings there may be among Irish political parties now or hereafter, we go on in the calm certitude of having done the clear, clean, sheer thing. We have the strength and the peace of mind of those who never compromise."[14] The paired words "clear" and "sheer" that Pearse had used to describe truth in poetry here bookend a middle term, "clean," which through its alliterative link with "clear," "calm," and "certitude" is brought into alignment with them thematically, accruing to Pearse's program a sense of its intrinsic, transparent rightness, and sanctifying its (unspoken, unclean) commitment to physical force. Pearse's path thus moves us not only from complexity to clarity, but also, almost unnoticed, from the hall of debate to the field of action. Violence, as Seamus Deane notes, "was regarded as a great and manly simplifier of problems which were by then, on every level, threatening to become almost infinitely complex (as indeed they were),"[15] and more recently Sarah Cole has elaborated on how Pearse's "story of blood and fecundity was one of certainties."[16] In the case of the 1916 Rising, the violent deaths of both volunteers and leaders—the latter executed shortly after their surrender to English officers—would indeed eventually produce in Irish opinion the transformative political clarity Pearse promoted.

It is no wonder that a revolutionary leader would claim a strategic position of stability. Holding the mirror up to post-Parnell Ireland was precisely what Pearse did not want: he did not want to reflect upon Yeats's "*hysterica passio*," the debate, compromise, betrayal, and disappointment that the 1890s and subsequent decades had bequeathed to the politics and culture of Irish nationalism. For the mirror was Joyce's cracked looking-glass of a servant, and staring into it had apparently not brought the country any closer to Home Rule, to say nothing of independence. In January 1900 "Clovis," writing in the *United Irishman*, bemoaned the unruly state of Ireland's national populace and imagined the cure of a redemptive liberator: "Her people uneasy, dissatisfied, apathetic, despairing, agitated by conflicting counsels and impulses, face the coming century without a leader whom they can trust or a plan which they can confidently follow . . . we await the coming of the chosen one."[17] The chosen one, in this case, would not be a new Moses, but a new Christ. As Matthew Kelly writes, "the Christological metaphors that became so characteristic of Patrick Pearse's later oratory are evident here, implicitly transfiguring Parnell, an earlier reification of the chosen one, into a sacrificed Christ. Packed with presentiment, this passage is also a call for clarity amid the confusion."[18] We cannot know whether Pearse saw Lady Gregory's play *The Deliverer* and was faced with the timorous, compromised, tragic citizens that she produced, or reproduced, on the Dublin stage. Certainly he would have rejected such a querulous vision. Rather, Pearse would transform the Irish narrative of liberation from a Parnellite, Protestant, Moses-centered narrative to a revolutionary, Catholic,

Christ-centered one; from a story of earthly struggle to one of spiritual martyrdom; from a story of ambivalence and hybridity to one that insisted, more than ever before, on purity.

De-Anglicization

Pearse's call for clarity and purity was part of a general cultural anxiety about the adulteration of Irish identity by Anglicization. Although his rhetoric is not Anglophobic in the same way as, for example, D. P. Moran's is, Pearse nevertheless displays a notable aversion to Englishness in Ireland.[19] On a fund-raising trip to the United States in 1912, Pearse wrote of St. Enda's, the school he established in 1908, "Our work is radical: it strikes at the root of anglicisation."[20] The new Ireland for which Pearse was educating his students would be a purely Irish Ireland, with little room for anything Anglo, including the Anglo-Irish who had been, and in fact still were, so central to Irish cultural nationalism. Indeed, the literary revival represented a particular affront to Pearse's vision of an Irish Ireland: as his former student and biographer Desmond Ryan writes, "Pearse's whole mental attitude was antagonistic to Anglo-Irish literature. The very words Anglo-Irish he detested and denied their validity."[21] At the core of Pearse's philosophy—and connected with his rejection of the English-language revival—was a belief that the Irish language was critical to national life. Irish education was accordingly integral to his school's mandate, despite the fact that outside of a few Gaeltachtaí (Irish-speaking areas), Catholics were as unlikely as Protestants to speak a language that had been nearly wiped out by famine and emigration. Yet the language question burned at the crux of the nationalist program, and soon became linked with ideologies of cultural and political separatism.

Meanwhile, the Irish language was also becoming rhetorically linked with Catholicism. One article in the *Leader*, entitled "Irish or Infidelity, Which?" claimed for example that "if Irish is compulsory [in the new Catholic University in Dublin], the University will be Catholic, that is to say, safe for Catholics; if Irish be not compulsory, and the University be open to a horde of un-Irish or anti-Irish students from everywhere, then, I say it will be impossible to save it from the modern spirit of materialism and unbelief."[22] The language would thus protect Catholicism from the "horde" of adulterating, modern, English heathens. A pamphlet some years later would apply the converse argument to identical ends, suggesting, "English is the language of infidelity."[23] If English was corrupt, Irish was pure, and vice versa: in a 1914 sermon in Cork, An tAthair Peadar Ua Leoghaire declared, "there is enmity between the Irish language and infidelity. They cannot keep house together. If Irish is inside, infidelity must remain outside."[24] Gradually the once interfaith, once ostensibly apolitical Gaelic League became, as Tom Garvin writes, "more Catholic, less Dublin-oriented, and more clericalist."[25] In 1915 its Protestant creator Douglas Hyde, whose iconic 1892 speech "The Necessity for De-Anglicising Ireland" could not guarantee his own claim on Irishness in a climate increasingly focused on religious and ethnic identity, would, as a result of the league's increasingly political stance, resign the presidency of the organization he had founded. Pearse, who edited the league's paper from 1903 to 1909, steered it firmly into the separatist movement, arguing in 1913 that its cultural project must give way to more vital political work, led by "men or movements that have sprung from the Gaelic League, or have received from the Gaelic League a new baptism."[26] The "new baptism" was, at least rhetorically, a Catholic one; as we will see, the language of baptism, of rising, of Christ sacrificed, would be marshaled into a typology that Pearse used to signal and reify the Catholicism of the nationalist project.

Other Irish-Ireland organizations and publications, such as D. P. Moran's *Leader*, were also unabashedly questioning (and rejecting) Protestant leadership in the new advanced nationalism.[27] Moran's conception of "the Battle of Two Civilizations"—the Gael vs. the Anglo-Irish—was, as Lyons has demonstrated, in essence the "intense conviction of the necessity to throw off every kind of attachment to things English."[28] The distinction between Gael and Gall expanded from cultural to religious sectarianism and what was increasingly seen as racial difference; the Gaelic movement was inexorably approaching Moran's claim that "the Irish nation is *de facto* a Catholic nation."[29]

Pearse, meanwhile, made calls for unity among Catholic, Protestant, and Dissenter, echoing his hero Wolfe Tone; according to Boyce, he was "ever mindful of the Protestant contribution to Irish nationalist thinking,"[30] and recent scholarship has further examined the inclusive elements of Pearse's thinking.[31] Nevertheless, Pearse's writings work to translate a nation of multiplicity into a singular unity, a unity that used certain Catholic tropes as shortcuts to clarity. This is not to say that Pearse aimed to create a Catholic revolution; rather, he signaled the newness, difference, and inevitability of his movement as a form of supersession: just as the Old Testament narrative was obviated by the New, the Protestant Mosaic analogy would be obviated by the Catholic Christological one—a formal, rather than religious, rejection of Protestant leadership.[32]

As Boyce writes, "the rising was not a rising against Protestants; but it was a rising without Protestants, or at least without Protestants playing the kind of leading role that they had played in 1798 and 1848."[33] Even Parnell, by this time recuperated as a national martyr by many Catholics as well as Protestants, was perhaps losing his luster as a guiding leader, as witnessed in the heartfelt yet static elegy rehearsed in Joyce's story of political malaise, "Ivy Day in the Committee Room." Pearse, writing in one of his final pamphlets, "Ghosts," claims Wolfe Tone, Thomas Davis, James Fintan Lalor, and John Mitchell as the four gospelists of Irish nationalism; he then continues, "Parnell must be considered. If one had to add a fifth to the four I have named, the fifth would inevitably be Parnell."[34] But there are only four gospels, of course, and thus Pearse exorcises the specter of a martyred Parnell, avoiding the problems of Parnell's Protestantism, his Ascendancy background, and his relationship with the married Katherine O'Shea. If Parnell still carried an adulterating taint, it is evaded by Pearse, who imagines a leader who is his very opposite: whereas Parnell, like Moses, was an aloof outsider, this deliverer, like Jesus, is of the people and lives among them;[35] whereas Parnell was sinful (and antinational) in his connection with the English O'Shea, this savior translates his sexual energies into national ones; whereas Parnell was an adulterer, this liberator is an innocent young virgin unsullied by a connection to England. At the conclusion of Pearse's play *The King: A Morality*, the martyr-child's death brings these words from the king who has chosen the boy—the "most innocent" among his schoolmates—as his nation's sacrifice: "O victorious child! I kiss thee, O white body, since it is thy purity that hath redeemed my people."[36] When in January 1914 one Ita O'Shea imagined the nation's new messiah, it was in terms similarly religious and transcendent: "He is intensely Irish in every fibre of his being. . . . He is the Incarnation of the Spirit of Ireland—the heir par excellence of her Past—destined to be the dominating figure of the spacious days of her not so remote future."[37] While Parnell had been a man "in whose veins there was not even a drop of Celtic blood" according to Joyce,[38] the new messiah would not only be "intensely Irish," but a divine *incarnation* of Irishness. This description owes not a little to Pearse's vigorous transformation of biblical rhetoric in Ireland—the transition from the Moses story to the Christ story that effectively wrested the narrative of Irish liberation out of Protestant hands.

The New Testament of Irish Nationality

The Abbey Theatre was a particularly potent site for the culture wars between the Protestant Ascendancy and Catholic Ireland. Initially seen, quite accurately, as a mainly Anglo-Irish venture, the Abbey became more truly national when it began producing Irish-language plays and Catholic playwrights as the first decade of the twentieth century pressed on. But Pearse's early comments on the Irish Literary Theatre (precursor to the Abbey) and the Anglo-Irish literary movement were famously harsh. "Let us strangle it at birth,"[39] he wrote in 1899, suggesting that literature in English would only confuse and stifle what he hoped would be an Irish language revival. Pearse later recanted, but only gradually. He was becoming friendlier with the Abbey group (in later years St. Enda's would stage plays there) in 1906 when he wrote, "Unlike most Gaelic Leaguers, we have a sincere admiration for much of the work of Mr. Yeats, Mr. Russell, and the other poets and dramatists of what, without irreverence, we may call the Celtic Twilight School. . . . But do Mr. Yeats and his fellows hold a place in the intellectual present of Ireland comparable to that held, say, by An tAthair Peadar or Conan Maol? . . . The Twilight People will pass with the Anglo-Irish Twilight . . . The future is with the Gael."[40] Pearse would repeat this prophecy in 1907, responding to the controversy over Synge's *Playboy* with the same dire—and as it would turn out, false—prediction: "as for Anglo-Irish drama . . . it is the beginning of the end."[41] Even as Pearse later changed his position on *The Playboy*, he continued to critique Yeats, Gregory, and Synge. In 1912 he could be found telling Joseph Holloway (who recorded it in his diary) that he "thought the Abbey was run too much on Ascendancy principles."[42]

Pearse had the highest words of praise, however, for one of the Irish Literary Theatre's early productions: Yeats and Gregory's spectacularly popular 1902 play *Kathleen ni Houlihan*. Pearse thought it "the most beautiful piece of prose that has been produced by an Irishman in our day."[43] The narrative begins on the eve of Michael Gillane's marriage—also the eve of the 1798 rebellion—when this young man chooses to sacrifice his life to aid an old woman, "Kathleen, the daughter of Houlihan,"[44] who has come to the house with "the hope of getting my beautiful fields back again; the hope of putting the strangers out of my house."[45] This coded language would have been clear to all who saw the play; the "four beautiful green fields"[46] are the four provinces of Ireland, and Kathleen herself is the land of Ireland (or the concept of Irish sovereignty) who can only be transformed from an old woman into "a young girl . . . [with] the walk of a queen"[47] by the renewing blood of young men who die on her battlefields. Traditional sovereignty myths such as this one had circulated for years in Irish culture, but Yeats and Gregory's updated version modernized and, equally important for an audience valuing both post-Victorian rectitude and nationalist purity, desexualized the story.[48] The short play powerfully articulated to the receptive Dublin audience the trope of blood sacrifice that would become so critical to Pearse's political philosophy. *Kathleen ni Houlihan*'s story of liberation was apocalyptic, unlike Gregory's Exodus narrative in *The Deliverer*: for the followers of Kathleen, there is no temptation by worldly things, no wandering in the wilderness, but rather an instantaneous deliverance, a miraculous unseen transformation through sacrifice. This is the "enchantment" that Cole describes as "the ideal of generative violence"; her description of Yeats's "Easter 1916," equally apt for *Kathleen*, shows how the text works by "erasing the body and occluding the moment of violence, replacing these with a statement of lovely transformation."[49] Even (or more to the point, especially) the financially rewarding, endogamous marriage that the Gillanes are preparing for offers no competition to the call of the nation and its magic.

The politicizing force of the play was remarked on by many contemporaries, most notably Stephen Gwynn in his frequently quoted assessment that "the effect of *Cathleen ni Houlihan* on me was that I went home asking myself if such plays should be produced unless one was prepared for people to go out to shoot and be shot."[50] *Kathleen*'s powerful effect as something akin to propaganda was suggested by Yeats himself, who famously asks in the late poem "The Man and the Echo," "Did that play of mine send out / Certain men the English shot?"[51] Yeats and Gregory would each, in later works, bring more skeptical, complicated perspectives to the question of how Ireland could gain her freedom, but would nevertheless rely in the coming years on *Kathleen* for their nationalist credentials (Yeats implored an audience rioting against Synge's *Playboy* to desist, as "the author of *Kathleen ni Houlihan* addresses you"[52]). Such was the power of *Kathleen* that it functioned not only as propaganda but also as religion: Countess Markievicz, who would later fight in the Easter Rising, described it as "a kind of gospel," while another republican saw it as "a sort of sacrament."[53] This was almost, but not quite, sufficiently monumental for Pearse, who was not content with qualifications such as "a sort of" or "a kind of." For him, the elements of the new liberation narrative would be truly equivalent to the sacred forms, would themselves be gospel and sacrament.

Pearse's equation of Christian religion and Irish nationalism has been well documented, perhaps most exhaustively by Cruise O'Brien, who (not uncontroversially) attributes today's troubles in Northern Ireland to Pearse's legacy of violence.[54] Recent scholarship has also taken up the theme, but Father Francis Shaw, writing for the fiftieth anniversary of the Rising, stated its basic tenet with precision in an earlier revisionist assessment (published only posthumously in 1972 when the date and the critique of Pearse were not so potent). Shaw, appalled at Pearse's unorthodox rhetorical strategy, claims that Pearse had "introduced a new idea, a startling one: the idea that patriotism and holiness are the same, that they are convertible concepts."[55] Kiberd similarly reads Pearse's translation of religion into nationalism as a straightforward technique of substitution: "he moved from faith in 'the kingdom of God' to faith in 'the kingdom of Ireland', employing the language of the former to launch his crusade for the latter."[56] Christian language, Kiberd suggests, was already powerful for the Irish people and particularly the poor; thus the substitution that Pearse enacts (Kiberd implies) is a natural one.[57] But Pearse's translations are in fact more strategic than this reading allows, as they specifically undermine and replace one form of religious language with another. The result is a move not simply from religious faith to faith in the nation, but a supersession of the previously privileged biblical language of the Hebrew Bible. The movement to the New Testament, or as Pearse repeatedly calls it, "The New Testament of Irish Nationality," is coded not only as the path to liberation for Ireland, but as a purifying transformation—a turn from the chaos of Old Testament forms and struggles to the clarity of Christian "redemption."[58] It is also a political turn, a way of excluding the problematically "Old" leadership—the Anglo-Irish, Protestant, Israelite-analogizing revivalists—and rhetorically ushering in the "New"—Catholic, Gaelic League, physical force separatists. Kiberd, in his more recent work on Pearse, has valuably noted the modernity, the powerful sense of newness, and the "drive towards futurity"[59] in Pearse's writings, and these are expressed perhaps most clearly in the supersession of Christian symbols over Hebrew ones.

Pearse's shift from Old to New Testament language is a form of biblical typology, a strategy that imbues the moment of national liberation with the status of ultimate divine fulfillment.[60] The terms within a typological system of reading take on profound religious and political value, for they refer not only to one's own historical moment, but to the biblical past, an imagined future, and all of sacred time. With its genealogy in medieval biblical hermeneutics, typology would perhaps seem out of place as a way of articulating anticolonial struggle in modern Ireland. But it was still a familiar way of thinking about the relationship between the Old and New Testaments in the nineteenth century, among both Catholics and Protestants; James Joyce learned it in school,[61] and Ian Paisley continued to offer sermons of this sort into the twenty-first century.[62] Along these lines Kathleen Biddick argues that "the purported 'secularization' of modernity . . . has never overtaken this core Christian conception of supersession."[63] Indeed, Northrop Frye's speculations on the lack of critical attention to typology (which Biddick's 2003 book *The Typological Imaginary* goes some way to correcting) suggest a kind of scholarly intransigence, despite the fact that "this structure of doctrine became increasingly the compulsory means of understanding the Bible."[64] Pearse's hypernationalist Christianity—and particularly his quasiheretical self-identification with Christ—were hardly doctrinaire; however they did correspond to an established system for reading typologically. Yet for Pearse, supersession operated as "applied typology," which, ironically, had historically been a Protestant technique.[65] It was not only that the Old Testament was fulfilled by the New, but that the Scriptures were fulfilled by the Nation. Pearse takes hold, then, of a largely Protestant form of reading, and within that very form enacts the transition that rewrites Irish nationalism as formally Catholic. This is all the more remarkable since, for Catholics in particular, the secularizing, or politicizing, of religious forms and language was not especially organic. As the Catholic writer W. E. Addis argued in an 1880 essay in the *Dublin Review*, Roman Catholicism denied nationalism, for "her universal empire had destroyed the spirit of patriotism. . . . Hence room was made for a religion 'which was from the first the denial of any earthly country.'"[66] And as Father Francis Shaw would point out in his essay quoted above, Pearse's politicizing of religious discourse was technically heretical rather than intrinsically natural.[67] Almost magically, though, the heresy was absorbed into a new orthodoxy, as Ireland's long-standing national investment in biblical narratives allowed Pearse's radical typology to become an acceptable truth, one constructed to seem both simple and ineluctable.

The Potency of Catholic Symbols

Pearse's pamphlets, speeches, and literary works all call upon Christian symbols, which he sees as able to both inspire awe and foreclose debate. Writing in 1913 of "this matter of symbols," Pearse approves that "the Church to which I belong, the wise Church that has called into her service all the arts, knows better than any other institution, human or divine, *the immense potency of symbols*: with symbols she exorcises evil spirits, with symbols she calls into play for beneficent purposes the infinite powers of omnipotence."[68] Pearse's most potent symbols—the crucified Christ, Mary, communion, baptism—may be ostensibly ecumenical, yet Pearse uses them to foreground a Catholic vision. Kiberd suggests that Pearse enlists the imagery "of a generalized mystical Christianity rather than something specifically Catholic in overtone,"[69] but by employing the symbols as types—in other words, as fulfillments of earlier Old Testament tropes, Pearse suggests not only their superiority over earlier symbolic systems (Exodus, particularly), but their associations with a Catholic rather than an Ascendancy Ireland. Parsing the distinctions between Protestant and Catholic language, imagery, and forms, Edna Longley offers a helpful schema: "Protestantism . . . eschews iconography, martyrology, mariolatry, saints, Christ on the Cross. . . . Orange insignia stick to the Old Testament, not only out of savage affinities, but because of the ban on representing the New. As a result, the Protestant equivalent of martyrology is a biblical narrative of persecution (paranoia rather than masochism)."[70] There is also a contrast, Longley writes, "between the verbal and the visual, text and image," in which the Protestant, verbal, Old Testament emblems "require exegesis, translation,"[71] unlike, Longely argues, the more immediately apparent Catholic symbols. However, Pearse's Catholic symbols only seem transparent; they encode religious and political meanings that do indeed need to be "read" precisely because they are presented as self-evident.

In the period of his conversion to the revolutionary movement, Pearse edited the short-lived *An Barr Buadh*, in which he published "Mionn" (Oath), his own nationalist rewriting of the Catholic Litany of Saints:

> In the name of God,
> By Christ His only Son,
> By Mary His gentle Mother,
> By Patrick the Apostle of the Irish,
> By the loyalty of Colm Cille,
> By the glory of our race,
> By the blood of our ancestors,
> By the murder of Red Hugh,
> By the sad death of Hugh O'Neill,
> By the tragic death of Owen Roe,
> By the dying wish of Sarsfield,
> By the anguished sigh of Fitzgerald,
> By the bloody wounds of Tone,
> By the noble blood of Emmet,
> By the Famine corpses,
> By the tears of Irish exiles,
> We swear the oaths our ancestors swore,
> That we will free our race from bondage,
> Or that we will fall fighting hand to hand
> Amen.[72]

The litany is a Catholic form, and the inclusion of Protestant Irish patriots in place of saints incorporates the former into a Catholic tradition, particularly through the resonances of Christ's sacrifice in "the bloody wounds of Tone" and the "noble blood of Emmet," which embody Christ's death on the cross and the transubstantiation. If it is appealing to read the presence of Emmet and Tone as nonsectarian, the unmistakable formal Catholic syntax encasing the figures seems rather to assimilate them into a Catholic identity, rather than accurately representing Tone's ecumenical views.[73] Moreover, it is possible, too, that the poem functioned as Catholic-nationalist pedagogy at

St. Enda's, where "An Old Irish Litany"—perhaps this very text, as updated by Pearse—was recited daily by the students, effectively making the text, if not part of Catholic religious ceremony, a display of Catholic form.[74] Pearse limns the space between the broadly Christian and the specifically Catholic, an ambiguity also reflected in the poem's conclusion with an echo of Exodus, where we are reminded that "our ancestors" identified with the narrative of Israelite liberation "from bondage."

In the late poem "The Rebel," Pearse imagines liberation for Ireland as contingent upon the very transition from Exodus to Calvary. The opening stanza includes the lines "My mother bore me in bondage, in bondage / my mother was born";[75] again, "bondage," and the phrases "the lash of masters" and "the task-work of strangers," consciously echo the language of Exodus. Lines that are spoken by a Moses-Parnell figure—"I speak to my people, and I speak in my people's name to the masters of my people. / I say to my people that they are holy, that they are august, despite their chains"[76]—reflect the parliamentary negotiation of the Parnellite politics of the 1890s. But if the words offer echoes of Moses debating with Pharaoh (or Parnell with Gladstone), this echo is superseded by the New Testament rhetoric that dominates the final lines of the poem: "And I say to my people's masters: Beware, / Beware of the thing that is coming, beware of the risen people, / Who shall take what ye would not give. Did ye think to conquer the people, / Or that Law is stronger than life and than men's desire to be free?"[77] Law, with its capital L, is not only the British rule of law in Ireland, but the Mosaic Law that Christ's sacrifice makes obsolete, which is made obsolete by the new life and freedom that "the risen people," or perhaps more accurately, the risen Pearse, would provide through his Christlike, Christ-fulfilling sacrifice.

The move from the Hebrew Scriptures to the New Testament is strategic in ways that reach beyond the Protestant/Catholic shift. In substituting Calvary for the desert wilderness of Exodus, Pearse avoids two problems: the forty years of waiting, and the recalcitrant citizens grumbling for the fleshpots (of English culture, English goods, English literature). Instead of the masses, as Northrop Frye writes in *The Great Code*, Jesus is "the individual form of the society of Israel."[78] Or as Deane writes of Pearsian messianism, "the single hero incarnates the potential of his race."[79] Metaphorically, then, Pearse underlines the particular need for unity in the Irish struggle by allowing all of Ireland to inhere in his own body, an idea already supported by the Young Ireland tradition whereby, as Marjorie Howes notes, "the individual and the nation [are] necessarily homologous."[80] The corollary is the suppression of Irish dissent and difference—difference of politics, but also of "race," religion, class, and culture. This was a distinct shift from Parnell's autocratic leadership, in which his very apartness created the separate energy of *the people*, whose role as (resistant) followers proved as critical as Parnell's role in leading (and failing) them. Under Connolly's socialist influence, Kiberd argues, Pearse was moved "beyond the notion of a single Christlike redeemer to the idea of a people as its own Messiah."[81] Yet the people-as-Messiah was imagined as singular rather than multiple, as perhaps Pearse's increasing connections to Lalor's labor movement and Connolly's socialism authorized the sense in which he himself might—as one of many equals—emblematize the nation.

In his 1913 article "The Coming Revolution," published in the Gaelic League's newspaper *An Claidheamh Soluis*, Pearse wrote that "the people itself will perhaps be its own Messiah, the people labouring, scourged, crowned with thorns, agonizing and dying, to rise again immortal and impassible."[82] The image of "the people labouring" is not the labor of Lalor's workers, however, nor is it the labor of Exodus, the labor of the wilderness. It is the work of sacrifice, of martyrdom—and more particularly, of crucifixion. The boundaries are clearly delineated, and the end is clear and inevitable (if also, as in *Kathleen ni Houlihan*, magical and invisible). Pearse writes that the revolution will not take place "without stress and trial, without suffering and bloodshed at any rate, it is not going to be achieved without work."[83] It is in this context that we have Pearse's much-quoted caveat: "We may make mistakes in the beginning and shoot the wrong people; but bloodshed is a cleansing and a sanctifying thing, and the nation which regards it as the final horror has lost its manhood. There are many things more horrible than bloodshed; and slavery is one of them."[84] Much has been written on the apparent bloodthirstiness of the above lines, either as appallingly violent (Father Shaw and the revisionists) or as participating in the widespread rhetoric of wartime Europe (Lee in his essay "In Search of Patrick Pearse," Deane in *Celtic Revivals*).[85] It is worth considering, though, the way in which this passage fits into Pearse's central narrative, in which Christ's bloodshed, his role as a sacrificial substitute who is without sin, is the "cleansing and sanctifying thing."[86] Pearse's death, modeled on Christ's, at once guarantees the success of his liberation narrative—its certainty of closure, that is—while it simultaneously obviates concern with the future realities of potential Irish discontent. Unlike Moses, Pearse's liberator does not try and then fail to reach the promised land, does not encounter in his people profound ambivalence about liberation and its responsibilities—perhaps does not need to attend to the mistakes of shooting "the wrong people." Rather, he succeeds in failure (death), through his sacrifice. The disappointment of not reaching the promised land is replaced with the promise of heaven for the Irish martyr. Pearse's journey to freedom, unlike Parnell's boundaryless "march of a nation,"[87] is synchronic rather than diachronic, ascending (a rising) vertically up to God, rather than forward on a winding path through the wilderness.

Pearse's self-sacrifice becomes a metonymy for (if not a guarantee of) Irish national liberation; his writings and actions offer a teleology that ends not with Christ, but with Pearse. Written just a month before the Rising, Pearse's final pamphlet, "The Sovereign People," concludes with a promise of the impending apocalypse: "the day of the Lord is here, and you and I have lived to see it."[88] When Pearse invokes apocalypse, even in traditional Christian terms, he is speaking not of the end of the world, but the end of English colonial rule in Ireland. In his pamphlet "Some Aspects of Irish Literature," Pearse argues that the great theme of Irish literature is sacrifice and redemption: "The curse of primal sin lies upon a people; new and personal sin brings doom to their doors; they are powerless to save themselves; a youth, free from the curse, akin with them through his mother but through his father divine, redeems them by his valour and his own death comes from it."[89] Pearse is speaking here not of the story of Christ, but of the mythic Irish hero Cuchulain, whose famed words gave Pearse the motto that he painted on the entrance to his school: "I care not though I were to live but one day and one night if only my fame and my deeds live after me." He says of the double-meaning of the narrative, "I do not mean that the *Táin* is a conscious allegory: but there is the story in its essence, and it is like a retelling (or is it a foretelling?) of the story of Calvary."[90] Although Pearse equivocates about which comes first chronologically, he hints that the *Táin* is a foretelling, an anticipation or "type" of the redemption that would occur with Christ. This is not then simply a "curious amalgam of Cuchulain and Christ,"[91] as it has often been read, but a reorganizing of these figures into a new typology (a "nativist anachronism," as Valente puts it[92]). One of the effects is the suppression of the original "foretelling" of Christ's story that is implied through a typological reading of the Hebrew Scriptures. In other words, it is no longer Exodus that provides a foretelling of Calvary, but Irish mythological history. Exodus is not only superseded, but entirely obscured.

Pearse's Passion Plays

In April 1911 Pearse brought his most successful play, *An País*, a Passion play performed in Irish, to the Abbey. It was remarkably well received, particularly compared with Dublin audiences' nonplussed response to Lady Gregory's Old Testament allegory *The Deliverer* performed just three months before. But unlike Gregory's embittered fusion of biblical and Irish politics, Pearse's play appeared to be less demanding: Edwards writes that "he succeeded through the straightforward adaptation of the dialogue of the Gospels to an Irish social ethos," including such Irish elements as women keening Christ at Calvary.[93] That the New Testament text was essentially unchanged made it no less of a political statement. Desmond Ryan wrote in 1918 of the performance, "The audience which, slowly and without applauding, passed out of the Abbey on the two nights of the performance had much to think of. The Irish medium, strange to most of it, had not veiled but intensified the meaning and pathos of the story. Some of us, too, thought, though to many it may seem an irreverence, that our national and individual struggle was in many ways a faint reflection of the Great One just enacted. It is not so? The Man is crucified as the Nation, and the Soul moves slowly, falteringly, towards the redemption."[94] For the boys and staff of St. Enda's onstage, and perhaps even the Abbey audience, it surely was so. The Irish struggle was hardly a "faint" reflection of the "Great One" to Pearse, and it is hard to imagine him using terms like "slowly, falteringly" about Irish redemption. Pearse himself played the minor role of a thief in the production, but nevertheless Edwards reads the performance as a momentous occasion in which Pearse began, more conclusively, to identify himself with Christ.[95] It is also a moment in which he reiterates the move away from Exodus: as Elaine Sisson notes, Pearse's introduction of the keening women only when act 3 begins allows him to formally register the introduction of "a Celtic influence, signalling a shift away from Judaism towards Christianity."[96] Finally, it seems the Passion play was a rehearsal, of sorts, for his sacrifice in the Rising, which Nicholas Grene describes as "an event planned with conscious theatricality."[97] What Cairns and Richards write of Pearse's other plays was equally true of the Passion play: it was "drama as a ritual pre-enactment of an advocated action,"[98] and in fact three of the staff members acting in the play were later executed for their roles in the Rising.[99] The audience seems to have anticipated the play's importance even at the time: there was a wide demand for photograph postcards of the actors in character, and Pearse himself viewed the event as a high point of the revival.[100]

But it was Pearse's play *The Singer*—written just months before the Rising—that most explicitly supports his identification with Christ. The play depicts its protagonist MacDara as one who will redeem Ireland through sacrifice: "some great hero that has come back again to lead the people against the Gall, or maybe himself an angel, or the Son of Mary Himself that has come down on the earth."[101] As MacDara walks alone into a doomed battle, he cries, "One man can free a people as one Man redeemed the world. I will take no pike, I will go into the battle with bare hands. I will stand up before the Gall as Christ hung naked before men on the tree!"[102] Christ on the cross was for Pearse a central symbol for Irish nationalism, and it is not surprising that he invokes it here in his most politically galvanizing dramatic scene. Encouraged, perhaps, by Pearse's use of the image, his sister Margaret wrote after his death, "His greatest devotion was to the tragedy of Calvary—to Christ Crucified, and to the Crucifix. He showed this very quietly, but very plainly, in the arrangements of the little Oratory at St. Enda's. He placed the Crucifix in the most prominent position on the altar, and would not allow it to be disturbed or outplaced by any statue or picture."[103] Pearse was identified with the Christlike MacDara even before the Easter Rising confirmed it; the character MacDara was, like Pearse, a teacher, a poet, an organizer. According to Robert Welch, Pearse delayed the play's production—originally intended for before the Rising—"on the grounds that its obvious message would provide the authorities with an excuse for interning the participants."[104] To his own mother in the days before his death, Pearse would invoke the Mariolatry of Catholicism: "People will say hard things of us now, but we shall be remembered by posterity and blessed by unborn generations. You too will be blessed because you were my mother."[105] Hours before his execution, Pearse again wrote to his mother mentioning a last poem "which would seem to be said by you about me."[106] The poem, "A Mother Speaks," extends the analogy between Mrs. Pearse and Mary: "Dear Mary, that didst see thy first-born Son / Go forth to die amid the scorn of men / For whom He died, / Receive my first-born into thy arms, / Who also hath gone out to die for men."[107] These lines recall Pearse's earlier translation of the traditional Irish poem "The Keening of Mary." In Pearse's translation, when Mary sees Christ on the cross he addresses her as "little Mother,"[108] and as Mrs. Pearse tells us in her memoir, this was her son's special term of endearment for her.[109]

In the days after the Rising, Cairns and Richards write, "post-execution posters on Dublin walls depicting Pearse in pieta position supported by Mother Erin, [indicate] how pervasive was the image of his self-willed immolation."[110] The form of the Rising, they insist, ensured that "the supremacy of Catholicism" would become the hallmark of the people-nation.[111] In the aftermath of the executions there was indeed, as Newsinger writes, a sort of "conversion" in which "the martyred dead of the Rising were canonized in popular consciousness":[112] one young man recalled "a feeling of sadness, and at the same time of holiness and exultation."[113] Speaking in 1920 the republican Terence MacSwiney, whose hunger strike in a British prison would end in his death, repeated the Pearsian idiom: "The liberty for which we today strive is a sacred thing, inseparably entwined with that spiritual liberty for which the Savior of man died, and which is the inspiration and foundation of all just government. Because it is sacred, and death for it is akin to the Sacrifice of Calvary, following far off but constant to that Divine example, in every generation our best and bravest have died."[114] MacSwiney, like Pearse, was a national hero after his death. Yet the years after 1916 would also bring critique, both covert and explicit. Most infamously impious to the national creation story was Sean O'Casey's 1926 play *The Plough and the Stars*, which juxtaposes Pearse's speechifying with the scene of a prostitute in a pub. Where O'Casey was frank in his repudiation of the sacrificial ethos, Lady Gregory was subtle—so subtle, in fact, that her critique seems to have gone unnoticed.

Gregory's Passion Play

When Pearse invokes the four honored patriots of his "New Testament of Irish Nationalism" in his pamphlet "Ghosts," and adds to this group the additional figure of Parnell, he writes, "Thus Tone, thus Davis, thus Lalor, thus Mitchel, thus Parnell. Methinks I have raised some ghosts that will take a little laying."[115] As I noted earlier, Parnell is only a provisional addendum, but it is Parnell's ghost in particular that has not been laid to rest even after the Rising and Pearse's sacrifice. Not long after Easter 1916, we begin to find resistance to Pearse's style of sacrificial messianism. And at the center of many of these antimessianic narratives—plays and other writings by Lady Gregory, Lennox Robinson, Seamus O'Kelly, and George Moore—we find Parnell. A now ironic and even cynical revenant,

Parnell reinserts struggle, ambivalence, and dissension into the story of liberation—and with him comes the return of the themes of Exodus. When Gregory returns to *The Deliverer*'s Kiltartan Israelites in her 1924 play *The Story Brought by Brigit*, like Pearse she offers a version of the Christ story as national drama. Yet if it seems that this is simply Gregory's attempt to assimilate Pearse's new Christ-centered narrative of liberation—the version that had been authorized by the new Free State—the play, while ostensibly about Christ's sacrifice, instead urgently returns to the turmoil of postcolonial politics and the story of Parnell betrayed. When Gregory interrogates the transformative power of the sacrifice of Christ/Parnell/Pearse, she reveals it not as a triumph, but as a terrible mistake.

In "Some Aspects of Irish Literature," Pearse had remarked on the spiritual connection between Jesus, Mary, and Ireland: "Christ and Mary have been incorporated in to the Gaelic clan; and the Irish peasant women can keen Christ dead with as real a grief as they keen their own dead . . . The strange intimacy that connects certain places in Ireland with the scenes of Christ's birth and life and death, and links certain Irish saints and heroes with the joy of the Nativity and the tragedy of the Passion—this is the true Irish mysticism."[116] In addition to mystical or imagined visitations, there were also genealogical folk traditions, such as the one Gregory records that "brings the Holy Mother and Child to our own country."[117] In the program note for the Abbey performance of *The Story Brought by Brigit*, Gregory explains this tale as the genesis for her play: "Our tradition and that of Gaelic Scotland speak of St. Brigit as 'the foster-mother of Christ,' and I have been told by poor women of Slieve Echtge that she succoured both the Blessed Mother and Child when they were brought here by a Heavenly messenger for safety in Herod's time, and that she 'kept an account of every drop of blood He lost through His lifetime.' So it is not going very far from tradition to suppose she may have been present at the end of His life as at the beginning, and have told the story in her own way, as she had seen it in the body or in vision" (398).[118] The *Irish Times* reviewer deduced that this account was simply "an excuse for giving a Kiltartan Irish flavour to the narration of the Passion story."[119] Gregory herself recalled that "I knew I could best write [the Passion story] through the voice, as it were, of our own people" (395), but she did far more than simply incorporate Kiltartan speech patterns. Where Gregory claims to write the story of Christ through an Irish perspective, her conceit is subtly disingenuous. The narrative does not simply have Irish flavor; it is an Irish allegory. Toward the end of the play, a woman tells Brigit, "indeed it is a heart-broken story you will have to bring back to Ireland" (337). The story, however, is already in Ireland—it is the story *of* Ireland.

The allegory may be less explicit, less specific, than the story of Parnell in *The Deliverer*, but it is undeniably an account of Ireland's colonial status. The same Kiltartan Israelites left to their continued oppression by the Pharaoh are now under the yoke of the Romans, a colonial context remarked on many years before by Yeats: "It is hardly an exaggeration to say that the spiritual history of the world has been the history of conquered races. . . . And has not our Christianity come to us from defeated and captive Judea?"[120] Jesus, from the start of Gregory's play, is presented not as a religious leader, but as a political activist and national hero. As Lucy McDiarmid points out, "Christ . . . has become an Irish felon, his followers 'rebels,' and his transgressions political."[121] As in Gregory's essay "The Felons of Our Land" (1900) and her play *The Gaol Gate* (1906), Christian iconography and republican ideals are fused.[122] According to Joel, *Brigit*'s romantic would-be rebel, Jesus's purpose is "to put out the Roman strangers and to take off their yoke. Haven't they enough countries in their hand without coming ploughing through the sea to meddle with our own?" (304). Within the first few moments of the play, Gregory thus invokes Ireland's colonial status through the now-archetypal language of *Kathleen ni Houlihan*, in which "strangers in the house" is coded to mean British interlopers. Joel describes the long history that has motivated him to follow a revolutionary leader come "to give us our freedom" (304): "I heard rebellion talked ever and always and I a child, in the high mountains and on the low ground. Our country a ruin, our people scattered" (305). As the *Freeman's Journal* reviewer noted, "The parallel . . . between the Roman domination of Palestine and the British occupation of Ireland is clearly drawn."[123]

But why write another allegory of colonialism in 1923, just months after the establishment of the Irish Free State? In her notes on the text, Gregory suggests one reason for the play's appearance at that particular time, although Yeats had been urging her for many years to consider a Passion play. "But it was only last summer, when my life seemed to have drifted into a quiet backwater, and I was much alone, that the great subject took hold of me, and so filled my mind that I was forced to get it into words, and into the form I am most used to, of a play" (395). The loneliness and sadness Gregory implies here are not surprising, considering the relatively recent death of her son in the Great War and of her beloved nephew Hugh Lane on the *Lusitania*—men also sacrificed to war. More directly relevant, perhaps, is the continued strife in an Ireland that had managed to reach the metaphorical promised land of independence. Gregory's scrapbook from this period registers the trauma visually: in a collection that includes exclusively broadsheet ballads from the 1880s up until the 1920s, suddenly Gregory inserts a dreadful memorial culled from the newspapers: photographs, obituaries, and last letters written by young men on the eve of their executions by the new Free State. It is a chilling archive of the brutal Civil War, as well as a graphic representation of the sacrificial ethos absorbed by both sides.[124]

The Free State had very little in it of milk and honey. Rather, Gregory found the situation in Ireland deeply troubling, even compared to the war in Europe: "this is a far sadder war, being brother against brother, friend against friend."[125] The first line of *Brigit* seems to acknowledge the despairing conditions in Ireland in the early '20s, when a messiah seemed impossible: "I think the time will never come when I will see him!" (303). The pathos of the play is also that, in 1923, the savior had *already* come, and it had made little difference. Ireland now was post-savior: post-Parnell, post-Pearse, but also post-Treaty with Britain and post-partition. Israelites in Gregory's Roman-ruled Judea are, like the Irish of the Free State, both saved and not saved, and Gregory shows them as chosen people living in a culture where bourgeois greed trumps true freedom. *Brigit* projects a knowingness about the challenges of emerging from a colonial relationship: "Ah, Freedom never put a penny in anyone's pocket" (304), says Daniel, the treacherous alcoholic pragmatist representative of the (male) citizenry. The oppressed, fearful, colonized psyche returns to haunt the postcolonial nation. In the Gospels the Jews fail to recognize the redemption they have been given, and Gregory suggests the Irish have made the same mistake; they are as oppressed after liberation as they were before it.

Like Gregory's Parnell play of 1911, dissension within Irish politics is a central theme of *Brigit.* Early in the play the Roman Marcus explains, in the language of 1916, "to tell the clean truth, a little Rising now and then is no harm at all. It gives us an excuse to get rid of disturbers and to bring more of our armies in. A Rising too is very apt to lead to splits, and splits are a great help when you want to keep a country down" (310). This passage includes within its condemning scope both the Parnell "split" in Committee Room 15 and the division of the country over the Anglo-Irish Treaty and the resulting Civil War. If the former is the rift that kept Ireland "down" by killing Home Rule, the latter was the raw wound in the Free State. But even if the social and political concerns of Ireland in 1923 differed from those of 1911, there is a remarkable sense of continuity, even repetition, in *Brigit* and *The Deliverer.* The plays are not so much a chronological series—a two-part narrative of the Irish-as-Israelites in the Old and New Testaments—as the same play repeated later, or a pathological return to the repressed story of Parnell. Much of the repetition takes place at a rhetorical level, with vocabulary that explicitly recalls the earlier play, such as the word "over-Government" (308). In *Brigit*, the hero "has power to free and to *deliver* his people" (306, my emphasis), and "is surely the man that will *deliver* Israel" (313, my emphasis); he is also a "mountainy lad" (322) according to Silas—linking him with Parnell, who was thought to have had ambiguous connections to the disenfranchised rural Irish rebels known as "mountainy men." It is, in fact, remarkable that the play has never been connected with the Parnell theme.[126]

Gregory had first anticipated and then witnessed the difficulties of devolution, and persisting problems of social hierarchy and economic injustice are central concerns in both plays. As Daniel in *Brigit* points out, even with freedom "the rich will be stiff and covetous, and the grabbers will grab all the same as at this day" (304). In the earlier play, after helping the deliverer make preparations for the exodus by taking stores from Pharaoh, Dan says, "I wish I didn't wipe the mortar from me awhile ago. There might some of the riches have stuck to my feet."[127] He seems very nearly the same character (with the same name) as the Daniel of *Brigit*, who returns from the Temple with Jesus noting the riches strewn about on the ground, saying, "my grief I had not a bit of wax spread upon the sole of my shoe before I was driven out the door" (316). Beyond the details, the larger theme of *Brigit* is essentially the same as that of *The Deliverer*: the people's betrayal of the man who has come to deliver them to freedom. Christ first appears in *Brigit* in a scene that virtually repeats that in *The Deliverer*, in which the King's Nurseling is lauded with praise by the crowd; but as in *The Deliverer*, fear and greed subsequently divert the people from their nationalist intentions. When Silas, a particularly insidious Roman/Unionist collaborator, describes the dangers of rebelling, the crowd evinces the same cowardice and lack of conviction that characterized the previous Israelites, and they turn away from Christ ("I wouldn't wish to go against the neighbours" [323]) just as they betrayed the King's Nurseling. Treachery is, as in *The Deliverer*, a case of selling out to the colonizing power and the religious authority of (Catholic) priests.

Gregory again references her Parnell allegory when Jesus laments, "Jerusalem, thou that killeth the prophets and stonest them that are sent to thee!" (312). This image of stoning recalls not only the biblical text of Exodus 17:4 but also *The Deliverer*, in which the Moses figure is stoned to death by the people. The King's Nurseling's death is further echoed in *Brigit* when Christ is described as "a bird of the high air cast down among wild cats of the clefts" (325–26), invoking the "King's cats" to whom the deliverer is finally thrown and who tear him apart. Likewise, the shouting crowd of *Brigit* is described as "the howling of wild dogs after their prey" (326), an allusion to Parnell's famous plea not to be thrown to the English wolves by his Irish party. In *Brigit* the character Joel particularly represents the betrayal of a once-faithful people: persuaded by Silas that Jesus is in fact in league with the Roman governor Pilate, Joel cries out for crucifixion. But when Christ is put on the cross, Joel realizes the error and attributes his actions to an inevitable Irish pathology: "That's the way of it! All the generations looking for him and praying for him. We wanted him, and we got him, and what we did with him was to kill him. And this is the way it will be ever and always, so long as leaves grow upon the trees!" (339). In *The Deliverer*, too, Gregory invokes a past of Irish perfidy: "That young man [the King's Nurseling] to have read history he would not have come to our help."[128] History, Gregory suggests, proves that the Irish always betray their leaders.

In addition to conjuring the revenant Parnell, Gregory's play uses the Gospel stories to address challenges of postcoloniality that were also central to *The Deliverer*: economic instability, Catholic bigotry, and the role of women. All of the women in *Brigit*, and only the women, are faithful to Christ, and when one of the weak, betraying men makes a sexist comment, Gregory means it to expose the widespread chauvinism in nationalist circles (323). Likewise, the hypocrisy of supposedly pious "Jews" (read Catholic Irish-Irelanders) is exposed when they attack Jesus for mixing with the nonreligious and the lower class: one decries Jesus as "He that goes eating and drinking with a low class that do not so much as wash their hands!" (309). Ireland's national drinking problem is what catalyzes the final betrayal: those who call out against Christ are culled from the pubs and bribed with drink to shout him down (327).

More subversive than these social critiques, Gregory's Passion play is an indictment of Pearse's vision of himself and his Rising as the salvation of Ireland. A moment before Christ reappears resurrected to his followers, Joel cries out, "my bitter blame upon the place where he died! I thought it had been he would have redeemed Israel!" (344). Saint Brigit, who seems to know this story already, tells Joel, "it is the whole of the Universe he has redeemed" (345), but even this Christian truth seems unconvincing in the context of such national misery. Within the logic of the play's allegorical narrative, the sacrifice at the end fails; even if Christ's death on the cross "redeems the world," it clearly does not redeem the nation. The death of the people's savior may mean eternal *Christian* salvation, but the nation is still oppressed. Had the Jews/Irish not betrayed Christ (as the Irish betrayed Parnell), had he lived, the play suggests, perhaps there *would* have been a leader to bring the nation together, and it would have been saved from Roman tyranny. With a Christ so reminiscent of Parnell, it is not surprising we are left with more disillusion than redemption. Gregory's play implicitly suggests what Father Francis Shaw would argue years later: "Christ was not born to set bondsmen free from any chains other than those of sin. In the Judea of his day, Christ was set down in a situation comparable to that of the Ireland of 1916. Christ made it unmistakably plain that he was not a national saviour, and his words to his disciples on the day of the Ascension expressed his sorrow that those who knew him and who loved him could continue so long in error."[129] As a national allegory, *Brigit* offers little more fulfillment than the bitter and hopeless *Deliverer*; rather, it demonstrates Gregory's ambivalence about both typology and analogy: unlike the clearly didactic *Deliverer*, this play includes both redemption (in its Christian sense) and the impossibility of redemption (for Ireland).

Like Pearse, Gregory is particularly concerned with highlighting the typological transition from Moses's Law to Christ's grace. In foregrounding that shift in *Brigit*, however, Gregory's purpose is to specifically critique Pearse and to reject blood sacrifice as a form of political agency. A soon-to-be follower of Jesus notes, "to love Him . . . and to love his neighbour as himself, is more than all burnt offerings and sacrifices" (312). And as Christ himself says in the play, "I will have mercy and not sacrifice" (312). In the years after 1916 the word *sacrifice* evoked images of young men following Kathleen to the battlefields; by 1924 the playwright who had offered *Kathleen ni Houlihan* as the archetype for national blood sacrifice had seen the grim consequences of this vision. When Joel proposes, "If we are killed itself, to die for our country is a good death to die!" (322), his bravado rings hollow in the context of the play's ironies and betrayals. The hollow sound is perhaps amplified, too, by the now-absent young men whose deaths Gregory had recorded in her scrapbooks. Yet for all of the cynicism about Ireland embedded in Gregory's version of the passion story—so different than Pearse's 1915 production—what *is* expressed earnestly is the concept of typological supersession implicit in the fulfillment of the Mosaic Law in Christ. As the character of Saint John explains, "The law was given by Moses, but grace and truth came by Jesus Christ" (313). Gregory, in reasserting the tenet that Christ's sacrifice indeed supersedes and fulfills Moses's law, also returns Christian typology to its original home in the New Testament. In doing this, she renders Pearse's nationalist typology—in which his personal sacrifice for Ireland fulfills and supersedes the universal Christ story—false: neither Christ's sacrifice, nor Pearse's, can redeem a single nation. For Gregory, national struggle was the work of women and men, not divine apocalypse, and Christ's sacrifice was for all people, not just the Irish, whose national struggle would remain unaffected by it.

But even as Gregory rejects Pearse's brand of holy nationalism, *Brigit* is still inevitably filled with Pearsian echoes, as any retelling of the Christ story would have been after the Easter Rising. When Saint Brigit tells the other women waiting by the cross not to worry for Christ's mother, for "there will be joy in her heart in the years to come, knowing that he has visited and redeemed his people" (337), it is likely that Irish audiences would have recalled Pearse's now-famous last words to his mother, that they would both "be remembered by posterity" and that she would be "blessed because you were my mother."[130] Moreover, when Christ is mourned in the play's final moments, it is with the above-mentioned poem "The Keening of Mary" that Pearse had translated and published.[131] Thus, as in *The Deliverer*, there is a tension between nationalist rhetoric and its critique, and Gregory uses biblical narratives to at once produce and cloak her commentary on

Irish politics. She seems to have learned from *The Deliverer* that the Irish didn't appreciate twist endings on their biblical stories, and for the most part, Abbey audiences received *Brigit* as a simple retelling of the Christ story; it was widely celebrated and considered by both Yeats and Douglas Hyde to be Gregory's best work.[132] There was some recognition of the play's political engagements, including Maud Gonne's slightly mysterious report to Gregory that "they are saying you have written a Republican play."[133] Gregory's unsparing analysis of English colonialism may read as Republican, but the play also critiques Irish bourgeois materialism and Pearsian blood sacrifice. And Gregory's characters need a political salvation that they seem unlikely to get in the world of the play, a world in which the Irish are by nature or experience unwilling to follow their deliverer. One otherwise appreciative reviewer notes the failure of the play's ending, writing that "the only part of the story which drags is that after Christ has passed to Calvary. The scene afterwards holds much that is beautiful, but it seems, nevertheless, as anti-climax."[134] This was apparently as close as anyone would come to recognizing the political implications of the anticlimactic reality of a nation still in bondage.

As with *The Deliverer*, audiences seemed disinclined to recognize the political critique coded within Gregory's play. Gregory records in her journal the response from Huntington: "I read your Passion Play last night, and I feel indeed that it is a beautiful and precious work. It has the inevitable quality, and it seems to depend, as religion should, upon the heart rather than upon the mind. There is the wonderful story just as it is known to children and simple people, and there are no clever new theories to upset our cherished conceptions."[135] Gregory's response to this, "a relief!"[136] is ambiguous; it may be simply that she is grateful for praise. But she may also be pleased not to have the more controversial elements of the play discovered, especially by someone who would use the phrase "clever new theories." For while Gregory was a devout believer, she was also an open-minded one. Perhaps the most astute observation of the play was by H. Speakman, who wrote to Gregory, "if tears still came to my eyes at the third reading of your play, it was not at Daniel crying 'Crucify him' nor at his going out with the nails, but at the lad *Joel* crying 'Crucify him'! Haven't I walked Ireland with a donkey cart?"[137] The tragedy of this betrayal—the betrayal of innocence—is, as Speakman recognizes, the central drama of the play.

An allusion toward the end of the play amplifies the text's concern with Irish betrayal. Joel, upon realizing his treacherous error in forsaking Christ, speaks with echoes of Pegeen Mike's final lament in Synge's *The Playboy of the Western World*. He cries out, "if he is or is not the Christ I cannot tell. But whether or not, he is the only whole gentleman in the world!" (340). The exclamation can be read as simply a playful citation: Christy (*Christ*-y) is first embraced, then rejected in Synge's play. Gregory perhaps wryly offers the idea of Christ's crucifixion as a version of *The Playboy*, instead of the other way around. More seriously, she offers a commentary on Ireland's pathological betrayal of its leaders, its prophets, and its artists. For Synge, like Christy Mahon, was also repelled and betrayed by the Irish, as they rioted against one of the best plays that Ireland would produce in the twentieth century.[138] In a reversal of his rejection of Synge's play some years before, Pearse had linked the playwright (now dead of Hodgkin's disease) to Christ. In 1913 he wrote, "when a man like Synge, a man in whose sad heart there glowed a true love of Ireland, one of the two or three men who have in our time made Ireland considerable in the eyes of the world, uses strange symbols which we do not understand, we cry out that he has blasphemed and we proceed to crucify him."[139] While Pearse's political program forced critique and ambivalence from his own works, his belated defense of Synge may offer compelling complications to the readings explored above if, along with Pearse himself, Synge the subversive artist is also represented as a Christ for Ireland. In the same way, Lady Gregory was moved not by Pearse's sacrifice of his own life for Ireland, but by his sacrifice of art for politics: "Poor Pearse," she wrote after the Rising, "whose interests had seemed to be in literature."[140]

Anti-Messianism

Pearse's death guaranteed his continuing presence in Irish national culture, and many believe that it is true (if fraught and complicated) that his sacrifice made the Irish Republic possible. But his ghost was not the one that haunted literary writers in the decade leading up to 1922. Rather, it was Parnell who would reappear, not as the saving messiah, but again as the betrayed one: a reminder that Pearsian messianism, like constitutional nationalism, had failed to liberate Ireland. Gregory's subtle dismissal of the sacrificial narrative would be rendered more explicit in plays by Lennox Robinson, Seamus O'Kelly, and George Moore, as each of them recast the messianic theme in an ironic register in which resurrection, Pearse's metonymy for national freedom, is retrospectively applied to Parnell. Yet if the resurrection (or attempted resurrection) of Parnell or his ghost brings no relief, it does bring back the ambivalence and difficulty of Exodus. A brief consideration of these texts—which in the years before the founding of the Free State question and ultimately reject Pearse's newly dominant typology—prepares us for the turn back to Exodus that Joyce's *Ulysses*, the subject of chapter 4, demands.

Unlike Pearse, the Parnell of Lenox Robinson's 1918 play *The Lost Leader* does not want to be resurrected like Jesus; he does not want the responsibility of leading a people who have proven so difficult. Upon recovering from the near-fatal illness that the world believes has killed him, this almost-sick-to-death-of-politics Parnell ("I remember as I lay dying I hoped there was no resurrection of the dead,"[141] he proclaims) makes a new start as the owner of a bed-and-breakfast in the promised land of the west of Ireland. Eventually he is revealed, through accidental hypnosis and pseudo-Freudian analysis, to be the true Parnell in hiding—and indeed, it was a popular myth (ruminated on by Leopold Bloom in *Ulysses*) that Parnell had never been seen in his coffin and might still be alive. Robinson's "Lucius Lenihan"/Parnell explains how, in 1891, a friend "showed me a way out, he showed me how I could live and yet be dead. . . . How I laughed afterwards to read of the crowds that followed my coffin, and in that coffin lay a poor Russian immigrant who had died unknown even by name, and whose body thousands followed to the grave. How Irish that was!"[142] In this scenario, Parnell's rejection of the roles of Moses and Christ is itself rendered ironic, since his plan has only been carried out by the aid of a Jewish body; the Russian immigrants in Ireland at that time were all Jews, and it is a gesture toward the biblical story that has failed. Robinson also subtly echoes Gregory's *The Deliverer*: in that play, Moses/The King's Nurseling kills an Egyptian with a hurley stick; here, the same weapon is used to kill the would-be deliverer himself. In *The Lost Leader*'s most cynical irony, just as Lucius/Parnell's existence is about to be revealed to the world (although Robinson adds some ambiguity about whether he is, in fact, Parnell), he is killed by his most fervent admirer. The old blind Houlihan—his very name evoking the unfulfilled promise of Yeats and Gregory's play—strikes down his hero by accident, in the midst of the crowd's bickering about which party Parnell would take up with in the new Ireland of the twentieth century. Parnell is destroyed (yet again) by the obstinacy of the Irish people.

Likewise looking back to Gregory's *The Deliverer* is Seamus O'Kelly's 1917 play *The Parnellite*, set in the 1880s and '90s. It ends with the murder by stoning of the eponymous hero Stephen, whose community turns against him after Parnell's involvement in the O'Shea divorce case is revealed. As Gregory had implied, the stoning of Moses-Parnell (or here, his stand-in), threatened but not carried out in the Hebrew Bible, is the culminating truth of the Israelite-Irish rejection of their deliverer, the psychological truth (as Freud later claimed) of their departure from Egypt. "To your tents, O Israel!" cries Stephen as he rallies for Parnell's no-rent manifesto; but once again, the people destroy him instead of allowing him to deliver them from oppression. Before he is killed, Stephen offers an image of Parnell, and himself, as Christ: the man who has given all for a people who betray him, "the man who has raised them from abomination, who has set your feet and my feet on a road which leads to the heights."[143] The traitors, Stephen says, "are of the breed of Judas Iscariot who sold Christ for thirty pieces of silver. . . . Men of Kilmacshane, throw the light of your torches on the heap of blackened ruins stark on yonder hill [where Stephen's house has been burned for his political activities]. There you can see the testimony of my sacrifice."[144] Earthly or apocalyptic, Old or New Testament, the response to Irish political messianism in both of these plays is one of skepticism and scorn. Yeats, too, had interrogated and rejected sacrifice and resurrection in his later plays, including *Calvary*, written during the Anglo-Irish War in 1919–20, and *The Resurrection*, in 1931. *Calvary* in particular, in which a resurrected Lazarus berates Jesus for taking "his death" is a covert but powerful indictment of Christological, Pearsian sacrifice, as are the Cuchulain plays.[145] Yeats and Gregory's *Kathleen ni Houlihan* would continue to be produced by the Abbey Theatre every year but one from its founding until 1922 (and indeed, most years up through the 1930s), yet both authors had moved on from their story of blood sacrifice to plays that rejected it.

Finally, there was the case of George Moore, whose anti-messianism first appeared just as Pearse was developing his new Christological ethos. In 1911 when Moore left Ireland for London and published the first volume of *Hail and Farewell*, his exposé of Ireland's literary revival, he was already both invested in biblical narratives and disillusioned with Ireland and its politics—two themes that would become connected in much of his future work.[146] That same year Moore, drawing on a new theory that proposed Jesus did not die on the cross but merely experienced a "cataleptic swoon,"[147] and "fearing that so tempting an idea might be pillaged,"[148] quickly published a roughly sketched dramatic treatment entitled *The Apostle: A Drama in Three Acts*. Moore worked on the idea for twenty more years, publishing at least six versions of three different texts, all of which imagine a scenario emerging from Jesus's ensuing earthly, human life.[149] In *The Apostle*, Jesus, who has survived the crucifixion, is shocked to learn that while quietly living in a desert monastery he has been deemed by a small sect the resurrected Son of God. Encountering the proselytizing Paul, this nondivine Jesus feels obliged to clear up the misunderstanding: "I go to Jerusalem to save the world from crimes that will be committed in the name of Jesus of Nazareth, if I deny not before the people the Godhead thou has thrust upon me."[150] Paul, however, cannot accept the humanity of Jesus; as Moore would write some years later in the introduction to his novelized version, *The Brook Kerith*, "we have grown so accustomed to these fond figurations of the messianic idea that any more human conception comes to us like a blasphemy."[151] Confronted by the man Jesus and not the savior, Paul cries out, "O Blasphemy! Blasphemy! Jesus of Nazareth, the great mediator between God and man, sitteth at the right hand of his father, and it is in his name that I strike thee down."[152] Paul strikes Jesus dead so that the truth will remain buried. Here is yet another echo of Parnell, the leader betrayed by a people and murdered by their unthinking and dogmatic religious zeal.

Moore's play came up against Joyce's wit in the latter's rant against its publisher Maunsel and Co., which had signed on to publish Joyce's *Dubliners* before bowing to self-censorship and the pieties of its printer. In his savage satire "Gas from a Burner" (1912), Joyce invokes Moore's drama as "a play of the Word and Holy Paul / And some woman's legs that I can't recall."[153] But for all his mockery, in this same poem Joyce offers his famous lines concurring with Moore's reading of Ireland's betrayal:

> This lovely land that always sent
> Her writers and artists to banishment
> And in a spirit of Irish fun
> Betrayed her own leaders, one by one.[154]

In fact, Moore and Joyce are much aligned here: both self-banished, both censored, and both bemoaning the Irish practice of refusing to see liberation—whether political or artistic—when it was at hand.

In 1916 as Pearse was acting out the Christ story and making it into Ireland's own, Moore, in his new novel, was doing just the opposite: unmaking Christianity at its source and showing how such an undoing might, in fact, offer a better sort of liberation. Moore made substantial changes to *The Apostle* in *The Brook Kerith* (which another of Moore's dust jackets proclaims, absurdly for today's readers, as "the best-known and possibly the best of George Moore's books"), a long naturalist novel that doesn't depend on irony for its effect. Here Jesus is not murdered by Paul, nor does he go to Jerusalem to preach the falseness of Paul's gospel.[155] Rather, Moore revises his story in a less cynical register that recasts the nondivinity of Jesus as a powerful spiritual alternative. As Moore writes in the novel's introduction, "we are not pagans, surely, because Jesus seems to us as great in his humanity as in the divinity which some credit him with."[156] Moore, like Pearse, offered up a Christian sacrilege, but Ireland reacted to the two heresies very differently: unlike Pearse's narrative of blood sacrifice, Moore's far less dramatic story was forgotten in Ireland and everywhere else. Yet Moore was also powerfully imagining a true leader—one who was not a martyr or a sacrifice or a ghost. His Jesus brings us some way toward another antihero who is at once Moses, Christ, and everyman, and who, like Moore's human Jesus, inhabits (if psychologically and metaphorically) the space of the desert: James Joyce's Leopold Bloom.

4

A Pisgah Sight of Palestine from Dear Dirty Dublin

James Joyce's *Ulysses* takes place on June 16, 1904, some weeks after a choral composition entitled "The Exodus" won the award for best sacred cantata in Ireland's national *Feis Ceoil* music festival. The cantata goes unmentioned in Joyce's novel, but it would not be out of place among other public performances of the Irish-Israelite analogy circulating through the text: the recitation of John F. Taylor's speech on Moses; Stephen's "Pisgah Sight of Palestine" parable; the Citizen's lament for Irish emigrants as "our lost tribes" (*U* 312). Yet if Exodus had been considered not only apt for the oppressed Irish but practically sacred before the turn of the century, things were changing in 1904. Sinn Fein founder Arthur Griffith argued that the new cantata, written by the future Easter Rising martyr Thomas MacDonagh and with music by Joyce's Italian voice coach Benedetto Palmieri, was too "foreign" to merit an Irish prize.[1] The Israelite analogy, with its strong link to Parnell, was already becoming contested as a way of imagining anticolonial struggle in Ireland; by the time Joyce's novel appeared in 1922—the same year as the birth of the Free State—the trope had disappeared almost entirely from Irish political and cultural discourse. During those intervening years of revolutionary war and finally devolution, Patrick Pearse had led the way in deconstructing the Parnell-as-Moses myth and producing a new narrative of Irish liberation that depended upon sacrifice, rather than on a long and difficult struggle through the wilderness. A New Testament version of the birth of the Irish nation had become dogma throughout the country, and in *Ulysses* Joyce memorializes the Exodus narrative after it had already been made obsolete. If the novel is many things, one of those is an account of the erasure of the Israelite analogy from Irish national life.

Exodus still had a rhetorical and ethical place in Ireland in 1904, and the trope circulates, with both historical accuracy and retrospective critique, through the pages of *Ulysses*. Writing from abroad, Joyce was remembering an earlier Ireland, and carefully reconstructing the post-Parnell Dublin he had known before departing for the Continent. In Joyce's hands the Exodus story is much more than a rhetorical flourish (and a tired one at that) that had happened to embellish Irish politics at the turn of the century. Rather, like Lady Gregory, Joyce finds in Exodus a narrative that exposes difficulties, explicates them, and finally reveals the process of Ireland's liberation to be a complicated one. Joyce was not interested in an account of liberation that simplified the difficult process of anticolonial struggle. To refuse to show life's realities, Joyce wrote, would "retard the course of civilization in Ireland by preventing the Irish people from having one good look at themselves in my nicely polished looking glass"—a look that would expose an Ireland he saw as characterized by "the odour of ashpits and old weeds and offal."[2] Although Joyce was speaking here of *Dubliners*, *Ulysses* too would be an exposition of the raw "real" Ireland, in which Joyce remade his polished mirror into the "cracked lookingglass of a servant" (*U* 7) and then named it the "symbol of Irish art" (*U* 7).[3] The servant is, among other possibilities, a figure for colonial Ireland, yet *Ulysses* not only depicts Ireland's servitude to England, but also imagines the difficulties in becoming free. Joyce had described *Dubliners* as "the first step towards the spiritual liberation of my country," and liberation—spiritual, intellectual, cultural, and not least national—would be central to *Ulysses* too.[4] But Joyce's novel does not conclude with the decisive arrival in the promised land, for it was in the wilderness itself where Irishness and Irish culture could be discovered as something inclusive, unfixed, evolving. Joyce's use of Exodus in *Ulysses* is, then, a provocation for how a dead metaphor might be given new life, and might give new life in turn.

Arthur Griffith's position in *Ulysses* is also a sort of provocation: he is, in Leopold Bloom's prescient vision, "the coming man" who would in 1922 become the first president of the Free State. But Griffith's vision of Irishness, his exclusion of the foreign and most particularly the Jew, is at odds with Bloom himself; as Joyce wrote of his hero, "only a foreigner would do — and Jews at that time were foreigners."[5] In 1904 Griffith was actively rejecting both the Exodus analogy and Ireland's Jewish communities; the moment in *Ulysses* when it is rumored that Bloom himself has given Griffith the idea for Sinn Fein is an irony that surely has Griffith's anti-Jewish stance at its origin.[6] So when Joyce reimagines this period from his self-imposed exile in Europe, his Odysseus is both Jewish and Irish, a hybrid affront to Irish Ireland. Moreover, Bloom embodies the way in which Exodus *is* a narrative for Ireland after all, for his journey is one of departure from biblical Egypt nearly as much as Homeric voyage. Elements of the Exodus story are present in *Ulysses* as analogy, metaphor, and metonymy; they help explain the struggles and triumphs of Stephen, Bloom, Parnell, the Irish language, and indeed Joyce himself. Exodus is also the principal model for national liberation in *Ulysses*, and it takes on new significance in light of two decades of postcolonial rereadings of Joyce. The Irish Joyce now rivals (and has perhaps replaced) the long-standing new-critical conception of an apolitical, cosmopolitan, classically modernist Joyce; the increased focus on nationality in Joyce's writings invites attention as well to the Jewish nation or race, which serves as both ancient and modern parallel to the Irish experience.[7]

Although the theme of Exodus in Joyce's writings has of course received critical attention, there has been a hesitation in theorizing the significance and contradictoriness of this material.[8] Most often, Joyce's use of biblically inflected nationalist rhetoric—the Irish as the chosen people, Parnell as Moses—has seemed to critics of *Ulysses* to be fodder for his parodies and little beyond that. In "Joyce and Nationalism," Seamus Deane writes of the Irish-Jewish analogy that "no matter how urgently we pursue this parallel we can come to no satisfactory conclusion about the bearing it has on the relationship between Stephen and Bloom, or on any other relationship between people in the novel."[9]

Deane thus concludes that the parallel is "arbitrarily introduced" and merely a "system of ordering."[10] Emer Nolan, too, reads *Ulysses*' "allegorical correspondences" as "mock-heroic parody . . . a kind of joke," and Neil Davison writes about Stephen's "Pisgah Sight of Palestine" that it is "little more than a bitter parody of a simile that once sustained a nation. But the Irish-as-the-lost-tribe-of-Israel is only that: a simile. It offers no help to the identity struggles of either Stephen or Bloom."[11] There is certainly parody and cynicism in Stephen's highly rhetorical invocations of Exodus, and Joyce's novel does address the fate of a trope that has become banal and even ironic, particularly given the anti-Semitism that, throughout the novel, accompanies analogies with Jews and Israelites. Yet it is a mistake to discount Stephen's parodies as unproductive, just as it is a mistake to confuse them with Bloom's accommodating, even promising, ideas about promised lands and liberation.

Lady Gregory's play *The Deliverer* had made the Exodus story vivid, had made its political resonance for Ireland disturbingly immediate. For Joyce, Exodus becomes most instructive not by reading it through Irish history, but through Jewish history, and specifically, as we will see in chapter 5, through Jewish forms of national memory. The Jewish memory of the Exodus allows Joyce to reimagine the departure from Egypt as a national narrative that is still political, still anticolonial, but also deeply personal and complex, reflecting back onto the Irish the ambivalence that Pearse's rhetoric had worked so hard to cover up. Ultimately, however, as we will see in this chapter, Joyce eventually moves beyond Exodus's Jewish origin, and the narrative of departure from (and indeed, *into*) bondage is much more than a way of understanding Bloom's ambivalent Jewish-Irishness—even as that remains a topic that requires our renewed attention. For if Jewish forms (of narrative, of reading, of remembering) allow Joyce to bare the core of Exodus, they also allow him to show its essential universality.

The Fleshpots of England and Ireland

When Leopold Bloom considers the Israelite Exodus from Egypt, he imagines it not as a journey to freedom but precisely the opposite:

"All that long business . . . that brought us out of the land of Egypt and into the house of bondage" (*U* 118). It is here, in Bloom's apparent slip, that Exodus generates meaning for Joyce—for like Bloom he understands national emancipation as a traumatic and fraught process. "That long business" (even listening to the story feels like a burden!), the story of the Exodus that Jews are required to retell every year at Passover, is a story not only of freedom and celebration, but of resistance to the responsibilities of nationhood. "The great paradox of Exodus," writes Michael Walzer, "and of all subsequent liberation struggles, is the people's simultaneous willingness and unwillingness to put Egypt behind them. . . . They yearn to be free, and they yearn to escape their new freedom."[12] The ambivalence can be found in the biblical text itself, most particularly in the wilderness episodes when the Israelites voice their longing for life in Egypt: "The whole congregation of the Israelites complained against Moses and Aaron in the wilderness. The Israelites said to them: 'If only we had died by the hand of the LORD in the land of Egypt, when we sat by the fleshpots and ate our fill of bread'" (Exodus 16:2). Filled with the meats and flavorings of Egypt—garlic, onions, leeks—fleshpots symbolize cultural seductions for the newly emergent (escaping or devolving) nation. They are a synecdoche for the difficulty of the birth of the nation, conjuring the memory of an alien culture that at once must be and cannot be left behind; they are code for whatever is foreign, material, and desirable; they represent the impossibility of an original, pure, essential national identity; they are, in short, the symbol of the antinational.

If fleshpots in *Ulysses* are potentially appealing, whether the "fleshhotpot" prostitutes of nighttown or Plumtree's Potted Meat (much more on these shortly), they were generally, and not surprisingly, invoked with scorn in contemporary political contexts. As a favorite symbol of cultural nationalists and religious leaders, fleshpots were typically associated with Egyptian (read English) materialism and cast as a threat to Irish nationality. This was the case, for example, in a 1915 novel by the Catholic writer Canon P. A. Sheehan, who writes of a "great race abandoning all the splendid, if phantasmal, idealism of the past, and hungering after the fleshpots of the successful but degraded nations of the earth. And there was no help. Not a voice was raised to recall the nation to its old sense of honour; not an organ of public opinion dared express a single sentiment that would breathe of the old and sacred independence that sanctified the individual, and saved the nation from corruption."[13] A 1911 article in the *Irish Review* had imagined in similar terms the corrupting factor of Irish dependence on England: "Nationalist Ireland should make up its mind as to what it really wants, whether it is Fleshpots or Freedom."[14] The author insists that "the Irish people . . . cannot have it both ways," and that they seem "busier about the content of the Saxon stall than concerned with the milk and honey that may entail sacrifice to win."[15] When the Free State was finally accomplished, the fleshpots were no less desirable, for they remained forbidden. Seán Ó Faoláin would write, in 1939, that De Valera's ideal of peasant life "is that of a dreary Eden, and the meager flesh-pots he offers to his as-yet unconverted Egyptians . . . are always associated by him in a melancholy way, with duty and patriotism."[16]

Clearly, amid such "melancholy" patriotism, a strategic incorporation of the fleshpots could be valuable. And Joyce, as we will see, had encountered some writers—both Irish and Jewish—who proposed the integration of fleshpots into national life. Although the language of Exodus is rarely present in Irish discourse after 1916, the fleshpots still made an occasional appearance. Within sight of the Free State, and advocating the treaty that would partition Ireland, Michael Collins would invoke fleshpots as potentially assimilable. By accepting the treaty, Collins insisted, "we are not going in for the flesh-pots of the British Empire—not unless we wish to. It is futile to suppose that all these tendencies would disappear under freedom by some other name, or that the government of an externally associated nation, or of a Republic, any more than a Free State, would be able to suppress them, and to force Gaelicism upon the nation."[17] For Joyce, bringing the fleshpots—or at least the memory of them—on the journey into the wilderness, into the new nation, is no less problematic because it is inevitable.[18] A careful reader of the biblical text and a cosmopolitan epicure, Joyce foregrounds fleshpots in *Ulysses* to show what had often been left unexplored (or intentionally suppressed) in earlier Irish uses of the Israelite narrative that focused on creating and maintaining cultural purity. Implicitly, then, Joyce also critiques the Pearsian fetishes of purity, clarity, and unity—those things that the fleshpots by their very presence disrupt. For above all, fleshpots are emblems of unconscious and ambivalent desire, or that which remains—like home without Plumtree's Potted Meat—always incomplete.

John Eglinton's Exodus

William Kirkpatrick Magee, writing under the pseudonym John Eglinton, is an unacknowledged early source for Joyce's Exodus theme in *Ulysses.* Eglinton understood the Israelites' ambivalence about their departure, and extrapolated to his own analysis of modern literature: "In the present case," he explains, "it was less Pharaoh who would not let the Chosen people go than the Chosen People who have wished to remain."[19] Eglinton knew the appeal of remaining in a place of comfort—he was also a cosmopolitan who proposed that "the consummations of the promised land would not exclude the generosities of the flesh-pots of Egypt."[20] Of the chorus of Anglo-Irish revivalists whom Joyce consistently ridiculed and rejected, here was one voice, at least, that Joyce treated with serious consideration. Eglinton is probably the most neglected of the important figures of the revival, best known for appearing as himself in the National Library scene in *Ulysses.* But he was a prolific essayist, and Joyce was clearly an attentive reader—this even as Joyce mockingly referred to the Presbyterian celibate and teetotaler as "Stiffbreeches."[21] Nevertheless, Eglinton had Joyce's respect as a writer and, perhaps equally important, as an antagonist of the pieties and narrow-mindedness that often characterized the period's cultural nationalism. As Bonnie K. Scott writes, Eglinton "maintained an attitude of critical aloofness and independent thought"—something, she notes, the young Joyce would have found attractive.[22] That Griffith had attacked Eglinton's "barbarous fetish of cosmopolitanism"[23] can only have made Eglinton more appealing to Joyce, who also rejected Griffith's racist provincialism.

Of Griffith Joyce wrote, in a now often-quoted letter, "what I object to most of all in his paper is that it is educating the people of Ireland on the old pap of racial hatred."[24]

Eglinton used the Exodus narrative as a structuring trope for his manifesto "Two Essays on the Remnant" (1892), which was reprinted in Justin McCarthy's widely read anthology *Irish Literature* in 1904 and had "attracted much attention."[25] Here Eglinton exhorts the "Chosen People"—"that curiously situated class of Idealists, who, as Israel took over the brick-manufacture of Egypt, have in this century been taking over the manufacture of literature"[26]—to go forth into the wilderness and abandon the nation that stifles their creativity. If such a prescription for artistic creation might have seemed unremarkable when Matthew Arnold articulated something similar in *The Function of Criticism at the Present Time*, it seems rather more confrontational in an Irish context at the start of the literary revival.[27] Indeed, Eglinton seems intentionally provocative in his depoliticizing of the Moses theme; he was writing, after all, just a year after the death of Parnell, when Exodus was *the* metaphor associated with Irish national freedom, and specifically Home Rule.[28] Joyce, for example, was still describing Parnell in 1912 as one who, "like another Moses, led a turbulent and unstable people from the house of shame to the verge of the Promised Land."[29] But in Eglinton's vision, wilderness is described not as a stage before freedom, but as an artist's alternative to the nation-state: "there comes a time when the Chosen People and the State, if either are to fulfill the conditions of their existence, must take different ways—when Moses, or in our own time Thoreau, Whitman, Tolstoi, and others, appear, to call them forth to build in the wilderness the City of God."[30] In other words, the way out of the state is through literature, and literature must free itself from the state. While Eglinton's rewriting of Exodus as nonpolitical appears at odds with Joyce's Parnellism, nevertheless the idea of escaping the bondage of the nation—in Stephen Dedalus's terms from *A Portrait*, flying by the nets of nationality in order to forge an artistic covenant—aligns well with the long-standing critical understanding of Joyce as apolitical; as Ira Nadel describes it, Joyce made a "covenant with art."[31] If that reading elides the importance of the nation to Joyce's work, it reminds us that Joyce was not looking to make Ireland into a promised land. And as for Eglinton, the notion of the wilderness as a productive space was one Joyce would relish and indeed develop in *Ulysses.*

That other literary Parnellite, W. B. Yeats, was unabashed in his dislike of Eglinton's theory, particularly the conception of an apolitical literary elite. Eglinton had advocated individualism only for the artist, with Wordsworth serving as the key figure (when Stephen thinks of Eglinton in *Ulysses*, he thinks, "Give me my Wordsworth" [*U* 198]). Writing in the *United Irishman* in 1901, Yeats chastises Eglinton for disavowing political revolution and offers up a comical version of his proposal:

> If John Eglinton had found any one of these people of the Remnant I can imagine what they would have said to one another. . . .
> "But what is the wilderness?"
> "The wilderness is a country life."
> "And when I get into the country what am I to do?"
> "Why! Read Wordsworth."[32]

More to the point, Yeats argues that social change, the "movement to destroy modern civilization," will not come, as Eglinton suggests, from "'liberated individuals' who separate themselves from the great passions, from the great popular interests, from religion, from patriotism, from humanitarianism."[33] In other words, for Yeats the liberation begun by Parnell (whom the poet had imagined in 1891 as the Exodus story's "tall pillar burning") was a journey for *all* the people in bondage, with all of their passionate ideologies; artists could not make the journey independent of the nation. If Yeats's position here seems somewhat out of character to us (for it is well noted how he remained always uneasy about the people, or "the mob"[34]), Eglinton does appear to have taken the criticism into account. While remaining ever skeptical of coercive patriotism, he perhaps somewhat regretted his early argument, and vigorously objected to Yeats's reprinting of a selection from *Two Essays on the Remnant* in 1905, admitting that his "metaphor is pressed to the point of being recommended as a gospel."[35] Moreover, Eglinton himself would later repoliticize Exodus when describing it as "the great national book of the Hebrews."[36]

In his shifting but sustained use of the Exodus trope, Eglinton directed Joyce to its literary and ideological flexibility, as well as its epic potential. Eglinton addresses the bards directly in the final section of his pamphlet, exhorting that they "desire only a leader, stronger than yourselves, to lead you forth into the wilderness! You will then sing no longer to a critical and moody public a brief, wine-flushed note, but to the memory of races—epics once more, and thronged with heroic forms."[37] Eglinton was advocating a national epic—not the melancholy "wine-flushed note" of Thomas Moore and his nineteenth-century predecessors, but implicitly the biblical scope and complexity of the Hebrew Bible that gave his pamphlet its title and theme. But could a national epic accommodate the dissent, cultural hybridity, even adulteration that Joyce saw in the birth of the Irish nation? David Lloyd has argued that the epic form resolutely insists on cultural purity, and "the process of hybridization . . . [is] at every level recalcitrant to the aesthetic politics of nationalism."[38] And yet in 1918 Israel Zangwill would write of the Hebrew Bible that "alone among epics it is out for truth, not heroics."[39] Here was a model that, while it tells the story of a nation, also admits the hesitation and refusal of the people.

When Eglinton assessed the Irish literary tradition at the beginning of the twentieth century, he found an absence of the very "heroic forms" that Joyce, perhaps in a direct response to Eglinton, would make central to *Ulysses*. As Eglinton wrote, "in the case of Ireland, no Moses has appeared to dominate [the Irish] with his spirit, nor Homer resolved them into epic unity."[40] Eglinton offered another challenge in 1911, writing that "if a masterpiece should still come of this literary movement we need not be surprised if it appears by a kind of accident and in some unexpected quarter," noting that the writer would be "of the type of Cervantes rather than . . . an idealizing poet or romance writer."[41] Joyce, self-consciously outside of the Irish circle (he famously declined Lady Gregory's request to include a letter of his in a book on the Irish literary movement), seems to have taken this to heart.[42] In *Ulysses*, during a discussion about the Irish epic that is yet to be written, the references to Cervantes ("a knight of the rueful countenance here in Dublin. With a saffron kilt? . . . And his Dulcinea?" [*U* 185]) evoke Eglinton's prediction. If it is only coincidence that Eglinton refers to the "Scylla and Charybdis of sensuality and ennui" in an early essay, and "Scylla and Charybdis" is the chapter of *Ulysses* in which he appears, there are nevertheless sufficient indications that Eglinton's literary vision was, to Joyce, worth considering.[43] Joyce's many Eglintonian allusions in the novel are intended not only for a sort of accuracy, since the assistant librarian is also a character, but as an answer to Eglinton's prophesy about the important Irish book of the future: *Ulysses* itself is the masterpiece that resolves Moses and Homer into a new sort of epic unity. Joyce, after all, took up Eglinton's challenge to lead Irish writers forth into the wilderness, and took his advice by setting forth from his Egypt—or at least leaving the particular bondage of Dublin, if only to bring all Ireland along with him to Trieste, Zurich, and Paris.

Zionism and the Irish Future

It was in Trieste that Joyce began to understand the Exodus story as a central trope not only of ancient Israel or contemporary Ireland, but of the nascent Jewish nationalism, and it seems clear that Joyce's encounters in that city with Jewish thinkers and Zionism inflected his ideas about nations and nationality.[44] Despite the obvious differences between Irish and Jewish realities in this period, debates about Jewish culture and national identity often mirrored Irish ones, and here too the fleshpots of Egypt could metaphorically embody the challenges of modernity and multiculturalism. Among the books in Joyce's Trieste library was Theodor Herzl's 1896 tract *Der Judenstat (The Jewish State)*, in which fleshpots take on new resonance; they are represented not as dangerous threats to national identity, but as that which can now be acculturated. Herzl notes that "daily customs can easily be transplanted," and declares that "when we journey out of Egypt again we shall not leave the fleshpots behind."[45] A cosmopolitan outlook, Herzl implies, would allow the new Jewish nation to include the fleshpots of Egypt, thus accommodating a newly globalized, but still

Jewish, identity. Thus he writes, "there are . . . French theatres in Russia, German operas in America, and best Bavarian beer in Paris."[46] Fleshpots, in other words, represent not only attachment to material culture and sensual pleasure, but also a more general openness to cultural exchange and contact. For Herzl fleshpots are the stuff of the modernizing world—and are therefore critical to the nation-state.

Fleshpots also appear in *Zionism and the Jewish Future*—an anthology Joyce owned that presented a far from unified sense of what a Jewish state should look like. One essay in the collection, by the editor Harry Sacher, describes how the German-Jewish emancipation movement contributed to the "decline and fall of the Commonwealth of Israel," arguing that "in the teachings of the German emancipation school [were] the formulas which sanctified the abandonment of Jewish nationalism and guaranteed the celestial bliss of Paradise along with the fleshpots of Egypt."[47] Fleshpots mean foregoing the Jewish nation, a problem Sacher also notices in the Russian case: "The best minds among the Russian Jews had discovered that there are things worse than persecution, and that emancipation, if it is the end of one problem, is the beginning of another."[48] Nevertheless, Sacher's solution is not isolation, but expansiveness: "If it be asked, How can any State admit variety of culture within its borders? the answer is that the devastation which is now upon the world arises from a failure to do so, and if the refusal be persisted in civilization is bankrupt. It will be one of the services of Zionism to give a wider and deeper rendering to nationalism, purging it of the grossness of intolerance, narrowness, arrogance, and aggression, which have made men doubt whether nationalism be not a scourge rather than a blessing."[49] This argument for a "wider and deeper rendering to nationalism," perhaps more than any other statement we encounter in Joyce's reading, describes the approach to nationalism in *Ulysses*: Joyce exposes, where he finds it, "intolerance, narrowness, arrogance, and aggression," and through Bloom—and beyond Bloom—he reveals the variety of cultures with which any Irish nation must necessarily contend. A similarly themed passage on Jewish nationalism appears in the same anthology, in Nachum Sokolow's "The New Jew: A Sketch." Sokolow writes that "if nationalism means hostility, the persecution of other nations, narrow-mindedness and racial fanaticism, I reject it. It is opposed to all my convictions, impulses, longings and interests as a Jew. But if nationalism means being at one with one's own people, then I am a Jewish nationalist."[50] It is a Bloomian definition, and a contemporary alternative to Gaelic Leaguer Father Peter Yorke, who insisted in 1899 that "if a wall of brass . . . was built one thousand feet high around Ireland it would be for the benefit of her people."[51] This is not to say that isolationism and essentialism were absent from contemporary Jewish discourse: we find a similar image at play in the revisionist Zionism of Ze'ev Jabotinsky, who imagined an "iron wall" around Jewish colonies in Palestine.[52] The idea that the promised land can be a walled nation is, however, at odds with the journey of Exodus, in which both the isolated deprivations of the wilderness and the remembered culture of the other define the people—perhaps as much as the land-to-be.

The Language of the Law and the Outlaw

The emerging Jewish nationalism that Joyce encountered in Trieste offered a further parallel with Ireland in its diverse approach to the language question. In the discussion on reviving the Hebrew language, positions in *Zionism and the Jewish Future* ranged from "linguistic unity . . . by itself does not create a nation" to something like the Gaelic League's ethos: "a people's language is its life-blood" and Hebrew is "an essential part of the Jew's being."[53] Obviously such conversations about a national language had resonance with Joyce in this period of intense Gaelic League activity, and they inevitably informed his representation of the Irish version of the debate.

The Gaelic League founder Douglas Hyde, in his famous 1892 speech on de-Anglicizing Ireland, had argued that "it should not be very difficult, with the aid of the foremost foreign scholars, to bring about a tone of thought which would make it disgraceful for an educated Irishman . . . to be ignorant of his own language—would make it at least as disgraceful as for an educated Jew to be quite ignorant of Hebrew."[54] Hyde's speech, which applies the Irish-Jewish analogy to the language question, is a likely source for one of the best-known political uses of Exodus in Joyce's Ireland: an apparently improvised speech given by John F. Taylor, a barrister and respected Dublin orator, at a meeting of the Law Students' Debate Society in October 1901. Taylor's words circulated in the memories of students and writers, and in various forms of print, for many years, and Joyce was very likely, as Ellmann tells us, present on the occasion of his speech.[55] In *Ulysses* when Professor MacHugh performs a version of the oration for the men in the newspaper office, Joyce is not simply showing off his mastery of the windy rhetoric that characterizes the "Aeolus" chapter, but condensing one of the most important debates around Irish cultural nationalism at the turn of the last century. The Hebrew/Irish-language analogy that organizes Taylor's argument was in fact used on both sides of the language debate, for and against the revival of Irish as a national language—a fact that Joyce's version of the speech implicitly understands.

Taylor's speech was clearly not, as some scholars have claimed, a particularly exceptional use of the Irish-Jewish parallel.[56] But notwithstanding the centuries of analogizing that came before, and in addition to Hyde's much-reproduced 1892 use of the trope on the specific point about language, a more immediate source was the Exodus imagery in the address directly preceding Taylor's, read by a Mr. Stephen Devitt. Just before Taylor takes the floor (and thus providing evidence in favor of the popular claim that Taylor's speech was extemporaneous), Devitt argues for instilling nationality in the people, "to teach them the history of their land . . . not merely the catalogue of battles, murders, and famines . . . but also that brighter period when Ireland was the pillar of fire that pointed the way to the nations yet buried in the gloom of the dark ages."[57] The pillar of fire would have recalled not only Exodus 13, but more particularly Yeats's elegy for Parnell, in which the memory of the dead leader "now is a tall pillar, burning / Before us in the gloom."[58] While Parnell is not mentioned explicitly here or in Taylor's speech, he haunts all of these texts, *Ulysses* included. It is both Moses and Parnell who have, as J. J. O'Molloy says "not without regret," "died without having entered the land of promise" (*U* 137). Also worth noting is that Taylor himself has died too:

as MacHugh rehearses the legend in *Ulysses*, Taylor "had come there, you must know, from a sickbed" (*U* 136), and like Moses and Parnell, will never find himself in the promised land.

Taylor's speech became Joyce's favorite section of the novel, and the only part he recorded on phonodisc.[59] Joyce's adaptation follows the original's famous conceit, in which an eminent Egyptian presents Moses with a case for accepting the boons of colonialism: "*—Why will you jews not accept our culture, our religion and our language? You are a tribe of nomad herdsmen; we are a mighty people. . . . You have but emerged from primitive conditions: we have a literature, a priesthood, an agelong history and a polity*" (*U* 137). Joyce may improve rhetorically on the speech, but he also obscures, or at least complicates, Taylor's real point—that the Irish language is a critical marker of national identity. In the account recorded in the *Freeman's Journal* the day after the meeting, surely the most accurate version, Irish takes on a spiritual significance: "Now as regards the language, suppose a great message was to be given to the human race, in what language was it likely to be given? What was the greatest message ever given to man? . . . Was that message in the language of Imperial Rome or the language of Intellectual Greece? No, it was given in the rustic dialect of the far-off land 'out of which no good could come.'"[60] Taylor concludes that sacred languages are defined by purity. He explains that a "great message" like that of the Hebrew Law "would come, not from a language encrusted with commercialism and materialism, but . . . from some pure language that was kept aloof and unsullied with contamination with the world." It was a position endorsed by the developing Irish Ireland consciousness: Irish was pure, and even, indeed, a preservative against adulteration. A sermon preached in 1914 insisted on its inherent quality of faithfulness, for "there is enmity between the Irish language and infidelity."[61]

Joyce's revision of the speech, which excludes the notion of purity, was perhaps inflected by John Eglinton's response to Taylor. Not long after the publication of "The Language of the Outlaw" in pamphlet form, Eglinton quite explicitly reversed this particular application of the Irish-Jewish analogy to the language question. In his 1906 book of essays *Bards and Saints*, Eglinton seems to be responding directly to both Hyde and Taylor when he writes, "After all it was amongst the 'lost sheep of the house of Israel'—amongst those who had lost the use of the Hebrew language—that the Jewish Messiah appeared. It was not the ancient language of the chosen people that gave expression to the most illustrious example of the fulfillment of a national dream, and it would be in keeping with the ironies of history if the fulfillment of the Gaelic dream should test the acumen of believers in a similar fashion."[62] Eglinton employs the same rhetorical strategy as Taylor, but in shifting his example from Moses to Jesus, he inverts it.[63] He imagines the displacement of a great (national) language by a banal (imperial) one in order to argue *against* the necessity of Irish as a national language. For Eglinton, the English language that gives voice to the national dream is also an underdog, but that is precisely because it is not "the ancient language of the chosen people"; it is neither unique nor pure, nor a language that will afford an easy signaling of "Irishness." The colonial language requires a negotiation with the way the very fact of otherness is involved in the emergence of national identity.[64] Perhaps Joyce was thinking of Eglinton's essay when he wrote in one of his notes for the "Cyclops" episode of *Ulysses* that "Jesus did not Speak Hebrew."[65]

Joyce was not especially interested in the revival of the Irish language—he had dropped out of Patrick Pearse's Irish language class, and had later written to his brother Stanislaus that "if the Irish programme did not insist on the Irish language I suppose I could call myself a nationalist."[66] But most obviously to any reader of *Ulysses*, purity of language is precisely the opposite of Joyce's aesthetic. So his reworking of the Taylor speech excises the call for linguistic purity, and substitutes for "aloof and unsullied" an alternative epithet for Irish: it is now "the language of the outlaw." This phrase was adopted by Joyce from a later source for Taylor's speech, a pamphlet by Roger Casement published (anonymously) in 1904 or 1905, and likely encountered by Joyce when it was reprinted in Griffith's *United Irishman* in 1906.[67] While Casement, like Taylor, is arguing for the necessity of reviving the Irish language, he finds value not in its purity, but in its status as the language of the oppressed: “The language of the outlaw gave the Law of God to man; the tongue of those who made bricks without straw was chosen for the shrine of Divine utterance on Earth while the speech of Pharaoh lies smitten, silent as the stones of his Pyramids.”[68] In *Ulysses* Joyce foregrounds the figure of the outlaw, punctuating Taylor’s original ending with the conclusion appended by Casement, so that “the tables of the law” are now “*graven in the language of the outlaw*” (*U* 137). If outlaw language might insist on its own sort of purity (as did some in the Gaelic League, for example), it nevertheless would be obliged to take on some qualities that resist purity: slipperiness, hidden meanings, adaptability. Language was always, for Joyce, a “changing thing”; it could not define nationality, which, he wrote, “must find its reason for being rooted in something that surpasses and transcends and informs changing things like blood and the human word.”[69] The substitution Joyce makes, eliminating Taylor’s “pure language that was kept aloof and unsullied” in favor of (Casement’s) “language of the outlaw” is a subversion that foregrounds the difficulty, the adulteration inherent in the departure from Egypt. While the original speech suggests that the Israelite-Irish require a pure language as a condition of independence and identity, Joyce’s invocation of an “outlaw” language is more ambiguous.

For Joyce, then, isn’t English, as well as Irish, an outlaw language? English is the language of the colonial state, and subsequently the colonial subject who speaks it must speak subversively, must always speak as the outlaw. Perhaps this is what Stephen realizes when ruminating on the word “tundish” in *A Portrait of the Artist as a Young Man*; of the English Dean of Studies he thinks, “his language, so familiar and so foreign, will always be for me an acquired speech. I have not made or accepted its words. My voice holds them at bay. My soul frets in the shadow of his language.”[70] Stephen, of course, does not turn to the Irish language, but expresses his “cunning” in English. In other words, Joyce embraces contradiction by writing in the language of Egypt and the fleshpots, not the language of the Ten Commandments—the language of the outlaw, not of the Law. In the Taylor passage, Joyce reproduces the rhetoric of a politics he rejects and simultaneously revises it to offer more inclusive possibilities. He reveals the inevitable disparity between language and identity, an irony made plain in the novel's first chapter when the Englishman Haines speaks Irish to an old milk-woman. She cannot understand her "native" language and guesses that he is speaking French (*U* 14): "I'm ashamed I don't speak the language myself. I'm told it's a grand language by them that knows" (*U* 14). In Taylor's speech, the Egyptian High Priest, who it seems was initially modeled on J. P. Mahaffey, Trinity College's officious enemy of Irish (he had described Irish literature as "either silly or indecent"), has ironically made his point: Moses may have stood up against a colonial culture, but the men in the newspaper office are, after all, speaking in English.[71]

When Joyce revisits the speech, rewriting its concluding lines toward the end of "Ithaca," it is to describe Bloom walking to his bath, carrying in his arms "the secret of the race, graven in the language of prediction" (*U* 629). The secret of the race (*which* race—the Irish, the Jewish, or the 1904 Gold Cup—remains ambiguous) is to be found in the nationalist newspaper, the *Freeman's Journal*: its pages of print and its very name aspire toward independence, but the words (like the words of Taylor's speech, spoken in that same newspaper's offices) are in English. The misapprehended "prediction" ironically forecasts the outcome of a horse race, not the promise of new covenant. Here is the outlaw language at work, with its inversions and surprises (Throwaway bests Scepter, against all odds). Still, we should remember that "Aeolus" is the episode of language as windy rhetoric. Exodus may blow out here—"Gone with the wind" (*U* 137), as Stephen thinks—but it will soon expand and be renewed: in a limited way with Stephen, and then in a far more substantial way with Bloom, who does in fact know something valuable about the secret of his race.

Stephen's Pisgah Sights

Taylor's speech activates Stephen's first extended consideration of Exodus. Like Eglinton and Herzl, Stephen envisions bringing the fleshpots on the journey to nationhood, but his approach is both more ironic and more oblique than his auditors, and perhaps his readers, are prepared to accept. "I have a vision too" (*U* 139), Stephen says, after hearing Professor MacHugh's performance. "DEAR DIRTY DUBLIN" is the headline for Stephen's parable, a deflated rereading of the heightened rhetoric of Taylor's analogy. In Stephen's story, "Two Dublin vestals . . . elderly and pious" (*U* 139) climb to the top of Nelson's pillar and have a picnic. Bread, headcheese, and plums make up their feast, after which they survey the city and spit plum seeds through the railing. Morton Levitt calls the narrative "inept and unfunny,"[72] a sterile modern version of Taylor's "borrowed fertility."[73] Or perhaps it is overly obtuse rather than inept: only when queried by Myles Crawford does Stephen reveal the story's biblical title, and thus its figuration of Exodus: "I call it *A Pisgah Sight of Palestine or The Parable of The Plums*" (*U* 143), he explains, rejecting the pretentious Virgilian title the Professor has proposed. And only then does MacHugh seem to understand and enjoy the tale: "Moses and the promised land," he says. "We gave him that idea" (*U* 143).

The idea, however, has already been suggested in the opening lines of the chapter, in which Nelson's pillar functions as a stand-in for the pillar of cloud that is the sign the chosen people must follow out of Egypt in Exodus.[74] In other words, the women of Stephen's parable are inevitably drawn to the pillar, rising up from the chaos of the city/wilderness ("Before Nelson's pillar trams slowed, shunted, changed trolley, started for Blackrock, Kingstown and Dalkey" [*U* 112]), which will afford them their Pisgah sight. Yet as Amardeep Singh notes, the "'Pisgah Sight of Palestine' in Joyce's anticolonial reading becomes the sight of a land—specifically, a nation space—which the viewer will never get to own."[75] So that although these colonial Dubliners are able to briefly point out the distinctive Catholic churches, they quickly become too dizzy to appreciate the view. They pull up their skirts, possibly even flashing, in the manner of Gerty MacDowell, anyone who might be looking up, and sit down to eat their plums. It seems a version of the Pisgah Sight—Moses's view of the Israelites' promised land—that is all banality. Whereas Stephen Sicari suggests that "their failure lies in their lack of imagination, in their inability to see the promised land right where they are,"[76] this is perhaps unfair. Even Stephen would admit that personal imagination is enslaved in colonial Dublin—and even he must go elsewhere to create a conscience for the nation. Stephen's parable has the virtue, if not of transparency (it is a parable, after all), then of truthfulness, in contrast to the overwrought "*peerless panorama*" of Ireland offered up for mockery by Ned Lambert earlier in the chapter, "*the peerless panorama of Ireland's portfolio . . . of bosky grove and undulating plain and luscious pastureland of vernal green, steeped in the translucent glow of our mild mysterious Irish twilight* . . ." (*U* 121). Deemed by Simon Dedalus to be "shite and onions!" (*U* 121), his son Stephen's vision shows a different reality, a view of banal Dublin-as-wilderness, rather than the pastoral (and notably depopulated) "mysterious Irish twilight" of the mythicized Irish west.

Anne Kearns and Florence MacCabe are unlikely Moseses, however. Their picnic, in addition to the plums, includes bread and "brawn," a sort of headcheese. They pun on the word, playfully asking each other, "have you the brawn" (*U* 139) as they struggle to climb the stairs to the top of the pillar. But the brawn offers another sort of joke, for it is, like the ubiquitous Plumtree's Potted Meat, a literal fleshpot: brawn is also known as "potted head." So the two women in the wilderness of Dublin, ignoring the view of the promised land—pulling up their skirts in the sight of the "Onehandled adulterer" (*U* 142), the statue of Nelson, are in fact carrying the fleshpots with them.[77] The titillating sexual element of fleshpots is there too, in the suggestion of oral sex, and especially nonprocreative (both postmenopausal and nonpenetrative) sex—and what's worse, with an English war hero. As in Bloom's encounter with Gerty, seed (or in this case, seeds) are spilled, rather than enlarging the nation through new generations. Finally, the women's abundant plums echo Plumtree's Potted Meat, that most ubiquitous of Dublin fleshpots. The joke offers a subtle punch line, but one that is refracted in multiple details. Stephen's "wise virgins" have inherited MacHugh's "noble" story, yet they climb not Mount Sinai but Nelson's phallic pillar, and are ineluctably associated with the fleshpots of Egypt even as they survey their promised land.

Stephen had already been thinking of his own fleshpots that morning, recalling his days in Paris: "Eating your groatsworth of *mou en civet*, fleshpots of Egypt" (*U* 41). Like Bloom's nonkosher kidney, Stephen's Parisian lung stew (another fleshpot-type food), if not his favorite, and eaten while "elbowed by belching cabmen" (*U* 41), symbolizes a challenge to national identity, an alternative to the "rasher fried with a herring" (*U* 39) he should properly be eating at home in Ireland. "Pintpots" (*U* 42) too, Stephen thinks about—pints of porter not native to the Irish Catholic economy, but rather produced and disseminated most notably by the Protestant Guinness family. As Willard Potts (whose own name lets him in on the pun) points out, Joyce was well aware of Protestant control of the alcohol trade. D. P. Moran, who called the industry "Bung," made it a particular target of his attacks in the *Leader*, and as Potts writes, "Joyce echoes Moran's terminology in *Ulysses*, where he refers to 'Bungiveagh and Bungardilaun' (*U* 287)":[78] Lords Iveagh and Ardilaun owned the Guinness Brewery. This is one kind of fleshpot, we sense throughout the novel, which Dubliners would be loath to leave behind, and Stephen's word "pintpots" thus embodies a particularly Irish paradox. As Moran preached it, English and Anglo-Irish productions, not only cultural but also commercial, were a threat to Irish Ireland.[79] Porter, seemingly a most Irish indulgence—and indeed, to the Citizen of "Cyclops," it is "wine of the country" (*U* 283)—is also condemned as an English tool of enslavement.

Moran might have been similarly concerned about Plumtree's Potted Meat, the fleshpot in *Ulysses* that most relentlessly flaunts both its figural and literal signaling of adulteration. As we learn in "Ithaca," this meat is manufactured and "put up in 4 oz pots" (*U* 636) by one George Plumtree, whose first name, "George," suggests he is an English Protestant, and whose surname, "Plumtree," is likewise decidedly English. "Beware of imitations" (*U* 636) we are warned by the label; yet, as Bloom recognizes, there is already something inherently adulterated about potted meat itself: "Lord knows what concoction. Cauls mouldy tripes windpipes faked and minced up. Puzzle find the meat" (*U* 163). But if the fleshpots of Egypt are dangerous not only for their otherness but also for their possible fraudulence, they nevertheless perfectly cohabit with the art of advertising. The catchy jingle for this "meatpot" insists that without it, life is inferior: "*What is home without / Plumtree's Potted Meat? / Incomplete. / With it an abode of bliss*" (*U* 72). Bloom repeatedly derides and rejects the slogan—"what a stupid ad!" (*U* 163) he thinks—and yet neither Bloom nor the reader succeeds in getting it out of their head. Here Joyce challenges us by literalizing the concocted, inauthentic ("faked") yet paradoxically appealing "fleshpots of Egypt" as actual fleshpots, and placing them strategically throughout the novel in places both apt and ironic: Stephen's memory of Paris, the pages of the *Freeman's Journal*, the top of Nelson's Pillar, Blazes Boylan's fruit basket, Bloom and Molly's bed. Even Molly's "met-him-pike-hoses," which replaces metempsychosis with a homophone suggesting sexual encounter ("met him"), brings us toward the further homophonic exchange of "meet him" (Boylan) with "meat him," since Boylan has, in a euphemism of the day, "potted his meat" in Molly Bloom. And potted meat is in fact the evidence of the act itself, as its crumbs on the bedclothes signal Boylan's usurpation of Bloom's marriage bed. Even before this final clue, we have earlier encountered the Plumtree's jar in the "bedded" wicker basket that Boylan sends ahead of his arrival, paired with "shamefaced peaches" and a bottle of port that later finds itself "half disrobed."[80]

The myriad overlapping associations of Plumtree's Potted Meat, plums, plumstones, stone, and fleshpots show how the latter, whether victual, cultural, or sexual, are a constant presence in Dublin; moreover, these terms also become metonymies that link Stephen and Bloom in their apparently discrete struggles with identity.[81] On the beach in the "Nausicaa" episode, Bloom thinks of Molly's adultery with Boylan: "I am a fool perhaps. He gets the plums, and I the plumstones" (*U* 359).[82] The plumstones that Stephen conjures in his "Parable of the Plums" likewise imply unconsummated desire, but they also evoke the stone Moses of Michelangelo, the lawgiver who has, like Moran in Dublin, forbidden the fleshpots: "stonehorned, stonebearded, heart of stone" (*U* 137).[83] Bloom, like Joyce himself, explicitly connects Moses with Parnell, whose betrayal he considers "in fact a stoning to death" (*U* 614), and it is Bloom who notices Parnell's monument in the cemetery and thinks, "Foundation stone for Parnell. Breakdown. Heart" (*U* 92). Here, finally, Joyce himself, and not his 1904 Dubliners, echoes Yeats's warning from "Easter 1916": "Too long a sacrifice can make a stone of the heart." Moses, with his "heart of stone," and Parnell, with his "foundation stone" and "broken heart," become ironically associated with Pearsian blood sacrifice, to which Yeats's "stone of the heart" alludes. Stephen will likewise summon (with an irony of which he cannot be aware) the ghost of Pearse in his second discourse on—or rather, as—Moses.

The memory of 1916, and in particular, Pearse's approval of stone, fixity, and certainty, infuses the moment when Stephen himself takes on the role of Moses some hours later in the "Oxen of the Sun" episode. His "sermon" is a straightforward parody of nationalist discourse that seems to have escaped proper notice under cover of its Latinate style. In fact, the antiquated prose is consistent with the biblically inflected political rhetoric of Ireland in the late nineteenth and early twentieth centuries. In a chapter characterized by its parade of English prose styles, Stephen's speechifying here feels strangely contemporary to the public discourse of Pearse's era. The sermon, as critics have noted, is a composite of Moses's song in Deuteronomy 32 and one of Thomas Moore's *Irish Melodies*, "Let Erin Remember the Days of Old."[84] Instead of trading out the heightened oratory of Taylor's "noble words" for the everyday of Dublin, Stephen does the opposite, translating the political message of Exodus back into its biblical style, as Pearse had frequently done. This second attempt by Stephen to speak of/for/as Moses also exposes something new, however: the irony of using the Irish-Jewish Exodus analogy in the midst of pervasive Irish anti-Semitism.

As in Moses's song, the people are chastised for losing their identity through adulteration with the "stranger": "Remember, Erin, thy generations and thy days of old, how thou settedst little by me and by my word and broughtest in a stranger to my gates to commit fornication in my sight and to wax fat" (*U* 375). "Stranger" in the Irish context meant English, most resonantly after Yeats and Gregory used it in their 1902 play *Kathleen ni Houlihan*, in which Ireland's goal is "getting my beautiful fields back again, the hope of putting the strangers out of my house."[85] But Stephen, like the Citizen of "Cyclops" who had used the same phrase to describe not English colonialism, but Jewish immigration ("we want no more strangers in our house" ([*U* 310), seems to ironically suggest through his subsequent allusions that the stranger who threatens Israel's purity is the Jew. In linking the English and the Jews as invaders/oppressors, both the Citizen and Stephen (for different reasons) draw on a discourse of Irish anti-Semitism that was developing in nationalist circles, particularly through the writings of Arthur Griffith in his paper *United Ireland.* As Reizbaum notes of the anti-Jewish boycott/pogrom in Limerick in 1904, "it only complicated matters further that the Protestant community supported the Jews throughout the trouble,"[86] thus reinforcing, by association with the imperialist, the image of the Jew as an invader of Catholic Ireland.[87]

Stephen next recalls Mr. Deasy's memorable anti-Jewish remarks in "Nestor." Deasy had told Stephen that the Jews were ruining England, and that "they sinned against the light" (*U* 34); Stephen now likewise rebukes his people (or at least his audience in the hospital, including Bloom) for having "sinned against my light." But rather than simply perpetuating such claims, Stephen seems to be addressing their irony in a culture still using the Israelite motif as its model for freedom. Stephen implores, "Look forth now, my people, upon the land of behest, even from Horeb and from Nebo and from Pisgah and from the Horns of Hatten unto a land flowing with milk and money" (*U* 375). The association with money brings us not only to the typical anti-Semitic accusation of Jewish moneylending, but back to Deasy, and Stephen's final vision in "Nestor" associating Deasy, rather than Jews, with money: "On his wise shoulders through the checkerwork of leaves the sun flung spangles, dancing coins" (*U* 36). The view from this Mount Pisgah is a cynical one that sees not the promised land, but the irony of Irish anti-Semitism. It is an irony already present, if not yet made explicit, in "Nestor," where Deasy recasts a culturally circulating claim of solidarity-in-suffering as an antagonism: Ireland never persecuted the Jews not, as Daniel O'Connell and Michael Davitt had claimed, because of shared persecution, but rather, as Deasy revises it, "because she never let them in" (*U* 36).[88]

Stephen's sermon is contained not only by the language of the Bible and the political tropes of contemporary Ireland, but also within a chapter defined by its rigorous attention to literary style, "Oxen of the Sun." But this particular moment, like Taylor's speech in "Aeolus," belongs not so much to literary as to cultural history, the heightened rhetoric of the podium and the newspaper. Fittingly then, the sermon is also a parody of Irish Ireland anxieties about cultural miscegenation. Here, on the verge of nationhood, Stephen channels not only Moses but Arthur Griffith, warning the people not to succumb to foreigners or fleshpots. Stephen also, as mentioned above, anachronistically channels Pearse's biblical style, as in Pearse's words about Ireland's dead patriots Tone and Mitchell: "these two shall teach you and lead you, O Ireland, if you hearken unto them, and not otherwise than as they teach and lead shall you come unto the path of national salvation."[89] But Pearse's nationalist messianism holds no promise here. Stephen acts out a parody of Taylor's Moses speech—and implicitly, if less specifically, Pearse's speeches as well—that is cynical rather than obscure, exhausted rather than creative.

Yet unexpectedly, in the midst of Stephen's sermon, the text returns to a mode of introspection that recalls the narrative style of "Proteus" and other early chapters of *Ulysses.* In the midst of speaking the political version of Exodus, Stephen is brought back to his own individual response to Moses: "First, saved from waters of old Nile, among bulrushes, a bed of fasciated wattles: at last the cavity of a mountain, an occulted sepulcher amid the conclamation of the hillcat and the ossifrage" (*U* 376). The passage works like an inversion of the parodic interpellations of "Cyclops," for here Exodus itself is the antidote to overdetermined political rhetoric. Stephen thus thinks about not only Moses the political speechmaker, but other, less public versions of the deliverer: as an infant, plucked from the waters; as a dead patriarch whose grave is hidden on a mountain. In "Proteus," seeing two figures picking cockles on the beach, Stephen had linked "the two maries" (*U* 45) with the two midwives of Exodus who defy Pharaoh's order to kill male Hebrew babies, and with the mother of Moses, Yocheved, and her daughter Miriam, who save the boy from the deadly edict by placing him in a basket of rushes; Stephen thinks, "they have tucked it safe mong the bulrushes" (*U* 45). In "Aeolus" Stephen had also thought of the life stages of Moses: "Nile. / Child, man, effigy. / By the Nilebank the babemaries kneel, cradle of bulrushes" (*U* 137). The baby Moses is, for Stephen, a link to the protecting mother: "*Amor matris*: subjective and objective genitive. With her weak blood and wheysour milk she had fed him and hid from sight of others his swaddlingbands" (*U* 28). Stephen's interest in Exodus emerges not only, then, from the political zeitgeist, but equally from its formal equivalence to the departure that has most obsessed Stephen since the first pages of *A Portrait*: individuation from the mother.[90] For Exodus is not only a narrative in which the nation finds its origin story; it is also a narrative of personal departure into identity, which, as Joyce knows (and Stephen seems to be learning) is also always ambivalent, always incomplete. Both the above lines and the ones in "Oxen" consider the shift from the vulnerable, maternally protected child Moses to the leader of a people, a passage that Stephen sees as a model for his own development as an artist. Like Moses, then, Stephen retains the mosaic ideal that he could grow to lead himself (at least) to freedom; for Joyce, this is akin to imagining the "spiritual liberation of my country."[91]

We can read Stephen's two public parodies of the Exodus trope as part of the antimessianism of *Ulysses*, the gesture that crumples the herald of the messiah, Elijah, into "a throwaway (subsequently thrown away)" (*U* 628). Yet when Stephen thinks about Exodus as a personal journey rather than a performance, he begins to consider its potential. It is Bloom, however, with his remarkable equanimity, who is best able to experience and accept the difficulty, the internal adulteration, the ambivalence of that passage through the wilderness. And so it is through Bloom that the Exodus narrative becomes most meaningful in the novel, even after it has ceased to be so in Ireland.

The New Bloomusalem

Bloom's recollection of a childhood Seder, the "mistake" that he repeats, nearly verbatim, in "Nausicaa"—"out of the land of Egypt and into the house of bondage" (*U* 361)—is commentary, not confusion. Commentary, that is, in the Jewish tradition of close, even relentless, textual analysis. Bloom's aphorism recalls a rabbinic interpretation of the Israelites "grumbling" in Numbers 11:4, "who shall give us flesh to eat? We remember the fish which we did eat in Egypt freely." As Michael Walzer writes, "some rabbis insisted that 'freely' meant 'free from commandments.' For the wilderness wasn't only a world of austerity; it was also a world of laws. . . . [And] against all this the people rebelled, remembering Egypt now as a house of freedom."[92] Even Bloom's recollection of the Passover song *Chad gadya* ("and then the lamb and the cat and the dog and the stick and the water . . ." [*U* 118]) invokes this sense of bondage-in-freedom. The text describes various animals and objects being consumed by yet bigger and greater ones ending with God, and one rabbinic interpretation suggests that "Israel is the kid [goat] which God bought for two zuzim, which are the two tablets of the Covenant."[93] God purchases the nation of Israelites through their bondage to his law.

Emer Nolan argues that Bloom "negates the promise of liberation by his significant verbal slip, his repetition of 'bondage.'"[94] Yet this reference to the double bind of liberation is intentional, for Bloom knows well the difficulty of Exodus, which is reflected in his own experience as a Jew in colonial Ireland. At the moment of nation-building, Bloom is divided in his identifications, particularly in regard to his ambiguous and ambivalent Jewishness: he is uncircumcised, has converted to Protestantism and Catholicism in turn, and frequents a Zionist porkbutcher.[95] As we learn in "Ithaca," Bloom feels remorse that "in immature impatience he had treated with disrespect certain beliefs and practices" (*U* 676), although these now appear to him "not more rational than they had then appeared, not less rational than other beliefs and practices now appeared" (*U* 676). According to Douglas Hyde's formula, Bloom's effective ignorance of Hebrew, his hodge-podge of misunderstood terms and misremembered phrases, is to be considered "disgraceful." If this word seems too strong, Joyce at least enlists us to contemplate it: consider, for example, how Bloom's ignorance of Hebrew is ostentatiously exposed to our judgment in his hilarious attempts to speak it in "Circe." There, Bloom recites the first letters of the Hebrew alphabet followed by a list of apparently random words he remembers: "Aleph Beth Ghimel Daleth Hagadah Tephilim Kosher Yom Kippur Hanukah Roschaschana Beni Brith Bar Mitzvah Mazzoth Askenazim Meshuggah Talith" (*U* 460). That he "reads solemnly" this Meshuggah (crazy) list reveals at once his aspiration and his shortcoming.

Bloom thus faces not only the cultural pieties of Irish Ireland nationalism and the fleshpots of English bourgeois culture, but the additional challenge of retaining his Jewish identity in the midst of an emerging Irish nation. He struggles not only to fit in as an Irish citizen, but more privately, to negotiate his failure in keeping Jewish laws and customs. A hallucination at the start of the "Circe" episode finds Bloom's father rebuking his assimilated son, who is holding meat from the fleshpots—a "cold sheep's trotter" and "lukewarm pig's crubeen" (*U* 413)—neither of them kosher. Rudolph asks an ashamed Bloom, "are you not my dear son Leopold who left the house of his father and left the god of his fathers Abraham and Jacob?" (*U* 416).[96] Bloom is chastised ("I told you not go with drunken goy ever" [*U* 416] and, "crestfallen," hides his parcels. Shortly after, when Bloom ponders his "wildgoose chase" (*U* 429) after Stephen, he thinks, "what am I following him for? . . . Go or turn? And this food? Eat it and get all pigsticky. Absurd I am" (*U* 429–30). Bloom rejects the literal fleshpots (feeding the meat to a dog "with regret"), but not the cultural ones, and he follows Stephen into Nighttown. Here, among other psychic dramas, he will be transformed into the slave of Bella/Bello Cohen. The name is not incidental: branded with a "C" by Bello, Bloom becomes identified with—or more precisely, claimed by—the priestly class of Israelites (identified by the name Cohen), the descendants of Moses's brother Aaron. Part of his masochistic performance in "Circe," then, is enslavement to Jewish identity: for Bloom, this is the meaning of "into bondage."

When Bloom is put on trial later in the episode, the Jewish pork-butcher from whom he bought his breakfast kidney appears as a mirage of possible reconciliation: Dlugacz "stands up in the gallery" amid a tableau of the Zionist planter's company Agendath Netaim, "holding in each hand an orange citron and a pork kidney" (*U* 440). The orange citron signifies both the ritual citron of Sukkoth (more on this in chapter 5) and the orange groves of Agendath Netaim—both not only markers of Jewishness, but of the land of Israel.[97] The pork kidney represents that which is *treyf*, or forbidden by kosher law. But each hand holds both the citron *and* the kidney. Weighing these two cultures against each other, Egypt and Israel, is rendered an impossibility, for both sides of the equation are repeated on each side of the scale. The irony of the image is further elaborated by the mocking caption spoken by Dlugacz himself, "Bleibtreustrasse" (*U* 440), or, "remain true street"[98]—the address of The Palestine Land Development Company in Berlin. To "remain true" to one discrete national identification is as impossible as weighing citron against kidney; the scales are balanced. But the balance cannot be achieved without a deep sense of irony, anxiety, and difficulty. The sudden metamorphosis of Bloom's lawyer into John F. Taylor, "pale and bearded, with sunken eyes" (*U* 440), recalls us to Taylor's rhetorical use of the Exodus narrative as political trope. Contrasted with Taylor's now-ubiquitous parallel and its association with Taylor himself (visibly ill and, like the analogy, apparently dying), is Bloom's experienced reality of Exodus—the negotiation of a multiplicitous past and present, the balancing of identities accepted and rejected, the continuing process of departure in forming identity, whether national or individual.

In "Ithaca" the advertising text for Plumtree's Potted Meat reappears, but Bloom ultimately rejects the slogan as not a worthy example of "the modern art of advertisement . . . to arrest involuntary attention, to interest, to convince, to decide" (*U* 636). Surely, though, this protests too much, because the lines hit close to home for Bloom.

In fact the slogan does all of these things, and moreover, it speaks a fundamental truth about fleshpots: that a home must include, whether literally, subconsciously, or imaginatively, the desire for what is outside it. Bloom's own incomplete home life, ten years removed from intercourse with his wife, is but one expression of his own unfulfilled desire, for as with food, the sexually forbidden is both a threat to, and a possible completion of, Bloom's identity. The English prostitute Zoe in "Circe" presents such a temptation, "*her odalisk lips lusciously smeared with salve of swinefat and rosewater*" (*U* 451); Virag's assessment of her *treyf* lipstick is "fleshhotpots of Egypt to hanker after" (*U* 483). But Zoe also speaks biblical Hebrew from the "Song of Solomon," and the line she recites to Bloom explicitly refers to the attractiveness of otherness: "*Schorach ani wenowach, benoith Hierushaloim*" (*U* 451) ("I am black, but comely, o ye daughters of Jerusalem"[99]). Molly, too, at once represents fleshpot and promised land, home and the betrayal of home. Although her own Jewishness is probable (she describes herself as "jewess looking after my mother" [*U* 721]), and she is also a figure of great local popularity, Gibraltar-born Molly is less Irish than Bloom. Both the *treyf*-Jewish Zoe, and the foreign–promised-land Molly—each of them, like Parnell's Katherine O'Shea, English as well as Irish—suggest that fleshpots, along with manna, are inevitably a part of what must be internalized for both personal and national development. And while Molly may be a desired fleshpot, her posterior is "redolent of milk and honey" (*U* 686), and the "plump mellow yellow smellow melons of her rump" (*U* 686), as Tindall notes, "[call] to mind the melonfields of . . . Agendath"[100]—evidence that her body signifies Bloom's Jerusalem.[101]

But Bloom is presented with a variety of promised lands: Agendath Netaim, Zion City, the New Bloomusalem. None is ideal, for throughout the text, promised lands have been figured as unstable places of wavering appeal. Agendath Netaim, "the model farm at Kinnereth on the lakeshore of Tiberias" (*U* 57), perhaps most clearly reveals Bloom's ambivalence. It is alternately a place of possibility, as Bloom reads in the prospectus—"Excellent for shade, fuel and construction. Orangegroves and immense mellonfields" (*U* 58)—and a nightmare, "a barren land, bare waste. . . . A dead sea in a dead land, grey and old. . . . the grey sunken cunt of the world" (*U* 59). From his first assessment, Bloom is of two minds: "Nothing doing. Still an idea behind it" (*U* 58). Alternatively, the appealing traits of the "new Bloomusalem in the Nova Hibernia of the Future"—ranging from "No more patriotism of barspongers" (*U* 462) to "Mixed races and mixed marriage" (*U* 462)—while undeniably promising for Bloom, are parodically undercut by the fact that this promised land is revealed to be "built in the shape of a huge pork kidney" (*U* 458). Joyce implies that even in the promised land, fleshpots may shape a nation.

Thus it is appropriate that in the New Bloomusalem, the fleshpot-coveting Bloom is the possible liberator of an oppressed but recalcitrant people. In a "momentary aberration of heredity, brought on by hallucination," it is revealed that Bloom's "native place" is "the land of the Pharaoh," that he "is an infant, a poor foreign immigrant who started scratch as a stowaway" (*U* 439). There is of course something comical here too: Bloom has already been labeled "Ikey Moses" by Mulligan, and heard the refrain from "A VOICE FROM THE GALLERY": "Moses, Moses, king of the jews, / Wiped his arse in the *Daily News*" (*U* 435). Bloom is also Moses by virtue of solving, after so many years, the riddle "where was Moses when the candle went out?" (*U* 681). He solves it by finally imagining *himself* as Moses—as Gifford notes, Bloom's answer is "in the dark."[102] These credentials may mark him as Moses, but like the Irish Parnell-Moses of Gregory's *The Deliverer*, Bloom is betrayed, made into a scapegoat:

> HORNBLOWER
>
> (*In ephod and huntingcap, announces.*) And he shall carry the sins of the people to Azazel, the spirit which is in the wilderness, and to Lilith, the nighthag. And they shall stone him and defile him, yea, all from Agendath Netaim and from Mizraim, the land of Ham.
>
> (*All the people cast soft pantomime stones at Bloom. Many bonafide travellers and ownerless dogs come near him and defile him. Mastiansky and Citron approach in gaberdines, wearing long earlocks, They wag their beards at Bloom.*) (*U* 469)

As in *The Deliverer*, the Parnell figure, Bloom, is stoned to death.[103] There is no choice here, as Joyce put it in his 1912 essay "The Shade of Parnell," between the leader's destruction by *either* the "English wolves" or the Irish themselves.[104] Rather, he is stoned by both Israelites and Egyptians, "all from Agendath Netaim and from Mizraim." In Bloom's case, at least the stones are "soft pantomime," but perhaps the more painful betrayal is from his Jewish childhood friends who wag their beards—signifiers of their resistance to assimilation—at the deeply assimilated Bloom, calling him "the false Messiah!" (*U* 469). The phrase recalls the sarcasm of the Citizen who had mocked Bloom: "That's the new Messiah for Ireland!" (*U* 323). Valente valuably observes here that "at just the moment Bloom's racial and sexual abjection achieve their ultimate articulation, he stands forth as the image of the group in his imposed otherness, *quintessentially Irish in the social construction of his Jewishness*."[105] A Jewish liberator of the Irish, Bloom amplifies the figure of problematic savior; however, it is this very difficulty that is instructive, even productive.

Throughout *Ulysses*, as Gibson reminds us, "Joyce suggests that Irish traditions be enlarged to include their self-betrayals, their will to self-sabotage,"[106] and Joyce was surely inspired by the Jewish tradition—of which Exodus is the archetype—of including dissent within normative culture.[107] Exodus necessarily includes something like heresy—that is, the departing Israelites' resistance to the formation of a monolithic, inflexible, contained tradition. Repeatedly we are confronted with the Israelites' persistent wishes to return to the fleshpots of Egypt, the idols of polytheism, the hybridity of a multicultural existence; we hear again and again the voices of hesitation, refusal, and the desire for something other than national identity.

The Exodus trope itself is, like Elijah the prophet, a throwaway that gets recycled in the novel: its repetition with a difference ultimately proposes the confluence of history, memory, and departure with *unsettlement* (both national and psychological), rather than fixed identity. Exodus as a political archetype can no longer promise much to the men in the newspaper office, to the Citizen, to Buck Mulligan and his fellow medical students; but Bloom embodies its meaning in understanding the challenges of nationality, and Stephen is perhaps on the verge of discovering the secret of the race as a form for capturing the birth-pang of the nation. Exodus is important not because it suggests a triumphal future; rather, it is the journey that matters, and Exodus is a viable narrative for liberation in Ireland because it can accommodate both the difficulty that attends the responsibilities of nationhood and the homologous difficulty of being a not-especially-heroic citizen of that nation, or any other. The Irish-Jewish Bloom is an exemplar of Exodus only on first view, heuristically, because of his Jewishness. Bloom, perhaps, is not any more attuned to Exodus than Stephen, than any other character in the novel, than any person living on the earth. Which is also to say that Exodus is neither especially Jewish nor particularly Irish; it is simply human.

5

A Bloomsday Seder

Joyce and Jewish Memory

Jews and Irish remember the past," Joyce wrote in his notes for *Ulysses*, suggesting that a similar experience of national memory was the reason to create, as he later described it, "an epic of two races (Israel-Ireland)."[1] Yet Irish national memory, which often appears in the novel as the reification of Ireland's "memory of the dead" (*U* 293), is countered with a different kind of national memory in the Jewish tradition. If Irish memory brings the dead into the present—*as if they were here*—Joyce also explores how forms of Jewish memory enlist us to remember the experiences of our ancestors—*as if we were there*. The latter mode is embodied in Bloom's observance, conscious and unconscious, of Jewish ritual—and most particularly of the Passover holiday that commemorates the Israelite Exodus and reenacts the moment of national origin. If Joyce resurrects Exodus to show us its expression of the essential human condition, it is through a specifically Jewish lens—an examination of Jewish collective memory—that he approaches the trope's universality. Likewise, it is through an individual experience of cultural memory—Bloom's unconventional yet paradoxically emblematic encounter with the Passover Seder—that Joyce powerfully reanimates the parallels between the Irish and the Jews, and shows us an Exodus story that remains relevant for Ireland in the twentieth century.

The value of the Exodus narrative for Joyce inheres in the fact that it is a national epic that includes resistance to the nation; he therefore sees Exodus as relevant beyond its articulation of the messianic hopes or political grievances that had for centuries characterized Irish uses of the theme. Joyce revitalizes the analogy by exploring the Seder, the ritual meal of Passover, and the Haggadah, the exemplary book of Jewish national memory that organizes the celebration. The historian of Jewish memory Yosef Hayim Yerushalmi describes Passover as "the great historical festival of the Jewish people, and the Haggadah [as] its book of remembrance and redemption. Here the memory of the nation is annually renewed and replenished, and the collective hope sustained."[2] Haggadah means "the telling," and the book is a compilation of biblical and post-biblical texts that recount the founding of the Jewish people. Whereas the Bible merely commands Jews to tell the Exodus story to their children, the Haggadah expands on this instruction: "Even though all of us were wise, all of us full of understanding, all of us elders, all of us knowing in the Torah, we should still be under the commandment to tell the story of the departure from Egypt. And the more one tells the story of the departure from Egypt, the more praiseworthy he is."[3] *Ulysses* tells the story of the Israelites (and by analogy, the Irish) going out from bondage, and it tells it again and again. If this enterprise is praiseworthy according to the rabbis, it also exposes the paradox of the Haggadah, which asks us to remember the nation's origins, but forgets the central struggles that the biblical text describes.

So Joyce also puts pressure on the Haggadah, whose evasive version of the Exodus both does and does not admit the nation's difficulties. If the Bible, as Yerushalmi explains, unabashedly describes Israelite recalcitrance, the Haggadah forgets these troubling memories.[4] The annual ceremony does not recount how the Israelites complain bitterly during their time in the wilderness, how they yearn to return to Egypt to eat of the fleshpots there, how they reject Moses, and finally, how they betray God by building and worshiping a golden calf. Rather, the Haggadah excises these instances of "desire and shame" that go against the grain of the liberation story.[5] Like perhaps most ritualized narratives of national origins, the Haggadah is, in a sense, a lie, one that recalls Ernest Renan's famous lines about a nation being a people who not only collectively remember, but who collectively have forgotten the traumas of their history: "*L'essence d'une nation est que tous les individus aient beaucoup de choses en commun, et aussi que tous aient oublié bien des choses.*"[6] In the case of the Haggadah, Jews annually and ritually forget the episodes in the wilderness where the Israelites murmur against Moses. They forget Moses, too—like Parnell, a problematic figure, at once Israelite and Egyptian prince, liberator, and disciplinarian—for he is effectively banished from the text, mentioned only in one biblical quotation (a far cry indeed from his ubiquity in *Ulysses*).[7] But against the Haggadah, and at the forefront of Joyce's mind, are arrayed the books of the Hebrew Bible and the midrash—the multiplicitous commentaries that admit and indeed explore the subversive aspects of the national story. As Jan Assmann writes in *Religion and Cultural Memory*, the biblical texts of Exodus speak not only "of memory [and] remembrance," but also "forgetting, and the repressed, of trauma and guilt."[8] Joyce brings these elements into tension with the canonical texts of Passover by merging them in Bloom's memory, and by using the praxis of the Haggadah (that is, its insistence on narrating the past as if one is living it) to tell of a more complicated and inclusive Exodus.

What the Haggadah requires at every Passover Seder—in which, as Yerushalmi writes, "ritual, liturgy, and even culinary elements are orchestrated to transmit a vital past from one generation to the next"—is both an exercise in cultural memory and an act of personal imagination: the text insists that "in every generation let each man look on himself as if *he* came forth out of Egypt."[9] For all of Bloom's ambivalence about Jewishness—or more precisely, because of it—he performs the act of memory that is asked of him at the Seder. As Irish colonial citizen and Jew, Bloom both experiences and meditates on the difficulties of the desert wilderness, the seductions of Egypt's fleshpots (victual, cultural, and sexual), and the possibility of not reaching the promised land. As Neil Gillman writes, Exodus "inhabits an eternal present; it is contemporaneous, it is happening today, to us."[10] Exodus is happening to Bloom on June 16, 1904, as it is to all the people of Ireland, who are in the midst of a cultural and political (and inevitably, personal) departure; thus Bloom can imagine without irony—and *as if he were there*—an old Irishwoman on the street as an Israelite departing Egypt, "thanking her stars she was passed over" (*U* 84). And it is the very act of imagining the experience of Exodus—not simply rehearsing the rhetoric of Erin as another Israel—that exposes its troubling ambivalence, instability, and hybridity: those very difficulties that have, paradoxically, been excised from the Haggadah. In other words, it is through a Jewish form of cultural memory that Joyce restores the relevance of Exodus for Ireland's own complicated story of liberation.

Bloom's Haggadah

The most important nineteenth-century Haggadah was published in Trieste,[11] the city where Joyce had his Jewish education and where he apparently extracted from Jewish friends information about Judaic tradition and ritual: Joyce's brother Stanislaus recalled their friend the writer Italo Svevo's insisting, "Tell me some secrets about Irishmen. You know your brother has been asking me so many questions about Jews that I want to get even with him."[12] Yet Joyce would have known of Passover in Dublin too, if primarily from its association with popular anti-Semitic folklore in the form of the blood libel (in which Jews are believed to use Christian blood to bake Passover matzo). In 1903 Michael Davitt's assertion of the prevalence of that "infamous legend" in Kishineff, where he had been reporting on anti-Jewish pogroms for the *New York Journal*, was reported by the *Irish Times*.[13] The following year saw the blood libel accusation itself appear in Ireland, as the redemptorist preacher Father Creagh invoked it in his inflammatory, pogrom-inciting speeches in Limerick.[14] But Passover, in its actual observance, was also remarked on in benign or even approving terms by newspapers like the *Irish Times*, which noted the rigor with which it was observed by Dublin's Jewish community: "all are alike enthusiastic in its observance to the minutest detail."[15] Even assimilated Jewish families, an earlier article suggested, might have participated (although surely Bloom's conversion would have placed him outside even this circle): "The Irish-born Israelite appears in daily life to have developed into an Irishman; visit him on the occasion of the

'Pessach,' and you see him engaged as vigorously in the observances enjoined in the Mosaic laws, as on the day when the Temple flourished in Jerusalem."[16]

Bloom's apparent recollection of a Seder as he watches a typesetter reading right to left (as in Hebrew) seems to indicate a high (even tedious, for the young Bloom) degree of observance: "Poor papa with his hagadah book, reading backwards with his finger to me. Pessach. Next year in Jerusalem. Dear, O dear! All that long business about that brought us out of the land of Egypt and into the house of bondage" (*U* 118). As with many of the other headlines of the "Aeolus" episode, the title of this section, "AND IT WAS THE FEAST OF PASSOVER," is an ironic exaggeration: the scene Bloom recalls is one in which his father reads not to a celebrating, feasting family, but just "to me"—a private recitation from father to son. Yet Rudolph Bloom, who has converted to Protestantism and intermarried, nevertheless does as the Hebrew Bible commands in Exodus 13:8: "thou shalt tell thy son on that day, saying, it is because of that which the Lord did for me when I came out of Egypt." Bloom's earliest memory similarly illustrates his father fulfilling this commandment, recounting a personal exodus "of migrations and settlements in and between Dublin, London, Florence, Milan, Vienna, Budapest, Szombathely" (*U* 676): a path winding, like that of the Israelites, to a new home-place. But Bloom's mother appears in *Ulysses* mainly as a parody of her own Catholicism, and surely there would be no family Seder in the home of Ellen Higgins Bloom. The more intimate retelling from father to son condenses the ritual and allows it to transcend religion, making room for Bloom and Stephen to share the story of Exodus in "Ithaca," the chapter that finally brings the pair together in the private space of the Blooms' home, and both formally and ritually enacts various moments of the Passover ceremony.

It would be an exaggeration to suggest that "Ithaca" itself is a kind of Seder, and yet the conspicuous presence of certain elements, from welcoming the stranger with literal and spiritual sustenance ("let all who are hungry enter and eat"[17]), to candle-lighting, hand-washing, question-and-answering, and the telling of the Exodus story (albeit in the unconventional form of Stephen's *Pisgah Sight of Palestine* parable) are evocative of the Jewish ritual—not observance exactly, but a sort of presence.[18] The most readily apparent of these correspondences is the chapter's catechetical questioning, a traditional Catholic form, of course, but also one that mirrors the central moment of the Seder, the "four questions." These are more accurately four versions of the same question, which might also be asked of Bloomsday itself: "why is this night different from all other nights?" The answer, for Bloomsday, surely is rooted in the affiliative, rather than strictly filial, union and disunion of Bloom and Stephen[19]—an encounter explored through the narrative of Exodus and its function in both cultural memory and history.

It is in "Ithaca" too that we finally see Bloom's own, clearly treasured, Haggadah. Passed down through the generations, now "ancient," it rests among the other contents of his second drawer, with the photographs of his father and grandfather and his father's suicide note. As inventoried by the narrator, it appears as "an ancient hagadah book in which a pair of hornrimmed convex spectacles inserted marked the passage of thanksgiving in the ritual prayers for Pessach (Passover)" (*U* 675). The place marked—and by eyeglasses intended to aid in close speculation—is significant. In the Passover prayer of *Hallel* thanks is given for the journey "from bondage to redemption"—a redemption, however, that both Rudolph Bloom and his son Leopold have approached ambivalently, if not antagonistically. Presumably this is the source of Bloom's ironically inverted formula for the Exodus journey, his commentary on its inevitable difficulty: "out of the land of Egypt and into the house of bondage." Two times in *Ulysses* Bloom revises the original passage (which occurs three times in the Haggadah) to mean its apparent opposite; he thereby suggests that Exodus is a story not only of freedom and celebration, but of the restrictions imposed by the responsibilities of nationality. This new formula can, moreover, be read as Bloom's (or more consciously, Joyce's) critique of the Haggadah itself, which excludes the forbidden but desired fleshpots of Egypt, and by excluding them forgets the tension and ambivalence at the nation's origin.

Unlike in the Haggadah's telling, in *Ulysses* the fleshpots are everywhere (as evidenced throughout chapter 4), and especially for Bloom, whose outsider status as a Jew places him in a sort of perpetual exodus, a liminal space between identities. "The Jew of to-day, but more especially the Dublin Jew," wrote E. R. Lipsett in 1900, "practically lives in two worlds, as far apart as the patriarchs and the Pharaohs are from telephones and electric tramways."[20] While Bloom's Irish eating habits (pork kidneys, in particular) function as an affront to Jewish kosher law, he is not without ambivalence in this regard: the "cold sheep's trotter" and "lukewarm pig's crubeen" (*U* 413) that Bloom purchases in "Circe" prompt a hallucinated accusation from his father: "Are you not my dear son Leopold who left the house of his father and left the god of his fathers Abraham and Jacob?" (*U* 416). Subsequently, Bloom "offhandedly," and in a rare untruth, explains to Mrs. Breen that these are "kosher. A snack for supper. The home without potted meat is incomplete" (*U* 424). Later in the episode the prostitutes of Nighttown, "fleshotpots of Egypt to hanker after" (*U* 483), are likewise temptations who threaten to unsettle Bloom's already divided identity. Yet the analogy of the discontented Israelite is applied to the average Dubliner too: as Stephen points out, even the ubiquitous Irish porter, brewed by the Anglo-Irish Guinness family, is a kind of fleshpot: a "pintpot" (*U* 42). And as I describe in chapter 4, Stephen's parable of two elderly ladies who view the promised land from the top of Nelson's pillar proposes that Anne Kearns and Florence MacCabe have in fact brought fleshpots (headcheese, or flesh in a pot) as their ironic snack of choice for a Pisgah sight of the future Irish state.

Next Year in Jerusalem

There may be no mention of fleshpots, but the Haggadah does not entirely occlude the less triumphal elements of the Jewish liberation story; its final words recognize that those who tell the story are not, after all, in the promised land: "This year we are here; next year may we be in the land of Israel. This year we are slaves; next year may we be free men."[21] Exile is, paradoxically, the inexorable coda to the narrative of liberation. Against the memory of home that the *Odyssey* provides, the Haggadah and the Exodus story insist on a memory of homelessness that is central to identity. As Assmann argues, the "counterfactual memory"—the memory of the desert that opposes life in the promised land—"ensures that people live in this world without feeling at home in it, a memory that far from making you feel at home, denies you a home."[22] In the Haggadah, then, we encounter, as Amnon Raz-Krakotzkin writes, "a document that may be seen as the foundation of exilic memory, [and which] embodies the notion of continuity within exile and of exile within the domain of revelation and also liberation."[23] To put it another way, Exodus is a narrative about homeland and place that simultaneously insists on the wilderness, or non-place, as the site of the nation. In remembering its origins in Exodus, exile is normalized, and made congruent with the national.

Wilderness also offers a possible antidote to the territorialism of the promised land: instead, the word, the text (and perhaps by extension, all language), is the origin of identity. It was, after all, in the wilderness that the Torah (the five books of Moses, containing the law) was given to the people, there that a covenant (with a book, not a land) brought a people into being. Both Marilyn Reizbaum and Ira Nadel have argued that Joyce was interested in Jewishness because it links language with exile; as Reizbaum writes, "Jewishness in this century, at least, informs a sense of the homelessness of language itself, or conversely, of the home that language may become."[24] Or as Nadel puts it, "for Joyce and the Jews the word is the promised land."[25] This is not to suggest, however, that the actual land is unimportant. As Daniel and Jonathan Boyarin write, it is precisely the tension between settlement and unsettlement that defines the Jewish sense of exile: "at the same time that one vitally important strain of expression within biblical religion promotes a sense of organic, 'natural' connectedness between this People and this Land—a settlement in the Land—in another sense or in a counterstrain, Israelite and Jewish religion is perpetually an unsettlement of the very notion of autochthony"; the Boyarins describe the Israelites as "a people that calls into question the idea that a people must have a land in order to be a people."[26] The quality of feeling not-at-home, the memory of being both powerfully attached to a land but not in it—whether literally or spiritually—is epitomized in the awkward way in which Bloom defines a nation: not only "the same people living in the same place," but "also living in different places" (*U* 317). The Citizen asks Bloom if he is "talking about the new Jerusalem" (*U* 318), but this misses the point: nationality is diasporic for Bloom. In fact, as Joseph Valente has suggested about the banter that surrounds Bloom's equivocal answer ("—By God, then, says Ned, laughing, if that's so I'm a nation for I'm living in the same place for the past five years. So of course everyone had a laugh at Bloom . . ." [*U* 317]), "the very mechanism for ridiculing Bloom's Hebraic placelessness underlines the fundamentally self-reflexive nature of the enterprise, insistently returning the muddled question of nationhood to the Dubliners' own place of residence, which is indeed, geopolitically speaking, a *self*-different interspace, the home as foreign country."[27] Bloom's—and not only Bloom's—every imagining of a stable, territorial Jerusalem, whether for Zionists or Irish nationalists, is at some point rendered reversible.[28]

"Is it," Enda Duffy has asked, "possible to imagine a nationalism without the primal scene of space, of national territory?"[29] If, as Duffy argues, this is a question that *Ulysses* asks of its readers, it is at least partly Jewish cultural memory that answers "yes." The national fantasy of "Circe" conjures the very space of the Israelite Exodus, with its Bloomusalem of forty thousand rooms evoking the forty years of wandering in the wilderness. Yet this promised land is "*built in the shape of a huge pork kidney*" (*U* 458), recalling, commemorating even, Bloom's forbidden fleshpots, and therefore implying the rejection of a land whose occupancy is dependent upon keeping God's covenant (if you betray God, you lose the land). Bloomusalem is, in this sense, a new monument—an Irish, not Jewish, form of cultural memory—to the murmuring of the Israelites who long to return to Egypt. It is a space that painfully recreates not only the emotional trials, but also the physical hardships of the wilderness: the old buildings and monuments have been demolished, and "the inhabitants are lodged in barrels and boxes" (*U* 458). Yet if such a space is hardly ideal, Joyce does not seem nostalgic for its alternative, and doubtless there is ethical value in the prospect of Bloomusalem's "mixed races and mixed marriage" (*U* 462). This sojourn in the wilderness, critically, allows Joyce to resist the most disturbing element of the Exodus story: the moment of (violent) arrival in Canaan that causes Edward Said, in his assessment of Exodus, to reject it.[30] The dislocations of Bloomusalem perhaps portend something that looks like Hardt and Negri's postnational world of global exodus.[31]

Even after Bloom finally returns to 7 Eccles Street, he continues to follow God's sign in the wilderness, the "pillar of the cloud by day" (*U* 679) that suggests he is still journeying, still not arrived. As Stephen and Bloom prepare to go into the back garden to relieve themselves, the catechizer asks, "In what order of precedence, with what attendant ceremony was the exodus from the house of bondage to the wilderness of inhabitation effected?" (*U* 650), and "with what intonation *secreto* of what commemorative psalm?" (*U* 651). The psalm, the 113th, appears at the start of the Haggadah's prayer of thanksgiving—the selection that, in Bloom's copy, remains wedged opened and available for consultation. Bloom and Stephen intone its opening lines, "When Israel came forth from Egypt, / the house of Jacob from a people of alien tongue," but not those that immediately follow: "Judah became God's sanctuary, / Israel His domain." It is fitting that the concept of domain should not figure in Bloom and Stephen's departure: the two men have now, after all, entered the "*wilderness* of inhabitation." Still, the domain here is not, in any case, the promised land we might envision; rather, as the Israelites depart from Egypt *they* become, themselves, a nation-space, a domain in which God will dwell. The psalm celebrates the birth of the nation, not the arrival in a land. At the novel's end, Bloom returns to his fleshpot-tainted bed (sweeping aside some crumbs of Plumtree's Potted Meat on the sheets), Stephen is still keyless and wandering, and this wilderness of inhabitation, or inhabitation in the wilderness, is, we sense, general all over Ireland. If the Irish nation can be imagined in the terms of Exodus, as a people departing, emerging, forging a relationship not with the soil or with boundaries but with their cultural memories and texts, then Joyce's departure from Ireland in order to forge Irish identity would no longer seem paradoxical (if indeed it still does). After all, for Joyce the Irish nation was best accessed, as we learn from the last words of *Ulysses*, beyond the monuments of Dublin, and in memories catalyzed by exile: "*Trieste-Zurich-Paris*." As for Bloom, "Longest way round is the shortest way home" (*U* 360).

Joyce's double epic concludes then not with triumphal homecoming, but a nevertheless hopeful state of exile. Similarly, the "linked double movement" of the Haggadah combines "the imagining of redemption and the experience of exile."[32] "Next year in Jerusalem," the aspiration that concludes the Passover Seder, appears in Bloom's "half dream" in "Nausicaa": "years dreams return tail end Agendath swoony lovey showed me her *next year in* drawers return next in her next her next" (*U* 364, my emphasis). Bloom's exile and yearning for return is laden with difficulty, as Molly merges with Gerty (who "showed me her . . . drawers"), who merges with Agendath Netaim, the Zionist financial scheme that could perhaps get Bloom to Jerusalem. Yet the nationalism of *Ulysses*—Irish and Jewish—is not messianic; it resists the very idea of redemption, even as it promises to remember the past. Thus Elijah, who it is thought will enter Jewish homes on the night of Passover to herald the messiah, becomes, through association with the advertisement that Bloom crumples and tosses into the Liffey, "a throwaway (subsequently thrown away)" (*U* 628), and the blood of the lamb that the throwaway announces—the Christological, but now also Pearsian sacrifice—is misread, at least initially, as the signifier Bloom ("Bloo . . . me?" [*U* 144]), who analyses, rather than fetishizes, the very idea of blood sacrifice. According to the biblical prophet Malachi, Elijah will "turn the heart of fathers to the children and the heart of the children to their fathers" (Malachi 4:6), but that future, like the messianic one, is neither realized nor imminent in *Ulysses*. No one can keep Stephen from his inexplicable departure.

The Nightmare of Jewish History

Over cups of cocoa, Stephen and Bloom compare the "points of contact [that] existed between [their] languages and between the peoples who spoke them," including "dispersal, persecution, survival and revival" as well as the anticipated end to exile, literal and figural: "restoration in Chanan David of Zion and the possibility of Irish political autonomy or devolution" (*U* 641). Shortly after this moment of what seems to be radical sympathy between two cultures, and perhaps two individuals—a moment in which "Jews and Irish remember the past" and imagine the future, we are confronted with the irony, and perhaps even the ultimate failure, of the Irish-Jewish parallel. As with Stephen's earlier performances in "Aeolus" and "Oxen of the Sun," the long-standing Irish-Israelite analogy is exposed, if not fractured, by the pressures of European history.

Bloom sings the opening lines of the Zionist anthem "Hatikvah," but a "defective mnemotechnic" (*U* 641) prevents him from recalling the song in its entirety. This is something that his Jewish grandfather had, in "Circe," warned him about ("exercise your mnemotechnic" [*U* 483], says Virag), and in effect, Bloom has given up the concluding aspiration of the song: "To be a free people in our land, / The land of Zion and Jerusalem." Much as this omission is in line with Bloom's antiterritorial ethos throughout the novel, his resistance to the obligations and exclusions of being "in our land," it also suggests that Bloom suffers from insufficient cultural memory: one must still remember the promised land, after all. In contrast, Stephen's response to "Hatikvah" illustrates a hyper-memory that persists through centuries. In singing "The Ballad of Little Harry Hughes," which, as Levitt writes, "is a Christian perversion of the Passover ritual," Stephen presents a distressing scene for both Bloom and the reader—one that is deeply at odds with the exercise in national parallels immediately preceding it.[33] The blood libel that the song recounts, the claim that Jews murder Christian children in order to bake their blood into matzo, is never far from the anti-Semitism that *Ulysses* exposes, but it is most immediately and strangely articulated in Stephen's dramatic performance here. In effect, by recounting the story of a Jew's daughter who murders little Harry, and thus reproducing the claim of Jewish monstrousness, Stephen provides the historically traditional version of Passover, not in Jewish memory, but in Western history. It is a history that, as Michael Davitt had so recently reported, makes diasporic Jews into tragic victims, not models of national self-determination. If the original victim is a Christian boy, the most resonant violence is against an entire Jewish community punished in retaliation.

Passover may normalize, however paradoxically, a diasporic national identity—one that surely has appeal in the face of territorial nationalism's violent exclusions—but it is also a cultural practice whose very presence in the Diaspora has occasioned a dark history of anti-Semitism.[34] Stephen may want to escape that nightmare, but nevertheless he interrupts Bloom's (faulty) memory, a vanishing longing for Jerusalem, with the historically—and in the novel, visually and musically—persistent "Ballad of Harry Hughes."[35] Whether self-consciously or not, Stephen ultimately forces us to confront our uncritical celebration of the solidarity of the oppressed, just as he did in "Oxen"; he reveals that analogies between peoples may be meaningful, but still they must happen within history, not outside it. The ballad brings a tolerated anti-Semitism into the present, and the dead boy haunts the space between Stephen and Bloom. As Margot Norris writes, this sabotaged climax "may . . . have an ethical effect": "By shocking the reader . . . Joyce forces us to explore why such outbursts are produced, to reexamine their historical origins, and to worry about their pernicious future effects not only on Leopold Bloom, but more widely on an entire European population."[36] Stephen's arcane follow-up, what Norris sees as his reading of Hughes as a "masochistic martyr" is perhaps, she writes, "a clumsy effort to save face, to mitigate the ballad's anti-Semitism in an effort to restore the geniality that the ballad has momentarily destroyed."[37] Along with Hughes (and in the model of Christ), Bloom and Stephen are both, in Stephen's commentary, "victims predestined," sharing in their victimization by history, and by each other.

But Stephen and Bloom are neither of them willing martyrs, and the implicit alignment of Hughes's (masochistic) sacrifice with the sacrificial ethos of 1916 connects the pathology of anti-Semitism with that of Pearse's blood sacrifice, for as Norris and Reizbaum have both noted, the Jew's daughter in her green dress is a link to Irish blood sacrifice.[38] There is no doubt, however, that Harry Hughes's death is a failed sacrifice; unlike Jesus, or in the later nationalist canon, Pearse, he offers no redemption (despite his later canonization as a martyr) but creates only more death; or rather, his death serves as the origin of one particular historical nightmare. Joyce wrote in "Ireland Isle of Saints and Sages" that Ireland must have done with self-immolation, the fetishizing of failure, and he valorizes neither the Jewish promised land nor Christ's sacrifice as a model for national liberation.[39]

The Secret of the Race

Hidden away—literally occulted, like Moses's grave, in the mountain of the text, we find a less explicit trope for remembering Exodus. It is to be found, in fact, in what has been singled out by Seamus Deane as among the most banal, "arbitrarily introduced"[40] details in the novel: Bloom's lemon soap. The lemon soap, however, is hardly random; it is a metonym for Bloom's Jewishness, linked throughout the novel with the citron, the lemonlike fruit used during the Jewish holiday of Sukkot, a commemoration of the wilderness period. As in the Passover Seder, the celebration of Sukkot dramatically recreates the experience of life in the desert; as Leviticus 23:42 instructs, "You shall live in booths [tents] for seven days . . . so that your generations may know that I made the people of Israel live in booths when I brought them out of the land of Egypt."

Bloom recalls the appealing citron of Sukkot after reading the Agendath Netaim prospectus and envisioning orchards in Palestine: "Nice to hold, cool waxen fruit, hold in the hand, lift it to the nostrils and smell the perfume. Like that, heavy, sweet, wild perfume. Always the same, year after year. They fetched high prices too, Moisel told me. Arbutus place: Pleasants street: pleasant old times. Must be without a flaw, he said" (*U* 58). Joyce most likely garnered his information on the citron's religious uses from his Triestine language pupil, the Zionist rabbi Moses Dlugacz (who gives his name to Bloom's pork butcher), who was apparently "an authority on the ritual use of citrons."[41] In the passage above, Bloom describes two Talmudic requirements: a citron's scent must be inhaled, and it must be perfect, "without a flaw."[42] When Bloom buys his lemon soap, he has had citrons on his mind, and performs precisely the religious act of purposeful smelling: "Mr. Bloom raised a cake to his nostrils" (*U* 82); he also holds the soap in his left hand, as the citron must be held in ritual use. Yet in the case of the moral conditions of the citron's acquisition, Bloom stumbles: he does not return to Sweny's as promised, recalling, "never went back and the soap not paid" (*U* 358). The soap, as symbol of observance and covenant, is countersign to the fleshpots, and Bloom's life in the wilderness moves between them. Unsurprisingly, then, throughout his day the soap continually makes Bloom uncomfortable: "I am sitting on something hard" (*U* 84); "Lose it out of that pocket" (*U* 118); "Ow. Soap feeling rather sticky behind" (*U* 274). "ONLY ONCE MORE THAT SOAP" (*U* 118) pesters the headline in "Aeolus" that succeeds Bloom's Passover reflection, and indeed, once more the soap brings itself to his attention, just as he has been thinking of his Jewish friend Citron, whose name recalls Sukkot. When Bloom smells the soap again, it is as a hybrid of Dublin soap and Jewish ritual fruit, "citron-lemon."

Bloom's lemon soap, a sticky symbol of the Exodus journey, is finally in "Ithaca" revealed, along with the newspaper in which he has wrapped it, as the "secret of the race" (*U* 629). The "secret" refers, literally, to Bantam Lyons's misunderstanding earlier in the day, when he thinks Bloom has given him a betting tip on the Gold Cup winner, the dark horse "Throwaway." But the *Freeman's Journal* is a "throwaway" (as Bloom says, "I was just going to throw it away" [*U* 82]) with another secret, for the soap hidden *within* the paper suggests the more consequential kind of race that the novel examines: the Irish or the Israelites of Joyce's "epic of two races," nations in the process of wandering toward freedom. In 1921 Joyce wrote to Frank Budgen, "O, my prophetic soul, when I put soap in Ulysses' pocket."[43] And it is, in fact, Bloom's pocketed soap that brings us back to the Jewish form of memory that insists we imagine and relive the difficulties at the nation's origin: insists, in fact, that we spend the seven days of Sukkot living in tents to remind us of life between bondage and the promised land. The festival of Sukkot, as Attias and Benbassa write, "is meant to lead to a rediscovery of the precariousness of life in the desert; it clearly signifies a refusal to rest, a liberation from subservience to place: for seven days, Israel must quit its stone houses and live in tents, in remembrance of the tents God gave the Hebrews as homes when they left Egypt."[44] Lemon soap, like the fleshpots of Egypt, is the (portable) mnemonic for a central theme of *Ulysses*: that human life happens in the wilderness, even when that wilderness is the city of Dublin.

In the Haggadah we are enjoined to imagine ourselves as Israelites journeying out of Egypt, and according to the Talmud the telling of that story must begin "in humiliation" and end "in glory."[45] That particular instruction, however, seems more suited to sacrificial messianism than the slow journey of Exodus. The text of the Haggadah does not explicitly address the instability of the years in the wilderness between oppression and freedom, but to truly imagine oneself leaving Egypt is to know the ambivalence, the difficulty of the departure. For Joyce, that unsettled space is more important to remember than every "next year in Jerusalem." In 1922 Ireland would find itself out of Egypt, but most certainly, as Leopold Bloom suggests, still very much in bondage.

Coda

The story of the Israelites' liberation from bondage in Egypt is both anticolonial and colonial, essentialist and inclusive, territorial and diasporic, racist and hybrid. In Ireland, as we have seen, Exodus signaled all of these things, and often simultaneously. Particularly during the years of the late nineteenth and early twentieth centuries, when the trope hovered like a pillar of cloud before the national imagination, it articulated arrivals and departures, the circumferences of identities, visions of the future. But even as the language and images of Exodus have disappeared from Irish consciousness—those pillars of cloud in Yeats and Joyce giving way to the crucifix of Pearse—elsewhere, the meaning of Exodus continues to inspire debate. Briefly, it is worth returning to one example that I set out in the introduction, for it surprises us with an unexpected reversal.

Edward Said, we can recall, deplored Michael Walzer's vision of Exodus as liberatory, instead pointing out its potentially genocidal and imperialist conclusion: the Israelites claiming the promised land as their own and driving out the Canaanite inhabitants. Yet in the last book Said published before he died, writing about the last book Freud published before he died, Said implicitly revises his position on Exodus. Through his reading of Freud's *Moses and Monotheism*, Said locates in the ancient story both hybridity and ambivalence, for in Freud's version Moses is not a Hebrew, but rather an Egyptian nobleman. Said writes that "in excavating the archaeology of Jewish identity, Freud insisted that it did not begin with itself but, rather, with other identities (Egyptian and Arabian) which his demonstration in *Moses and Monotheism* goes a great distance to discover, and thus restore to scrutiny."[1] Indeed, these other identities are also precisely what Joyce restores to scrutiny in his insistence on the fleshpots of Egypt in *Ulysses.* Such approaches to Exodus by Joyce, Freud, and (eventually) Said are not, however, simply descriptive; they can also be read as prophesies or warnings about what happens when the story of Exodus shifts its focus from departure to arrival. For when nations reach their promised lands they tend not to acknowledge hybrid beginnings, origins in wilderness, or inclusive identities. This was true of the new Jewish state of Israel just as it was of the Irish Free State.[2]

Said's rereading of Exodus brings me to what Jonathan Boyarin sees as the critical question about Walzer's *Exodus and Revolution*, "whether the Exodus narrative autonomously 'works' in history or whether it is merely available for effective rhetoric in a wide variety of situations. If it is merely available, how important is it in shaping action?"[3] The Irish case teaches us how Exodus "works" in two ways: first, as it did in the nineteenth century, bringing a diverse nation into imagined unity of purpose (as Eddie Glaude notes of the African American case, solidifying a "sense of communality needed for conjoint action"[4]). Exodus might, in this case, help a people see when change is necessary (the departure from Egypt), but not necessarily do the more challenging work of revealing the difficulties of liberation (the grumbling in the wilderness). In twentieth-century Ireland, the biblical analogy patently did not "work" this way, and Exodus was replaced by the New Testament Christ story that, whatever its own dangers for the nation, did. Where Exodus did its best work, then, was in texts like Gregory's *The Deliverer* and Joyce's *Ulysses*, texts that were willing to plumb the biblical narrative for its submersed but frank and unsettling story of ambivalent, impure, ironic origins. It should come as no surprise that Exodus, the birth of a nation as no immaculate conception, proved to be not simply an exhausted metaphor that would disappear by 1922, but rather an exhaustive and even exhausting one in Joyce's hands, one that he could reanimate for a final, gloriously impious, retelling. "All that long business . . . that brought us out of the land of Egypt and into the house of bondage"

(*U* 118), Leopold Bloom puts it; or in other words, Exodus is a way of describing struggle that makes every straight path into a winding one. "The New Bloomusalem" in *Ulysses* is not a land that fulfills a singular promise, but one that is premised on compromise; it includes not only milk and honey, but English potted meat, Irish exiles, and Jewish Dubliners.

NOTES

BIBLIOGRAPHY

INDEX

Notes

Introduction

1. Thomas Moore, *Moore's Irish Melodies: The Illustrated 1846 Edition* (1846; repr., Mineola, NY: Dover Publications, 2000), 157.

2. Quoted (qtd). in George Boyce, *Nationalism in Ireland*, 3rd ed. (London: Routledge, 1995), 249.

3. George Bernard Shaw, *The Drama Observed*, ed. Bernard F. Dukore (University Park: Pennsylvania State Univ. Press, 1993), 100.

4. Brendan Behan and Alan Simpson, *The Complete Plays* (New York: Grove Press, 1978), 263.

5. Joep Leerssen, *Remembrance and Imagination: Patterns in the Historical and Literary Representation of Ireland in the Nineteenth Century* (Cork: Cork Univ. Press in association with Field Day, 1996), 5.

6. See, for example, C. L. Innes, *Woman and Nation in Irish Literature and Society, 1880–1935* (Athens: Univ. of Georgia Press, 1993). Innes illuminates how, as with Exodus, the figure of Kathleen was appropriable on both sides of the colonial conflict.

7. Some of the broad foundational studies of Exodus as a political paradigm include Lincoln Steffens's *Moses in Red: The Revolt of Israel as a Typical Revolution* (Philadelphia: Dorrance and Co., 1926); Lewis Feuer's *Ideology and the Ideologists* (New York: Harper and Row, 1975); Michael Walzer's *Exodus and Revolution* (New York: Basic Books, 1985); and most recently, John Coffey's *Exodus and Liberation: Deliverance Politics from John Calvin to Martin Luther King Jr.* (Oxford, UK: Oxford Univ. Press, 2014).

8. Bruce Feiler, *America's Prophet: Moses and the American Story* (New York: HarperCollins, 2009), 308. See also Eddie S. Glaude, *Exodus!: Religion, Race, and Nation in Early Nineteenth-Century Black America* (Chicago: Univ. of Chicago Press, 2000); Melanie Wright, *Moses in America: The Cultural Uses of Biblical Narrative* (New York: Oxford Univ. Press, 2003); Gary S. Selby, *Martin Luther King and the Rhetoric of Freedom: The Exodus Narrative in America's Struggle for Civil*

Rights (Waco, TX: Baylor Univ. Press, 2008); Anna Hartnell, *Rewriting Exodus: American Futures from Du Bois to Obama* (London: Pluto Press, 2011); Robert Patterson, *Exodus Politics: Civil Rights and Leadership in African American Literature and Culture* (Charlottesville: Univ. of Virginia Press, 2013); James P. Byrd, *Sacred Scripture, Sacred War: The Bible and the American Revolution* (Oxford, UK: Oxford Univ. Press, 2013); Eran Shalev, *American Zion: The Old Testament as a Political Text from the Revolution to the Civil War* (New Haven: Yale Univ. Press, 2013); and Rhondda Robinson Thomas, *Claiming Exodus: A Cultural History of Afro-Atlantic Identity, 1774–1903* (Waco, TX: Baylor Univ. Press, 2013).

9. Coffey, *Exodus and Liberation*, passim.

10. Elie Kedourie, *Nationalism*, 4th ed. (Oxford, UK: Blackwell, 1993), 69.

11. Ibid., 70.

12. Benedict Anderson, *Imagined Communities: Reflections on the Origin and Spread of Nationalism*, revised and extended ed. (London: Verso, 1991), 149n16.

13. Anthony D. Smith, for example, points to where Kedourie, Anderson, Ernest Gellner, Tom Nairn, and Eric Hobsbawn describe paradigms in which "nations and nationalism are treated as wholly recent and novel phenomena, and a secular, anthropocentric, and anticlerical modernity is always counterposed to tradition and traditional society with its emphasis on custom and religion." See Smith, *Chosen Peoples: Sacred Sources of National Identity* (Oxford, UK: Oxford Univ. Press, 2003), 10. For Conor Cruise O'Brien, the Jewish nationalism of the Bible is the first example of what he terms the nationalism of "collective emotional force," as opposed to the modern "nationalism-as-ideology." Conor Cruise O'Brien, *God Land: Reflections on Religion and Nationalism* (Cambridge, MA: Harvard Univ. Press, 1988), 2.

14. Tony Claydon and Ian McBride, "The Trials of the Chosen People: Recent Interpretations of Protestantism and National Identity in Britain and Ireland," in *Protestantism and National Identity: Britain and Ireland, c.1650–c.1850*, ed. Tony Claydon and Ian McBride (Cambridge, UK: Cambridge Univ. Press, 1998), 8.

15. Tom Garvin, *Mythical Thinking in Political Life: Reflections on Nationalism and Social Science* (Dublin: Maunsel, 2001), 45.

16. Garvin, *Mythical Thinking*, 51. Jean-Christophe Attias and Esther Benbassa describe the final four books of the Pentateuch as "a veritable biography of the nation" in their book *Israel, the Impossible Land* (Stanford, CA: Stanford Univ. Press, 1993); on this point, Attias and Benbassa cite Ilana Pardes, *The Biography of Ancient Israel: National Narratives in the Bible* (Berkeley: Univ. of California Press, 2000).

17. "L'essence d'une nation est que tous les individus aient beaucoup de choses en commun, et aussi que tous aient oublié bien des choses." Qtd. in Anderson, *Imagined Communities*, 6.

18. John Wright, *Ireland the Restorer of Israel under the Protection of Louis Napoleon, Addressed to the Catholic Hierarchy and Population of Ireland: An Appendix to a Project for Constructing Railways in Algeria* (London: Myers, 1853), xii.

19. Ibid., xxv (emphasis in original).

20. Walzer, *Exodus and Revolution*, 93.

21. Although he does not mention Said's comments on Exodus, R. S. Sugirtharajah writes that "what postcolonialism does is to read the narrative from the Canaanite point of view, and discern the parallels between the humiliated people of biblical and contemporary times." Sugirtharajah, *Postcolonial Criticism and Biblical Interpretation* (Oxford, UK: Oxford Univ. Press, 2002), 118. I would disagree that the only postcolonial use for Exodus is in the "Canaanite" perspective, and elsewhere Sugirtharajah himself suggests an expanded reading; he writes that "postcolonial biblical criticism . . . [makes] ambivalence and paradox clear and visible" (101), suggesting that all aspects of Exodus might be relevant in a postcolonial context.

22. Walzer, *Exodus and Revolution*, 96.

23. See, for example, Glaude, *Exodus!*; Albert Raboteau, "African-Americans, Exodus, and the American Israel," in *African-American History: Essays in History*, ed. Paul E. Johnson (Berkeley: Univ. of California Press, 1994); Eric J. Sundquist, *Strangers in the Land: Blacks, Jews, Post-Holocaust America* (Cambridge, MA: Belknap, 2005), especially chap. 2, "The Black Nation Israel," 95–169. On Latin American liberation theology, Walzer cites the following as most explicitly engaging with Exodus: J. Severino Croatto, *Exodus: A Hermeneutics of Freedom*, trans. Salvator Attanasio (Maryknoll, NY: Orbis, 1981); and J. Andrew Kirk, *Liberation Theology: An Evangelical View from the Third World* (Atlanta: John Knox, 1979).

24. Walzer, *Exodus and Revolution*, 91.

25. Jonathan Boyarin makes a similar point, that if Said acknowledged this analogical connection, he "might be less puzzled at the sympathy for Zionism of someone like Martin Luther King." Jonathan Boyarin, "Reading Exodus into History," *New Literary History* 23, no. 3 (Summer 1992): 530.

26. Northop Frye, *The Great Code: The Bible and Literature* (San Diego: Harcourt, 1982), 50.

27. I am simplifying a more complex argument that Rose develops about the relation of the Holocaust to Zionism in *The Question of Zion* (Princeton, NJ: Princeton Univ. Press, 2005). She writes of Zionism that "as a unique national movement, [it] had the opportunity to forge a model of nationhood, neither belligerently nor preemptively, but ambivalent, uncertain, obscure, something close to . . . disquieting and transformative space. But did not take it" (86).

28. In his book on partition in Ireland and Israel/Palestine, Joe Cleary notes, "in the early twentieth century, Israeli Zionists maintained a complex and contradictory identification with both white settler and anti-colonial nationalism." Although

Cleary sees in Zionism mainly the former, in those years Irish nationalists saw mainly the latter—a perspective that then reverses after the establishment of the Israeli State. See Cleary, *Literature, Partition and the Nation-State: Culture and Conflict in Ireland, Israel and Palestine* (Cambridge, UK: Cambridge Univ. Press, 2002), 6.

29. Paul Gilroy, *The Black Atlantic: Modernity and Double Consciousness* (Cambridge, MA: Harvard Univ. Press, 1995), 207. It is also the case that Exodus was no longer as unproblematically available as a liberation narrative after the Six-Day War in 1967.

30. Elizabeth Cullingford, "Phoenician Genealogies and Oriental Geographies: Joyce, Language and Race," in *Semicolonial Joyce*, ed. Derek Attridge and Marjorie Howes (Cambridge, UK: Cambridge Univ. Press, 2000), 233.

31. See Donald Akenson, *God's Peoples: Covenant and Land in South Africa, Israel, and Ulster* (Ithaca, NY: Cornell Univ. Press, 1992), 99–100; 137–38.

32. Walzer, letter to the editor, *Grand Street* 5, no. 4 (Summer 1986): 249.

33. Wright, *Moses in America*, 8.

34. Declan Kiberd, *Inventing Ireland* (Cambridge, MA: Harvard Univ. Press, 1995), 255.

35. Examples include Abby Bender, "Irish-Mexican Solidarity and the San Patricio Battalion Flag," *Genre: Forms of Discourse and Culture* 36, no. 3 (Fall/Winter 2003): 271–93; Elleke Boehmer, *Empire, the National, and the Postcolonial, 1890–1920: Resistance in Interaction* (Oxford, UK: Oxford Univ. Press, 2002); Luke Gibbons, *Transformations in Irish Culture* (Cork: Cork Univ. Press in association with Field Day, 1996); Joseph Lennon, *Irish Orientalism: A Literary and Intellectual History* (Syracuse, NY: Syracuse Univ. Press, 2004); Bruce Nelson, *Irish Nationalists and the Making of the Irish Race* (Princeton, NJ: Princeton Univ. Press, 2012); Kevin Whelan, "The Green Atlantic: Radical Reciprocities between Ireland and America in the Long Eighteenth Century," in *A New Imperial History: Culture, Identity, Modernity 1660–1840*, ed. Kathleen Wilson (Cambridge, UK: Cambridge Univ. Press, 2003): 216–38.

36. Alicia Suskin Ostriker, *The Nakedness of the Fathers: Biblical Visions and Revisions* (New Brunswick, NJ: Rutgers Univ. Press, 1994), 135.

37. Accordingly, God dictates laws that emphasize the importance of discrete categories and divisions. The laws of Leviticus, for example, require the separation of things considered unalike, and as Mary Douglas has shown, proscriptions dictated against that which would fit into no category—that which is "neither fish nor flesh" (*U* 307), as the Citizen refers to Bloom in *Ulysses*. See Douglas, *Purity and Danger: An Analysis of Concepts of Pollution and Taboo* (New York: Frederick A. Praeger, 1966).

38. Qtd. in Basem L. Ra'ad, "Primal Scenes of Globalization: Legacies of Canaan and Etruria," *PMLA* 116, no. 1 (Jan. 2001): 98.

39. Foucault further writes that "what is found at the historical beginning of things is not the inviolable identity of their origin; it is the dissension of other things. It is disparity." Michel Foucault, *The Foucault Reader*, ed. Paul Rainbow (New York: Pantheon Books, 1984), 78–79. As Avivah Gottlieb Zornberg notes, such "counter-narratives" are revealed in the Jewish tradition of midrash: "The public, overt, triumphal narrative of redemption is therefore diffracted in the midrashic texts into multiple, contradictory, unofficial narratives which, like the unconscious, undercut, destabilize the public narrative." Zornberg, *The Particulars of Rapture: Reflections on Exodus* (New York: Doubleday, 2001), 3.

40. Attias and Benbassa, *Israel, the Impossible Land*, 17.

41. Zornberg, *The Particulars of Rapture*, 197.

42. References to *Ulysses* will be cited parenthetically in the text. James Joyce, *Ulysses* (Paris: Shakespeare and Co., 1922). For identical pagination, see the Oxford World's Classics edition, ed. Jeri Johnson (Oxford, UK: Oxford Univ. Press, 1993, reissued 2008).

43. Andrew Gibson, *Joyce's Revenge: History, Politics, and Aesthetics in "Ulysses"* (Oxford, UK: Oxford Univ. Press, 2002), 18.

44. Walzer, *Exodus and Revolution*, 73. Herbert Schneidau noted in the 1970s the particular literary appeal of the Bible's "ambivalence toward culture of any kind, but particularly one's own" (4); he writes, "it would appear that the word that might best describe the thrust of Biblical thought is *demythologizing*" (12). Schneidau, *Sacred Discontent: The Bible and Western Tradition* (Berkeley: Univ. of California Press, 1976).

45. Jacqueline Rose, *The Last Resistance* (London: Verso, 2007), 78.

46. Susan A. Handelman, *The Slayers of Moses: The Emergence of Rabbinic Interpretation in Modern Literary Theory* (Albany: State Univ. of New York Press, 1982), 144.

47. Freud, *Moses and Monotheism*, trans. Katherine Jones (New York: Vintage Books, 1939), 52.

48. Yosef Hayim Yerushalmi, *Freud's Moses: Judaism Terminable and Interminable* (New Haven: Yale Univ. Press, 1991), 84.

49. Nahum N. Glatzer, ed., *The Passover Haggadah* (New York: Schocken Books, 1953), xvi.

50. Douglas Hyde, "The Necessity for De-Anglicising Ireland," in *The Revival of Irish Literature: Addresses by Charles Gavan Duffy, K. C. M. G., Dr. George Sigerson, Dr. Douglas Hyde* (London: T. Fisher Unwin, 1894), 141.

51. Ibid.

52. Ibid., 121.

53. Frantz Fanon, *The Wretched of the Earth* (New York: Grove Press, 1963), 225.

54. Arthur Burrowes, "Fleshpots and Freedom," *Irish Review* (Nov. 1911): 418.

55. Ibid., 420.

56. Ibid., 418.

57. Ibid., 420.

58. Amardeep Singh, "A Pisgah Sight of Ireland: Religious Embodiment and Colonialism in *Ulysses*," *Semeia* 88 (Fall/Winter 2001): 146.

59. However in some periods, such as after the Flight of the Earls in the seventeenth century, the distance from the "promised land" was in fact literal, as leaders of the Irish community had been exiled to the continent.

60. Harry Berger, *Situated Utterances: Texts, Bodies, and Cultural Representations* (New York: Fordham Univ. Press, 2005), 136.

61. Attias and Benbassa, *Israel, the Impossible Land*, 25.

62. Jean-Christophe Attias and Esther Benbassa, *The Jew and the Other*, trans. G. M. Goshgarian (Ithaca, NY: Cornell Univ. Press, 2004), 2. "The fundamental experience of wandering in the desert," write Attias and Benbassa, "is no less central in Jewish memory than is possessing and then losing the land" (19).

63. Reuven Hammer, trans. and ed., *The Classic Midrash: Tannaitic Commentaries on the Bible* (New York: Paulist Press, 1995), 68.

64. Everett Fox, ed., *The Five Books of Moses: Genesis, Exodus, Leviticus, Numbers, Deuteronomy; a New Translation with Introductions, Commentary, and Notes, The Schocken Bible*, vol. 1 (New York: Schocken Books, 1995), 394. The Tabernacle can also be read, as Berger provocatively suggests, as denoting "a vague, stylistic return to Egypt at the end of Exodus in the building of so elaborate a portable structure" (129).

65. Zornberg, *The Particulars of Rapture*, 200.

66. Maeera Schreiber, "The End of Exile: Jewish Identity and Its Diasporic Poetics," *PMLA* 113, no. 2 (Mar. 1998): 274.

67. According to Hardt and Negri, "Circulation is a global exodus, or really nomadism; and it is a corporeal exodus, or really miscegenation." Michael Hardt and Antonio Negri, *Empire* (Cambridge, MA: Harvard Univ. Press, 2000), 364.

68. Ibid., 216 (emphasis in original).

69. In a different way, Irish philosopher Richard Kearney's concept of Ireland's "fifth province" also evokes the wilderness of Exodus. It is "a place of mind rather than of territory, a symbol rather than a *fait accompli*." Kearney, "Towards a Postnationalist Archipelago," *Edinburgh Review: New Writing and Critical Thought* 103 (2000): 28. Kearney, moreover, offers some good, Joycean advice: "In the face of resurgent nationalisms in these islands and elsewhere, fired by rhetorics of purity and purification, we do well to remember that we are all mongrelised, interdependent, marvelously mixed up" (34).

70. Benedict R. Anderson, "Exodus," *Critical Inquiry* 20 (Winter 1994): 315.

71. Buber writes, "If 'Israel' was already in origin the name of a people, then it is only . . . at the exodus from Egypt, not in Egypt itself, that the people comes into

actual existence." From *On the Bible: Eighteen Studies*, in *Exodus*, ed. Harold Bloom (New York: Chelsea House Publishers, 1987), 45–46.

72. Walzer, *Exodus and Revolution*, 12.

73. Kerby Miller, "Emigration, Capitalism, and Ideology in Post-Famine Ireland," in *Migrations: The Irish at Home and Abroad*, ed. Richard Kearney (Dublin: Wolfhound Press, 1990), 101.

74. Gibbons, *Transformations in Irish Culture*, 165.

75. Even before Moore, whose work is discussed in chapter 1, the trope of Jewish exile was especially popular with the Gaelic poets. Seán Ó Neachtain, the eighteenth-century poet, would write of Irish exile, "And because the Jewish people were the Children of God . . . they were greatly oppressed in a way that no other people were except the Irish . . . since their religion and their native land were lost to them, and although the Irish lost their land, their faith endures . . . And again, O great God of glory, summon your dear Irish children home to the native land of their ancestors." Qtd. in Peter McQuillan, *Native and Natural: Aspects of the Concepts of 'Right' and 'Freedom' in Irish* (Cork: Cork Univ. Press, 2004), 45.

76. Citing this phrase, Vincent Cheng notes, "rhetoric linking soil, nation, and race . . . is a quasi-religious discourse in which the rural countryside is transcended into a holy ground of originary and inherited sacredness." Cheng, *Inauthentic: The Anxiety over Culture and Identity* (New Brunswick, NJ: Rutgers Univ. Press, 2004), 49. "Inherited" is a key word here: as recent cultural criticism in Ireland has pointed out, the language that links land and blood has made it possible to construct Irish citizenship based on genealogy instead of residency in Ireland. In 1900 Yeats dismissively called the *Nation*'s motto "the trying phrase of 1845." W. B. Yeats, *Prefaces and Introductions*, ed. William H. O'Donnell (Basingstoke, UK: Macmillan, 1988), 49.

77. George Bernard Shaw, *John Bull's Other Island*, in *Selected Plays*, vol. 2 (New York: Dodd, Mead, 1949), 562.

78. Shaw, *Drama Observed*, 511.

79. Ibid., 100. Shaw offers yet another comparison of the Irish and the Jews in *Back to Methusaleh* in *Selected Plays*, 156.

80. Shaw later edited the above-quoted statements in a passage that can be found on many anti-Semitic websites today: "The Jews are worse than my own people. Those Jews who still want to be the chosen race (chosen by the late Lord Balfour) can go to Palestine and stew in their own juice. The rest had better stop being Jews and start being human beings." *Literary Digest*, Oct. 12, 1932.

81. Roy Foster, *W. B. Yeats: A Life*, vol. 2, *The Arch-Poet, 1915–1939* (Oxford, UK: Oxford Univ. Press, 2003), 165.

82. Qtd. in ibid., 468. In the diaspora—for example, New York City—we find a comic exposition of the theme in the 1912 song "If It Wasn't for the Irish and the Jews" by Jean Schwartz and William Jerome. For many more examples of Jewish-Irish

parallels outside of Ireland, see George Bornstein, *The Colors of Zion: Blacks, Jews, and Irish from 1845 to 1945* (Cambridge, MA: Harvard Univ. Press, 2011).

83. John Eglinton, *Irish Literary Portraits* (London: Macmillan, 1935), 3.

84. John Eglinton, *Two Essays on the Remnant* (Dublin: Whaley, 1894), 12.

85. Eglinton, *Irish Literary Portraits*, 3–4. Eglinton is not quite accurate on the language issue, although he makes this argument more than once.

86. "Dr. Douglas Hyde in Athlone," Jan. 25, 1902. Cited by Tom Garvin, "Priests and Patriots: Irish Separatism and Fear of the Modern, 1890–1914," *Irish Historical Studies* 25, no. 97 (May 1986): 74.

87. Qtd. in Cormac Ó Gráda, *Jewish Ireland in the Age of Joyce: A Socioeconomic History* (Princeton, NJ: Princeton Univ. Press, 2006), 179.

88. Cormac Ó Gráda, "Lost in Little Jerusalem: Leopold Bloom and Irish Jewry," *Journal of Modern Literature* 27, no. 4 (Summer 2004): 20, 21–22, 23.

89. Ó Gráda, *Jewish Ireland*, 190.

90. Ibid. Some years later in Dublin, Robert Briscoe, a Jewish member of the IRA, would help train the Zionist leader of the Irgun Vladimir Jabotinsky in "the methods we had found most effective in guerrilla war." Robert Brisco with Alden Hatch, *For the Life of Me* (Boston: Little, Brown, and Co., 1958), 264. In 1961 Briscoe would become the first of two Jewish lord mayors of Dublin.

91. Leslie Yodaiken, "The Song of Young Zion in Erin," *The Young Zionist*, [n.d.], The Leslie Daiken Collection, Manuscripts Department, National Library of Ireland, 10–11.

92. Ibid., 11.

93. Ibid. Yodaiken hereby gives evidence that Diaspora, which Shaw viewed so positively, was more properly thought of as exile by the Jewish community in Ireland. As Hasia Diner notes, "The Jewish Dramatic Society designed for itself a seal, which depicted a romanticized image of a wanderer with a staff, and included the Yiddish phrase 'With a staff in the hand / Without a home, without a land'" (8). Many Irish Jews would immigrate to Israel in later years, and the Jewish community in Ireland has today dwindled to very small numbers. Diner, "The Accidental Irish: Jewish Migration to an Unlikely Place," paper presented to the Shelby Cullom Davis Center for Historical Studies, Princeton Univ., Apr. 4, 2003.

94. Lady Gregory [here with W. B. Yeats], *Selected Writings*, ed. Lucy McDiarmid and Maureen Waters (New York: Penguin, 1995), 311.

95. Attias and Benbassa, *The Jew and the Other*, 4. Jonathan Boyarin reminds us, in a distant but related example, of how the fact of difference is also part of the liberator's appeal: "It is significant that (perhaps like Moses the Egyptianized liberator) the hero of the *Exodus* film, the 'new Jew,' the product of liberation from Zionism, is blond and blue-eyed Paul Newman." Boyarin, "Reading Exodus into History," 540.

96. James Joyce, *Selected Letters of James Joyce*, ed. Richard Ellmann (New York: Viking Press, 1975), 271.

97. John Eglinton, *Anglo-Irish Essays* (1918; repr., Freeport, NY: Books for Libraries Press, 1968), 22.

98. Ibid.

99. David Lloyd, *Anomalous States: Irish Writing and the Post-Colonial Movement* (Dublin: Lilliput Press, 1993), 114.

100. Herbert Howarth, *The Irish Writers 1880–1940: Literature under Parnell's Star* (London: Rockliff, 1958), 304.

1. British Israelites, Irish Israelites, and Ireland's Jews

1. Mairéad Carew, *Tara and the Ark of the Covenant: A Search for the Ark of the Covenant by British Israelites on the Hill of Tara (1899–1902)* (Dublin: Royal Irish Academy, 1986), 11.

2. Ibid., 47, 89.

3. *London Times*, June 27, 1902. Lady Gregory, with whom Yeats had been staying at Coole Park, typed a letter from Yeats to Wilfred Scawen Blunt on July 4 detailing the Tara adventure. Although Gregory appears not to have traveled to Tara, she uses the Exodus motif perhaps more than any other revivalist writer, and was certainly well aware of the controversy. See William Butler Yeats, *The Collected Letters*, vol. 3, ed. John Kelly and Ronald Schuchard (Oxford, UK: Clarendon Press, 1994), 214.

4. William Butler Yeats, *The Collected Poems of W. B. Yeats*, ed. Richard J. Finneran (New York: Scribner Paperback Poetry, 1996), 77.

5. Stephen Gwynn, *The Fair Hills of Ireland* (Dublin: Maunsel, 1906), 239–40. In a contemporary incarnation of the Tara incident, it was modernization that threatened: the M3 motorway running from Dublin into County Meath. Carew and many other Irish writers, artists, and public figures protested the project, to no avail. When the road was eventually opened in June 2010, Colm Tóibín echoed the language of a century ago: "The desecration of the landscape around Tara is shameful, short-sighted and beyond belief. In a time when Ireland needs places which have a sacred aura and a special beauty more than ever, it is sad to see those who have misruled our country ganging up on our heritage." See Tarawatch.org, accessed Sept. 16, 2010.

6. Gwynn, *The Fair Hills of Ireland*, 245.

7. William Butler Yeats, *Later Articles and Reviews: Uncollected Articles, Reviews, and Radio Broadcasts Written after 1900*, ed. John P. Frayne and Madeleine Marchaterre (New York: Scribner, 2004), 100.

8. It is, after all, the God "who stood by Moses" who may save Kathleen in the final stanza of James Clarence Mangan's famous poem. The poem is discussed below.

9. Eglinton, *Anglo-Irish Essays*, 35–36.

10. Kim McCone, *Pagan Past and Christian Present in Early Irish Literature* (Maynooth, IRL: Maynooth Univ. Press, 1990), 30.

11. Ibid., 72. McCone goes so far as to claim that the words *Thuatha De* suggest the chosen people, and thus explicitly evoke the Israelites. Not all scholars agree, however; see the review of McCone by Patrick Sims-Williams in *Éigse: A Journal of Irish Studies* 29 (1996): 179–96. For other accounts of how biblical narratives and Hebrew law were important in early medieval Irish texts, see essays by Damian Bracken, "The Fall and the Law in Early Ireland," and Hilary Richardson, "Biblical Imagery and the Heavenly Jerusalem in the Book of Armagh and the Book of Kells," in *Ireland and Europe in the Early Middle Ages: Texts and Transmission*, ed. Próinséas Ní Catháin and Michael Richter (Dublin: Four Courts Press, 2002).

12. For an extensive discussion of these origin myths, see Joseph Lennon's chapter "Origin Legends and Pseudohistories" in *Irish Orientalism*, 5–57, and for the specific Noahic genealogies, see his note 12, p. 385. For an example of how these genealogies continued to be valued into the late nineteenth century, see the subheadings on "The Division of the World by Noah" and "The Milesian Irish Nation" in John O'Hart's forcefully anti-English *Irish Pedigrees; or, the Origin and Stem of the Irish Nation*, 5th ed., vol. 1 (Dublin: James Duffy and Co., 1892), 7–12.

13. Of the early connections made between Moses and St. Patrick, Philip O'Leary writes, "throughout the *Life of St. Patrick*, Muirchú explicitly stresses the resemblance between Patrick and Moses with regard to Patrick's background, personality, and the events that occurred during his mission." O'Leary, *The Prose Literature of the Gaelic Revival, 1881–1921: Ideology and Innovation* (University Park: Pennsylvania State Univ. Press, 1994), 288. On the connections between Irish and Jewish law, John Hennig writes, "*Uraicept*, the fundamental Irish law was said to be derived straight from the law given to Moses." Hennig, "The Literary Tradition of Moses in Ireland," in *Tradition: Studies in Ancient and Medieval History, Thought, and Religion*, vol. 7 (New York: Fordham Univ. Press, 1949–51), 253. See also McCone, *Pagan Past and Christian Present*, 31.

14. Hennig, "The Literary Tradition of Moses," 253.

15. The *Saxum Jacobi*, or Stone of Jacob, was, as Emer Nolan writes, "widely mentioned . . . in works that assert the antiquity and pedigree of Irish-Gaelic Civilization." The stone was also known by other names, as Nolan points out: "The Liagh Fáil, the stone of destiny, the fatal stone, the stone of Scone, or Jacob's Pillow." Nolan's note on the stone also helpfully lists the early Irish sources in which it appears, from Keating to Vallancey. See *Memoirs of Captain Rock, the Celebrated Irish Chieftain, with Some Account of His Ancestors. Written by Himself*, ed. Emer Nolan (Dublin: Field Day, 2008), xviii, 219n5. See also Bernard Shillman, *A Short History of the Jews in Ireland* (Dublin: Eason, 1945), 3.

16. Martin Freeman, trans. and ed., *The Annals of Connaught (A.D. 1224–1544)* (Dublin: Dublin Institute for Advanced Studies, 1944), 709. Qtd. in Samantha A. Meigs, *The Reformations in Ireland: Tradition and Confessionalism, 1400–1990* (New York: St. Martin's Press, 1997), 58–59.

17. Qtd. in Meigs, *Reformations in Ireland*, 59.

18. Lennon, *Irish Orientalism*, 34. The Book of Invasions consists of a collection of texts, thus Keating explains, "all the books of invasion of Ireland, state that Gaedheal was in Egypt during the time of Moses being in the headship of the children of Israel in Egypt." Geoffrey Keating, *Foras Feasa ar Éirinn*, vol. 1, trans. John O'Mahony (New York: P. M. Haverty, 1857), 233.

19. Lennon, *Irish Orientalism*, 35.

20. Ibid.

21. Ibid., 37.

22. Keating, *Foras Feasa ar Éirinn*, 1:257.

23. In Keating's version, the escaping Israelites encamp at the edge of the Red Sea, where they await the parting of the waters. Niul, the father of Gaedheal, meets Moses's brother Aaron, who tells him the story of the Israelites' exodus. When Niul returns to his people,

> He told them all that had befallen the children of Israel. And that same night a serpent came upon Gaedheal as he was swimming, and wounded him so that he was at the point of death; and others say that it was from the desert it came and wounded him in bed. His people told Niul to take the lad to Moses; and he took Gaedheal into the presence of Moses. Moses prayed to God, and applied the rod he held in his hand to the wound, and thus healed it. And Moses said that, in what place soever the stock of that youth would settle, there no serpent would ever have venom, and this is verified in Crete, an island in Greece, in which some of his posterity are; it is without serpents as Ireland is. (2:18–19)

Gaedheal becomes linked to Moses not only through their physical contact, mediated by the divinely empowered rod of God through which Moses heals him, but also by the paralleling of their experiences. Most obviously, both are sons to Pharaoh's daughters (Pharaoh's daughter Scota gives birth to Gaedheal; Moses is born of Hebrew parents and adopted). Like Moses, who was set adrift in a basket of rushes in order to evade Pharaoh's death-sentence for male Hebrew babies, the leader of the Gaelic people is also fatally threatened in his youth—possibly while in the very same waters of the Nile.

24. Colin Kidd, *British Identities before Nationalism: Ethnicity and Nationhood in the Atlantic World, 1600–1800* (Cambridge, UK: Cambridge Univ. Press, 1999), 65.

25. Ibid.

26. McCone, *Pagan Past and Christian Present*, 77.

27. Frederic Jameson, *The Political Unconscious: Narrative as a Socially Symbolic Act* (Ithaca, NY: Cornell Univ. Press, 1981), 28–29. What I am calling typology (as in Frye, and theological criticism generally), and what Auerbach calls "figura," Jameson terms, descriptively, the "four levels of scripture." Jameson, *Political Unconscious*, 29.

28. Frye, *The Great Code*, 172.

29. For the most recent and sophisticated explication of the tensions between spiritual and political uses of Exodus, see Coffey, *Exodus and Liberation*, passim.

30. Cruise O'Brien, *God Land*, 26.

31. Ibid., 3–4.

32. Erich Auerbach, *Scenes from the Drama of European Literature* (Minneapolis: Univ. of Minnesota Press, 1984), 51, 52. See also David S. Katz, who imagines the incentive for this type of reading: "While it is true that figural history was in some ways ahistorical . . . at least it was the history of everyone, not just that of the Jews." Katz, *God's Last Words: Reading the English Bible from the Reformation to Fundamentalism* (New Haven: Yale Univ. Press, 2004), 80.

33. The extent to which the native Irish thought of themselves as a proper nation in this period remains the subject of vigorous debate. When did Gaelic Irish writers, and particularly bardic poets, begin to think of Ireland as a nation, a unified "imagined community?" A (necessarily simplified) summary of the debate may be helpful here. While Marc Caball extends the position of Breandán Ó Buachalla and Brendan Bradshaw in arguing for an emergent Gaelic national consciousness in bardic poetry, historians Tom Dunne and Nicholas Canny read bardic literature as local and unconscious of a broader sense of nationality in response to English colonialism. Literary critic Joep Leerssen takes a measured approach, "not, indeed, to deny [bardic poetry] explicitly and categorically all sense of Gaelic nationality, but to advance a verdict of 'not proven'; to call into doubt, rather than to prove wrong, the all-too-easy reading of bardic poetry as being nationally motivated or inspired." Leerssen, *Mere Irish and Fíor-Ghael: Studies in the Idea of Irish Nationality, Its Development and Literary Expression prior to the Nineteenth Century* (Cork: Cork Univ. Press in association with Field Day, 1996), 152. Also see Marc Caball, *Poets and Politics: Continuity and Reaction in Irish Poetry, 1558–1625* (Cork: Cork Univ. Press in association with Field Day, 1998), 8–9; and also Caball's review of Michelle Ó Riordan's book *The Gaelic Mind and the Collapse of the Gaelic World*: "The Gaelic Mind and the Collapse of the Gaelic World: An Appraisal," in *Cambridge Medieval Celtic Studies* 25 (Summer 1993): 87–96.

34. Walzer, *Exodus and Revolution*, 17.

35. Seán Ó Tuama, ed., and Thomas Kinsella, trans., *An Duanaire, 1600–1900: Poems of the Dispossessed* (Mountrath Portlaoise, IRL: Dolmen Press, 1981), 105–7.

36. Lughaidh Ó Cléirigh, *The Life of Aodh Ruadh Ó Domhnaill: Transcribed from the Book of Lughaidh Ó Cléirigh*, ed. Paul Walsh (Dublin: Irish Texts Society, 1957), 143–45. Also quoted in Marc Caball, *Poets and Politics*, 110. Lochlainn Ó Dálaigh's poem on the downfall of the Gaedhil ("Cáit ar ghabhadar Gaoidhil?") is similar: "It is the wrath of God scourging [the Irish] before all—that is the (real) cause of their expulsion . . . The sons of Israel of the bright weapons, when His wrath was kindled against them, many's the plague with which He visited His fury (upon them) to chastise them in the midst of all." *BBC History: Wars and Conflict: The Plantation of Ulster*, Dónall Ó Baoill, "A Poem on the Downfall of the Gaoidhil," 2010, accessed Apr. 21, 2010, http://www.bbc.co.uk/history/british/plantation/bardic/poem08.shtml. There are many more examples of this trope noted in the following: Ó Buachalla, "Poetry and Politics in Early Modern Ireland," *Eighteenth Century Ireland* 7 (1992): 163; Caball, "The Gaelic Mind and the Collapse of the Gaelic World: An Appraisal," *Cambridge Medieval Celtic Studies* 25 (Summer 1993): 94; Caball, *Poets and Politics*, 107–12. Also see Ó hÓgáin, *The Hero in Irish Folk History* (Dublin: Gill and Macmillan, 1985), 126; and Roy Foster, who mentions O'Sullivan Beare and Peter Lombard, Catholic writers of the early seventeenth century, as employing the Irish-Israelite analogy. Foster, *Modern Ireland, 1600–1972* (London: Allen Lane, 1988), 43.

37. Breandán Ó Buachalla, "James Our True King: The Ideology of Irish Royalism in the Seventeenth Century," in *Political Thought in Ireland since the Seventeenth Century*, ed. Paul Walsh (Dublin: Irish Texts Society, 1957), 26. Caball suggests something similar: "The proactive political implication of Gaelic parallels with the Jews must be stressed in the context of early modern crown aggrandisement. The belief that the Gaelic Irish might yet be liberated by a messianic hero, as Moses had done in the case of the Hebrews, illustrates how poets imparted an unquestionably forward-looking codicil to a potentially passive and acquiescent interpretative framework." Caball, *Poets and Politics*, 110.

38. Ó Cléirigh, *Life of Aodh Ruadh Ó Domhnaill*, 145.

39. Niall MacKenzie, "'Dougal MacCullony, I am glad to see thee!': Gaelic Etymology, Jacobite Culture, and 'Exodus Politics,'" *Scottish Studies Review* 2, no. 2 (Fall 2001): 43.

40. See also Bernadette Cunningham, "Native Culture and Political Change in Ireland, 1580–1640," in *Natives and Newcomers: Essays on the Making of Irish Colonial Society, 1534–1641*, ed. Ciaran Brady and Raymond Gillespie (Dublin: Irish Academic Press, 1986), 157–58; and Meigs, *Reformations in Ireland*, 60.

41. Cunningham, "Native Culture and Political Change," 157–58. Of course, this hopeful idea of finding a liberator in O'Donnell was written after the 1607 "Flight of the Earls," and, as Cunningham notes, "the 'prophesy' was already demonstrably false."

42. Caball, *Poets and Politics*, 112.

43. Ibid., 5.

44. This was clearly the case in what Jerrold Casway locates as another form of biblically based "embryonic nationalism" in "Gaelic Maccabeanism"—in which Owen Roe O'Neill and his officers "modeled themselves after the Maccabean 'freedom fighters' of ancient Judea." Casway, "Gaelic Maccabeanism: The Politics of Reconciliation," in *Political Thought in Seventeenth-Century Ireland: Kingdom or Colony*, ed. Jane Ohlmeyer (Cambridge, UK: Cambridge Univ. Press, 2000), 176. Maccabeanism itself finds its origin in the Exodus story, which the Maccabees took as a model.

45. Ó Buachalla, "James Our True King," 26.

46. Cruise O'Brien notes that although counter-reformation countries also adopted typological practices in imagining that the Old Testament prefigured their own nations, "in the main, identification with Israel and the new nationalist typology remained a Protestant property, and a constant theme in Protestant discourse." Cruise O'Brien, *God Land*, 27. However, the lack of attention to Ireland's Catholic typological imagination may be a result of inaccessibility of Gaelic sources: many are only recently (if at all) available in translation.

47. Raymond Gillespie, "Political Ideas and Their Social Contexts in 17th Century Ireland," in Ohlmeyer, *Political Thought in Seventeenth-Century Ireland*, 116. For a discussion of the Bible in Irish, see John Quigley, "The History of the Irish Bible," *Irish Church Quarterly* 10, no. 37 (Jan. 1917): 49–69.

48. There is substantial evidence that these biblical motifs were encountered by the Irish abroad, particularly in European seminaries. As Casway writes, "Hebraic studies were so important for Irish seminaries that the first Irish College at Salamanca required all theological students to learn Hebrew. But no religious order relied more heavily on the languages and traditions of ancient Judea than the Franciscans, whose biblical focus was stirred by the far-sighted political thinking of John Duns Scotus." Casway, "Gaelic Maccabeanism," 186. Caball suggests that the simultaneous English and Irish use of the Israelite analogy "is a useful reminder of the contemporary intellectual currency of the Gaelic interpretation of socio-political flux"; he makes the point to counter "[Michelle] O Riordan's overly neat portrayal of the Gaelic mind as antiquated and medieval" in his review of *The Gaelic Mind*, 94.

49. MacKenzie, "'Dougal MacCullony," 44–45.

50. Katz, *God's Last Words*, 41.

51. For a wide-ranging discussion of the English as Israelites, see Coffey, *Exodus and Liberation*, passim. See also Tom Claydon and Ian McBride, introduction to *Protestantism and National Identity: Britain and Ireland, c.1650–c.1850*, ed. Tom Clayden and Ian McBride (Cambridge, UK: Cambridge Univ. Press, 1998), 11; and Cruise O'Brien, *God Land*, 26.

52. Thus Linebaugh and Rediker propose a literally circular movement: that an Exodus-style "liberation theology that had originated in the English Revolution, then spread west to the plantation and African American . . . finally returned to London in the 1780s and 1790s." Peter Linebaugh and Marcus Rediker, *The Many-Headed Hydra: Sailors, Slaves, Commoners, and the Hidden History of the Revolutionary Atlantic* (Boston: Beacon, 2000), 290.

53. Tom Garvin, *Mythical Thinking in Political Life: Reflections on Nationalism and Social Science* (Dublin: Maunsel, 2001), 32.

54. Paul J. Korshin, *Typologies in England, 1650–1820* (Princeton, NJ: Princeton Univ. Press, 1982), 79. Frye argues, "the Protestant Reformation was an intensifying of the original revolutionary impulse in Biblical religion, and a renewed emphasis on the typological importance of the Old Testament one of the results." Frye, *The Great Code*, 86. See also Korshin, *Typologies in England*, 31; Walzer, *Exodus and Revolution*, passim; Coffey, *Exodus and Liberation*, passim; and Akenson, *God's Peoples*, passim. The critical insistence on the Protestant nature of applied typology is typically attributed to the Protestant focus on the Hebrew Scriptures. See Margaret Keller and Philip O'Leary, eds., *The Cambridge History of Irish Literature* (Cambridge, UK: Cambridge Univ. Press, 2006), 208. However, this commonplace is perhaps partly informed by the impressive scholarship on Protestant typology in Puritan America, to the exclusion of similar analyses of Catholic typologies.

55. Thomas Carlyle, ed., *Oliver Cromwell's Letters and Speeches* (London: Chapman and Hall, 1893), 19, 34. Qtd. in Walzer, *Exodus and Revolution*, 3–4.

56. Katz, *God's Last Words*, 59.

57. J. Hull, *An Exposition upon a Part of the Lamentations of Ieremie: Lectured at Corke in Ireland* (London: Alsop, 1618), 197–201. Qtd. in Alan Ford, "The Protestant Reformation," in *Natives and Newcomers: Essays on the Making of Irish Colonial Society, 1534–1641*, ed. Ciaran Brady and Raymond Gillespie (Dublin: Irish Academic Press, 1986), 70. Ford concludes that "the moral to be drawn from the biblical experiences of the Israelites was that the chosen people must maintain their purity despite the temptations surrounding them" (69–70).

58. Hull, *An Exposition*, 197–201. Qtd. in Ford, *Natives and Newcomers*, 72.

59. Tadhg Ó hAnnracháin, "'Though Hereticks and Politician should misinterpret their goode zeale': Political Ideology and Catholicism in Early Modern Ireland," in Ohlmeyer, *Political Thought in Seventeenth-Century Ireland*, 159.

60. John Temple, *The Irish Rebellion* (1646; repr., London: R. Wilks, 1812), 55.

61. Jarlath Killeen, *Gothic Ireland: Horror and the Irish Anglican Imagination in the Long Eighteenth Century* (Dublin: Four Courts Press, 2005), 39.

62. Temple, *Irish Rebellion*, 74.

63. Sir William Petty, *Collected Works of William Petty*, ed. T. Hutchinson (New York: Routledge, 1998), 199. Qtd. in Nicholas Canny, *Kingdom and Colony: Ireland*

in the Atlantic World, 1560–1800 (Baltimore, MD: Johns Hopkins Univ. Press, 1988), 111. English sarcasm had little if any effect on Irish uses of the trope. Writing out of deep social, economic, and political dismay, Jonathan Swift in "A Short View of the State of Ireland" (1727) continued to compare the pitiful state of the Irish to their biblical predecessors in bondage: "'Ye are idle, ye are idle,' answered Pharaoh to the Israelites, when they complained to his Majesty, that they were forced to make bricks without straw." Jonathan Swift, *A Short View of the State of Ireland* (Dublin: G. Faulkner, 1727), 14.

64. Edward Rogers, *Some Account of the Life and Opinions of a Fifth-Monarchy Man* (London: Longmans, Green, Reader, and Dyer, 1867), 49.

65. Seamus Deane, ed., *The Field Day Anthology of Irish Writing*, vol. 2 (Derry, IRL: Field Day, 1992), 999.

66. A. M. Sullivan, *The Story of Ireland: A Narrative of Irish History, from the Earliest Ages to the Present Time* (Dublin: A. M. Sullivan, 1867), 385.

67. Ibid., 382.

68. W. C. Taylor and William Sampson, *History of Ireland, from the Anglo-Norman Invasion till the Union of the Country with Great Britain* (New York: Bradley, 1833), 297.

69. Katz, *God's Last Words*, 40.

70. Charles O'Conor, *Dissertations on the Ancient History of Ireland* (Dublin: G. Faulkner, 1753), x. Qtd. in Kidd, *British Identities before Nationalism*, 34. Other links between the Irish and ancient peoples—Scythians and Phoenicians, particularly—also proliferated in the eighteenth and nineteenth centuries. Scythian (read, in most cases, "uncouth") origins were frequently invoked by Anglocentric writers attributing a "barbarian" genealogy to the Irish they had colonized. Alternatively, Phoenician origins, like biblical ones, were used by the Irish to signal a more cultivated pedigree. See Leerssen, *Remembrance and Imagination*, 73; and Lennon, *Irish Orientalism*, 2–25 and passim. However, even the "barbarian" Scythian origins were at times recuperated in positive terms by both Keating and later Maria Edgeworth. See Elizabeth Cullingford, *Ireland's Others: Ethnicity and Gender in Irish Literature and Popular Culture* (Notre Dame, IN: Univ. of Notre Dame Press in association with Field Day, 2001), 104–6.

71. Joep Leerssen, *Remembrance and Imagination*, 72. See also Lennon, *Irish Orientalism*, 29.

72. Taylor and Sampson, *History of Ireland*, 299. James Joyce became attached to such theories of the Semitic origin of the Irish language. In "Ireland, Island of Saints and Sages," he writes, "[The Irish] language is oriental in origin, and has been identified by many philologists with the ancient language of the Phoenicians" (*The Critical Writings*, ed. Ellsworth Mason and Richard Ellmann [Ithaca, NY: Cornell Univ. Press, 1989], 156).

73. The idea that Anglo-Saxons were the descendants of the lost tribes gathered "doctrinal coherence" only in the 1870s and 1880s, just as the century's interest in race was increasing. For more on the racialization of biblical genealogies, see Colin Kidd, *The Forging of Races: Race and Scripture in the Protestant Atlantic World, 1600–2000* (New York: Cambridge Univ. Press, 2006), 209.

74. Kidd, *Forging of Races*, 204.

75. Thomas Rosling Howlett, *Anglo-Israel, The Jewish Problem and Supplement: The Ten Lost Tribes of Israel Found and Identified in the Anglo-Saxon Race* (London: Spangler and Davis, 1892), 90.

76. Ibid.

77. Ibid.

78. Edward Hine, *Forty-Seven Identifications of the British Nation with the Lost Ten Tribes of Israel founded upon Five Hundred Scripture Proofs* (London: W. H. Guest and S. W Partridge and Co., 1874), 84. Hine elaborates: "There are two distinct elements in the population of Ireland. The first is the so called Norman element which is part of ourselves and most certainly as we are so also they are purely Israelitish. . . . But the second element most certainly is not Israelitish but Gentile neither are they the original inhabitants of Ireland. The aborigines of that land are almost if not wholly extinct and this Gentile portion now in Ireland and who swarm in certain parts of all our large cities not only in the United Kingdom but in America and in all our Colonies are literally and positively no other than the descendants of the Canaanites, the seven nations that were in Canaan prior to the possession of that land by our forefathers in times of old." Ibid., 82.

79. Ibid., 27. Qtd. in Kidd, *Forging of Races*, 213.

80. Ibid., 82.

81. Theobald Wolfe Tone, *The Writings of Theobald Wolfe Tone, 1763–98*, vol. 2, *America, France and Bantry Bay, August 1795 to December 1796* (Oxford, UK: Oxford Univ. Press, 2001), 301.

82. Lloyd, *Anomalous States*, 90. Protestants in particular now felt the need to legitimate their claim to Irish culture and history by connecting their past to that of the Gaelic Irish. For an example, see Joep Leerssen's detailed exposition of Samuel Ferguson's review of Hardiman's *Irish Minstrelsy*, in *Remembrance and Imagination*, 181. See also Margaret Kelleher and Philip O'Leary, eds., *Cambridge History of Irish Literature* (Cambridge, UK: Cambridge Univ. Press, 2006), 604–5.

83. See Ian McBride, *Scripture Politics: Ulster Presbyterians and Irish Radicalism in the Late Eighteenth Century* (New York: Clarendon Press, 1998).

84. Padraic Colum, ed., *Anthology of Irish Verse* (New York: Boni and Liveright, 1922), 128. This text was first published in the *Irish Penny Journal* on January 16, 1841. See also Stephen Regan, ed., *Irish Writing: An Anthology of Irish Literature in English, 1789–1939* (Oxford, UK: Oxford Univ. Press, 2004), 145–46.

85. Marjorie Howes, "Tears and Blood: Lady Wilde and the Emergence of Irish Cultural Nationalism," in *Ideology and Ireland in the Nineteenth Century*, ed. Tadhg Foley and Sean Ryder (Dublin: Four Courts Press, 1998), 152.

86. Lady Jane Wilde, *Poems*, 2nd ed. (Glasgow: Cameron and Ferguson, c.1871), iii.

87. Antoinette Quinn, "Introduction to Lady Wilde," in *The Field Day Anthology of Irish Literature*, vol. 5, ed. Angela Bourke (New York: New York Univ. Press, 2002), 900.

88. Ibid., 901.

89. Ibid., 35, 36, 180.

90. Ibid., 36.

91. Ibid., 178.

92. Howes, "Tears and Blood," 163. Howes's fascinating essay suggests that Wilde's "leaders are heroic, Christ-like, or God-like." And in their fraught relationships to the often recalcitrant masses, which Howes elaborates, the leaders seem, perhaps above all, to be Moses-like. This similarity is confirmed not only by Wilde's frequent explicit recurrence to Moses, but also by the implicitly Mosaic epithets she uses to describe leaders. These are, as Howes locates them, "poet-prophet," "poet-priest," "prophet-leader," and "patriot leader," 163.

93. Wilde, *Poems*, 35.

94. Gulielmus Dubliniensis Humoriensis, *Memoir of the Great Original Zozimus (Michael Moran), the Celebrated Dublin Street Rhymer and Reciter: with his songs, sayings, and recitations* (Dublin: McGlashen and Gill, 1871), 5.

95. Ibid., 8. Moran perhaps invokes a particular Moses for Ireland: Daniel O'Connell, who was known as "The Liberator" and more pointedly as the "Irish Moses." An Australian newspaper carried a reflection on O'Connell upon his death in 1847 that noted his shortcomings measured against the biblical model: "It has not rained manna during the famine; when the drought came, the 'Irish Moses' could not obtain water by striking a rock." *Courier*, Oct. 20, 1847, 4. See also Kelleher and O'Leary, *Cambridge History of Irish Literature*, 580; Hugh Kearney, *Ireland: Contested Ideas of Nationalism and History* (New York: New York Univ. Press, 2007), 87.

96. William Butler Yeats, *Celtic Twilight* (Gerrards Cross, UK: Colin Smythe, 1981), 31.

97. Ibid., 31. Paul Muldoon suggests that Yeats would have appreciated "the transgression implied in the presenting of 'contaygious' for 'contiguous.'" Muldoon, *To Ireland, I* (New York: Oxford Univ. Press, 2000), 135. "Humoriensis" sternly warns us away from this version, stating that it is "burlesque . . . not true to the character of Zozimus." Humoriensis, *Memoir of the Great Original Zozimus*, 4. However, as we might expect, it is this comic version that Joyce alludes to in *Ulysses* (Mr.

Dixon tells the story of when "lord Harry was cleaning his royal pelt to go to dinner after winning a boatrace" (*U* 382).

98. Frank Harte, ed., *Songs of Dublin* (Cork: Ossian, 1993), 81. Because Yeats quotes only selections from the ballad, I have cited additional lines from Frank Harte's collection of Dublin songs.

99. Yeats, *Celtic Twilight*, 31.

100. Jeffery W. Vail, *The Literary Relationship of Lord Byron and Thomas Moore* (Baltimore, MD: Johns Hopkins Univ. Press, 2000), 99.

101. Emer Nolan, *Catholic Emancipations: Irish Fiction from Thomas Moore to James Joyce* (Syracuse, NY: Syracuse Univ. Press, 2007), 3.

102. Moore's biographer Ronan Kelly describes how, at "a huge gathering in Boston in 1865," "'Sound the Loud Timbrel,' one of the Sacred Songs prophesying emancipation, had proved especially popular with the abolitionist movement, and when the news came through that Lincoln's amendment had been ratified, Moore's words were sung with a new emotion." Ronan Kelly, *Bard of Erin: The Life of Thomas Moore* (Dublin: Penguin Ireland, 2009), 276.

103. Moore's national-melodies style was an early influence on Byron's *Hebrew Melodies*, but the borrowing between the poets, particularly in regard to motifs of Jewish nationalism, would go in both directions. See Vail, *Literary Relationship of Lord Byron and Thomas Moore*, 92–102; and Thomas L. Aston, *Byron's Hebrew Melodies* (Austin: Univ. of Texas Press, 1972), 65–105.

104. Thomas Moore, *The Journal of Thomas Moore*, vol. 1, ed. Wilfred S. Dowden (Newark: Univ. of Delaware Press, 1983), 340.

105. Stephen Gwynn, *Thomas Moore* (London: MacMillan and Co., 1905), 185.

106. Moore, *Moore's Irish Melodies*, 157.

107. "The Parallel" can thus be interpreted as adapting the Israelite analogy to the "imperial sentimentality" that Nolan notes Moore has often been accused of; it is possible, Nolan writes, for "political allegories" to "transform an activist project of mass politicization, such as that attempted by the United Irish movement, into a merely passive longing for the indefinitely deferred dawn of freedom in Ireland" (*Catholic Emancipations*, 5). Interestingly, it is in one of the poems in *Sacred Songs*, "War Against Babylon!" that Moore describes violent rebellion—never mentioning Ireland, but surely invoking it: "Swarm we, like locusts, o'er all her fields, / 'Zion,' our watchword, and 'vengeance' our cry!" See Moore, *Irish Melodies and Sacred Songs* (New York: Oakley, Mason, and Co., 1869), 178.

108. As Nolan writes in her introduction to the text, "it defies any easy generic classification," being "part history, part fiction, and part satire." Moore, *Captain Rock*, xviii. Hamilton, whose work includes pamphlets entitled *Heathen Ceremonies of Rome* and *Tracts upon Some Leading Errors of the Church of Rome*, was odd source material for the Catholic, nationalist Moore.

109. Moore, *Captain Rock*, 12.

110. Ibid. It is worth pointing out that one possible, if ironic, source of Moore's apparently ambivalent response to Hamilton, and to biblical material in general, was the increasing push made by Protestant evangelists for Catholics to read the Bible. Just as Moore was writing elaborate allegories from material in the Hebrew Scriptures, many Protestants, including Hamilton, were working to address supposed Catholic biblical illiteracy. The project was part of what has been called the "Second Reformation" in Ireland—or more pointedly, as Irene Whelan terms it in her book on the subject, "The Bible War." Hamilton, for example, was vociferous in arguing that the Catholic Irish did not know the Bible. In a petition to the British parliament in 1845, he gathered 1,042 signatures from the archdiocese of Dublin to show that "in the national system in Ireland the value and importance of the Holy Scriptures are not properly recognized, inasmuch as the study of them, or even of extracts or portions of them, is made subject to the sanction of parents and patrons" (George Hamilton, Application 674, in *Parliamentary Papers, House of Commons and Command, Parts 1–2*, "Public Petitions delivered June 21, containing petitions presented June 11–13, 1845," accessed July 7, 2009, https://books.google.com.

But if the Catholic Irish did not read scripture as diligently as their Protestant countrymen and women did (and surely they did not), they were at the very least familiar with the story of an oppressed and then liberated tribe who came forth from Egypt. So was the "Bible War" a source of Catholic anxiety about using biblical analogies—and one of the factors that would eventually turn Catholic nationalism away from Old Testament narratives? Possibly, but it seems problematic to make too much of this; after all, Moore was hardly the only Catholic using the Israelite and other biblical analogies in the nineteenth century. See Whelan's *The Bible War in Ireland: The "Second Reformation" and the Polarization of Protestant-Catholic Relations, 1800–1840* (Madison: Univ. of Wisconsin Press, 2005).

111. Other Irish writers would also begin to dismiss the biblical genealogy: Sir William Wilde, in his essay "On the Ancient Races of Ireland," writes, "The old annalists bring [the early Irish invaders] direct from the Ark, and in a straight line from Japhet. The coming of Pharaoh's daughter from Egypt with her ships may be also considered apocryphal." The essay is appended to Lady Wilde's book *Ancient Legends, Mystic Charms, and Superstitions of Ireland: To which is appended a chapter "On the Ancient Races of Ireland" by the late Sir William Wilde*, vol. 2 (Boston: Ticknor and Co., 1887), 361.

112. Cormac Ó Gráda, *Jewish Ireland in the Age of Joyce: A Socioeconomic History* (Princeton, NJ: Princeton Univ. Press, 2006), 10. Popular memory recalls the Jewish population as refuges from pogroms, an idea that is called into question by recent scholarship that finds, in the case of Lithuania, economic factors more likely. Ó Gráda, *Jewish Ireland*, 14.

113. Cullingford, *Ireland's Others*, 99. Kidd's comparison of how English colonists treated both the Gaels and the Amerindians is likewise apt; with both cultures, "their pasts were appropriated, sanitised and rendered useful to the colonial cause, but as a real contemporary people they were despised, downtrodden and excluded." Kidd, *British Identities before Nationalism*, 180. In *Ireland's Others*, Cullingford explores several Irish analogies with other groups and the ironies that such figurations produce. She notes how, when the Northern activist Bernadette Devlin McAliskey came to the United States, she "was horrified by the racism she encountered among Irish-Americans, because her political education in the Northern Irish civil rights movement had convinced her that Irish and blacks everywhere should be on the same side of the barricades." Cullingford, *Ireland's Others*, 159. Cullingford concludes, "a literary, as opposed to literal, interpretation of the analogy is easier to defend" (ibid., 160). See also Aamir Mufti's *Enlightenment in the Colony: The Jewish Question and the Crisis of Postcolonial Culture* (Princeton, NJ: Princeton Univ. Press, 2007); and Brian Cheyette's review of the latter, "The Boy Singer Goes Global," *Times Literary Supplement*, Mar. 21, 2008.

114. Gibson, *Joyce's Revenge*, 50.

115. Ibid.

116. Ibid.

117. Ibid. It was, unsurprisingly, problematic for nationalists that Irish Jews identified primarily with Unionism—many Jews had family and congregational affiliations in England and felt connected to it. See Ó Gráda, *Jewish Ireland*, 188–89. And as Hasia Diner notes, while the Catholic Irish hated Cromwell, he was "a hero in all renditions of Jewish history, the individual responsible for bringing to an end the four-century-old Jewish expulsion from England." Diner, "Accidental Irish," 53.

118. There have been a number of recent scholarly works on Jews in Ireland, and particularly on this episode. Ó Gráda suggests that the term "pogrom" is not really appropriate, while Keogh writes that it is. See Ó Gráda, *Jewish Ireland*, 193; and Dermot Keogh, *Jews in Twentieth-Century Ireland: Refugees, Anti-Semitism and the Holocaust* (Cork: Cork Univ. Press, 1998), 26.

119. *United Irishman*, Apr. 23, 1904. Qtd. in Dominic Manganiello, *Joyce's Politics* (London: Routledge, 1980), 131.

120. Ibid.

121. Marilyn Reizbaum, *James Joyce's Judaic Other* (Stanford, CA: Stanford Univ. Press, 1999), 60.

122. Palmieri was Joyce's voice coach for several lessons that year. See Ellmann, *James Joyce* (Oxford, UK: Oxford Univ. Press, 1959), 151. I am indebted to Paddy Hawe for his generosity in sending me the libretto, concert program, and information on the background of MacDonagh's composition.

123. Johann A. Norstedt, *Thomas MacDonagh: A Critical Biography* (Charlottesville: Univ. Press of Virginia, 1980), 44.

124. Thomas MacDonagh, *The Exodus: A Sacred Cantata* (Dublin: Doremi and Co., 1904), 37.

125. Norstedt, *Thomas MacDonagh*, 45.

126. *United Irishman*, June 4, 1904. Qtd. in Norstedt, *Thomas MacDonagh*, 46.

127. Ibid. MacDonagh had certainly observed the connection between the Irish and contemporary Jews (by 1904, something of a cliché), noting that they were alike in their suffering. See Boyce, *Nationalism in Ireland*, 310. In this he was perhaps influenced by the chain of speeches recounted below in notes 135–38.

128. In *The Resurrection of Hungary: A Parallel for Ireland* (1904), Griffith describes how Hungarian Count István Széchenyi "led his country within sight of the promised Land." Qtd. in Gibson, *Joyce's Revenge*, 120.

129. Gibson, *Joyce's Revenge*, 48.

130. Qtd. in Neil R. Davison, *James Joyce, "Ulysses," and the Construction of Jewish Identity* (Cambridge, UK: Cambridge Univ. Press, 1996), 37.

131. Davitt had also written an exposé on the Kishinev pogroms of 1903, a series of articles eventually published as *Within the Pale: The True Story of Anti-Semitic Persecutions in Russia* (London: A. S. Barnes and Co., 1903).

132. Francis Sheehy-Skeffington, *Michael Davitt: Revolutionary, Agitator, and Labour Leader* (London: T. Fisher Unwin, 1908), 268.

133. Ibid.

134. Fanny Parnell, "Michael Davitt," *Pilot* 43 (Dec. 19, 1880): 1.

135. Michael Davitt, "Ireland and the Jews: A Letter to the Editor," *Freeman's Journal*, July 13, 1893. Qtd. in Keogh, *Jews in Twentieth-Century Ireland*, 20.

136. Louis Hyman, *The Jews of Ireland from the Earliest Times to the Year 1910* (Shannon: Irish Univ. Press, 1972), 196. Qtd. in Ira B. Nadel, *Joyce and the Jews* (Iowa City: Univ. of Iowa Press, 1989), 186.

137. For full text of the letter, see Jewish Historical Society of England, *Transactions—The Jewish Historical Society of England*, vol. 4 (London: Jewish Historical Society of England, 2009), 151. Qtd. in Shillman, *Short History*, 75.

138. Rev. L. Way, a letter in *The Jewish Expositor and Friend of Israel* (London: B. R. Goakman, 1820), 228 (emphasis in original).

139. Reading through the reports from the local associations suggests a strong Irish interest in the project—whether out of actual love for Jews is, of course, debatable. The note on the "Formation of an Association at Sligo, in Aid of the Irish Auxiliary Society" includes the following report: "The feeling excited at Sligo, in favour of the cause was truly uncommon. It pervaded all classes of society, unlike any thing I have as yet heard of. The houses at which the Rev. Mr. Bushe and Mr. Nixon remained, were continually crowded, and during the whole days they remained in

Sligo, they were literally occupied from morning to night, speaking to the people concerning Judah and Jerusalem." Mar. 14, 1821.

140. The conventionally anti-Semitic discourse of parasitism that did, in fact, accompany the arriving Jews had been elaborated much earlier by James Harrington. In 1656 he had proposed that Ireland, or "Panopea, the soft mother of a slothful and pusillanimous people," would be made most useful for the British Empire "by planting it with Jews"; not because of any sympathy or imaginative connection between the Irish and the Israelites, but rather to entirely replace the Irish, for "To receive the Jews after any other manner into a commonwealth were to maim it; for they of all nations never incorporate, but taking up the room of a limb, are of no use or office to the body, while they suck the nourishment which would sustain a natural and useful member." James Harrington, *The Oceana and other works of Iames Harrington, with an account of his life by Iohn Toland* (London: T. Becket and T. Cadell, 1771), 33–34.

141. *United Ireland*, Mar. 9, 1901. Qtd. in Carew, *Tara and the Ark of the Covenant*, 80.

142. "There is legend that an emissary of the Anglo-Israelite Society once approached a rich cynic with a demand for a subscription to further his identification of the inhabitants of these isles with the ten Lost Tribes, and that the cynic expressed his readiness to contribute $5 if they would undertake to lose the other two." *Spectator*, May 23, 1914.

143. More than sixty reviews are preserved in the James Owen Hannay papers, Trinity College Dublin; I am very grateful to Felicity Cable for her work in transcribing the relevant ones. The lost tribes of the title make no "real" appearance in the novel, either—a fact pointed out by more than one reviewer (*Times*, *Daily News*, *Literary Monthly*). If the British Israelites still had an interest in Ireland past the Tara excavation, they seemed, from the Irish perspective, mostly a curiosity. Even other marginal groups, such as the Church of Ireland Jews' Society (aimed at converting Jews), seemed nonplussed. At their annual meeting in 1907, the chairman of the Jews' Society explained that "he did not understand the great searchings that were going on as to where the ten lost tribes were, nor did he understand the great desire that existed to identify the British race with these lost tribes," further stating the view that such people were "trying to put themselves in the place of the chosen people." *Irish Times*, Apr. 10, 1907, 9.

144. Hannay's early novels were, as Eileen Reilly writes, "intended as serious commentaries upon Irish society and politics," and their strong anticlericalism elicited incensed responses from Catholic nationalists. As a result, Hannay was pushed out of his leadership position in the supposedly nonsectarian Gaelic League in 1906. The fiction Hannay published after the Gaelic League incident (and after riots surrounding one of his plays) offers more gentle satire, and, as Reilly argues, "farcical and far fetched" plots made the novels more acceptable—the case, surely, with *The*

Lost Tribes, which appears to take little interest in politics of any sort. Reilly, "'The Very Best Kind of Fiction': James Owen Hannay ('George A. Birmingham') and the Gaelic League," in *Encountering Ireland: Poetry, Politics and Prose since 1880*, ed. Alan Marshall and Neil Sammells (London: Sulis Press, 1998), 50, 56. The novel is, one reviewer claimed, "always genial and kindly, always free from sting and offense." *Irish Independent*, May 11, 1914, 7.

145. James Owen Hannay, *The Lost Tribes* (New York: Thomas Nelson and Sons, 1915), 30, 5.

146. In British Israelite belief, the lost tribes are lost, as even Mr. Dann knows, "in the time of the Assyrian Empire" (2)—well before the Roman era when Jesus lived.

147. Hannay, *Lost Tribes*, 65. Presumably Mrs. Dann is not referring to a true Miracle Play about a saint, but a Mystery Play (the terms are often interchanged; this may or may not be another version of Mrs. Dann's dilettantism); she seems to imagine a Passion Play that dramatizes Christ's sufferings. Mrs. Dann's interest in casting does not last long, however: just one Catholic handyman and one Protestant police sergeant are targeted as "Jews" during the course of the four-hundred-page novel.

148. Hannay's biographer hints at a developing anti-Semitism in this period, which may also have inflected his choice of these particular Jews as representative.

149. Hannay, *Lost Tribes*, 78.

150. Ibid., 55.

151. Ibid., 327.

152. Ibid., 58.

2. Lady Gregory, Parnell, and the Irish Deliverer

1. Joyce, *Critical Writings*, 228. The clinical diagnosis—a myocardial infarction, or in plain terms a heart attack—is offered by the physician-critic J. B. Lyons, in *'What Did I Die of?': The Deaths of Parnell, Wilde, Synge, and Other Literary Pathologies* (Dublin: Lilliput Press, 1991), 99.

2. Deane, *Field Day Anthology*, 2:310.

3. Seamus Deane, Declan Kiberd, and Gregory Castle have shown how writers like Gregory, Yeats, and Synge were obliged to produce texts that shifted "the grounds of Irish identity from race to locality." Gregory Castle, *Modernism and the Celtic Revival* (Cambridge, UK: Cambridge Univ. Press, 2001), 6. See also Declan Kiberd, *Inventing Ireland* (Cambridge, MA: Harvard Univ. Press, 1995), 107.

4. Seamus Deane, "Heroic Styles: The Tradition of an Idea," in *Theorizing Ireland*, ed. Claire Connolly (New York: Palgrave Macmillan, 2003), 16.

5. Eglinton, *Anglo-Irish Essays*, 9.

6. William Butler Yeats to John Butler Yeats, Nov. 24, 1910, in William Butler Yeats, *The Letters of W. B. Yeats*, ed. Allan Wade (New York: Macmillan, 1955), 555.

7. F. S. L. Lyons, "The Parnell Theme in Literature," in *Place, Personality and the Irish Writer*, ed. Andrew Carpenter (New York: Harper and Row, 1977), 70.

8. Hennig notes that O'Connell was also described as Moses; he cites O'Connell's funeral oration by Father Ventura ("like Moses, O'Connell *liberavit gentem suam a perditione*") and mentions several other examples. Hennig, "Literary Tradition of Moses in Ireland," 259. Gladstone interestingly uses the same rhetoric; see note 37 in this chapter.

9. William O'Brien, *The Parnell of Real Life* (London: T. F. Unwin, 1926), 151. Qtd. in Conor Cruise O'Brien, *Parnell and His Party, 1880–1890* (Oxford, UK: Clarendon Press, 1968), 246.

10. See Michael Valdez Moses's essay "The Irish Vampire: *Dracula*, Parnell, and the Troubled Dreams of Nationhood," *Journal X: A Journal in Culture and Criticism* 2, no. 1 (Fall 1997): 67–111. Another inhuman, mysterious Parnell—an Egyptian one, no less—is captured in the "The Irish Sphinx," a political illustration by "Conn" in the *Weekly Irish Times*, Sept. 29, 1883. The image is reproduced in Lawrence W. McBride, *Images, Icons and the Irish Nationalist Imagination* (Dublin: Four Courts Press, 1999).

11. One of his contemporaries called it "extraordinary": "One was not accustomed to it. All Irish agitators talked. He didn't. He listened with wonderful patience. His reserve was a revelation." See R. Barry O'Brien, *The Life of Charles Stewart Parnell, Part 1* (New York: Harper and Brothers, 1898), 137.

12. Exodus 4:10.

13. Michael Davitt, *The Fall of Feudalism in Ireland* (London: Harper and Brothers, 1904), 467. Qtd. in Malcolm Brown, *The Politics of Irish Literature: From Thomas Davis to W. B. Yeats* (Seattle: Univ. of Washington Press, 1973), 304.

14. Ibid., 652.

15. Ibid.

16. Considering Parnell's political career in context, it is worth noting Cruise O'Brien's observation that "there [were] political, as opposed to just mythical/cultural, reasons for the Parliamentary Party to choose an outsider to lead them." And it was not just a case of a Protestant landowner fitting in among the other MPs at Westminster—although certainly "Parnell's social superiority was one of his claims to leadership." O'Brien also points out that tensions between Fenians and ex-Fenians in the Irish Party created a space for a newcomer who had no political history. O'Brien, *Parnell and His Party*, 4, 6.

17. Joyce, *Critical Writings*, 162.

18. Brown, *Politics of Irish Literature*, 373. O'Grady's contribution is also recognized in John Kelly, "Parnell in Irish Literature," in *Parnell in Perspective*, ed. D. George Boyce and Alan O'Day (New York: Routledge, 1991), 253. Another compelling reading of Parnell is found in Joseph Valente's analysis of manliness as a way of explaining

Parnell's "tenacious hold . . . on the imagination of his compatriots." Valente, "The Manliness of Parnell," *Éire-Ireland* 41, nos. 1–2 (Spring–Summer 2006): 64.

19. Standish O'Grady, *The Story of Ireland* (London: Methuen and Co., 1894), 212.

20. Ibid., 211–12.

21. Yeats, *Collected Poems*, 279.

22. Augusta Gregory, *Collected Plays of Lady Gregory*, Coole Edition, vol. 2, ed. Ann Saddlemeyer (New York: Oxford Univ. Press, 1970), 304. Further references to the play appear parenthetically in the text.

23. Lyons speculates that this group was "the first generation to have grown up in the realization that the ascendancy of the caste to which they belonged was no longer secure and inevitable." F. S. L. Lyons, *Ireland since the Famine* (London: Weidenfeld and Nicolson, 1971), 229.

24. Susan Harris, *Gender and Modern Irish Drama* (Bloomington: Indiana Univ. Press, 2002), 30. The various ways in which Irish "purity" (or Anglophobia, according to Lyons) was encouraged in such publications, and more broadly in arenas of culture, language, religion, sexuality, and economics, have been well documented. See, for example, P. J. Matthews, *Revival: The Abbey Theatre, Sinn Féin, the Gaelic League and the Co-operative Movement* (Cork: Cork Univ. Press in association with Field Day, 2003).

25. David Krause, for example, separates nationalists, on the one hand, from literary figures interested in "the higher nationalism—the search for the truth about human beings," on the other. Krause, *The Regeneration of Ireland: Renaissance and Revolution* (Bethesda, MD: Academic Press, 2001), xii, 46.

26. Lyons, *Ireland since the Famine*, 228.

27. O'Donnell was the writer of perhaps the most important of the anti-*Countess Cathleen* pamphlets, "Souls for Gold: Pseudo-Celtic Drama in Dublin" (London: Nassau Press, 1899).

28. Reverend George O'Neill, "The Inauguration of the Irish Literary Theatre," *New Ireland Review* 11, no. 4 (June 1899): 249. Qtd. in Ben Levitas, *The Theatre of Nation: Irish Drama and Cultural Nationalism 1890–1916* (Oxford, UK: Clarendon Press, 2002), 44 (my emphasis).

29. Harris, *Gender and Modern Irish Drama*, 69. If such frank attitudes were unappealing to the nationalists of Irish Ireland, they were not the mainstay of the revival either. The romanticized peasant of Yeats's early writings was far more in evidence than the fraught and ambivalent colonial citizen.

30. Lyons, *Ireland since the Famine*, 232–33.

31. Ben Levitas, "Yeats and the Ireland of Synge's Time," lecture, New York Univ., Apr. 1, 2004. Lucy McDiarmid and Maureen Waters usefully contest a view of the apolitical Gregory in their introduction to her *Selected Writings* (xl).

32. Deane, *Field Day Anthology*, 2:310.

33. Joyce's father, John Stanislaus Joyce, was a staunch Parnellite. When at age nine Joyce wrote a poem denouncing Healy ("Et Tu, Healy") his father had it printed privately; no copy survives. See Ellmann, *James Joyce*, 33. Joyce conveys his father's brand of Parnellism in the Christmas dinner scene of *A Portrait of the Artist as a Young Man*, in which the cry of "Poor Parnell! My Dead King!" makes a powerful impression on the "terrorstricken" Stephen. James Joyce, *A Portrait of the Artist as a Young Man* (New York: Penguin Books, 1993), 39.

34. Qtd. in Cruise O'Brien, *Parnell and His Party*, 290. It seems Healy also contributed the second-most memorable metaphor associated with Parnell, that of the "howling pack" calling for his destruction—a favorite of Joyce. The metaphor was also invoked repeatedly by *United Ireland* readers, in poems such as that by Michael Hogan, "The Bard of Thomond." Here is the first stanza of "Call off the Dogs": "Parnell is buried and Erin is dead! / Sound the dirge to earth's farthest bounds; / Ireland's *Leader*—England's dread— / Was eaten up by his Irish hounds" etc. *United Ireland*, Oct. 24, 1891. Healy was also first to describe Parnell as the "uncrowned king of Ireland." See Deane, *Field Day Anthology*, 2:369.

35. Qtd. in Cruise O'Brien, *Parnell and His Party*, 289. After Parnell's death the statement was reprinted in *United Ireland* on Oct. 24, 1891. It had also been printed in a pamphlet by the Irish National League of Britain, entitled "The Last Irish Defection."

36. *Freeman's Journal*, Nov. 26, 1890. Qtd. in Cruise O'Brien, *Parnell and His Party*, 302.

37. *United Ireland*, Nov. 7, 1891.

38. Qtd. in Barry O'Brien, *Life of Charles Stewart Parnell*, 1:130. William Michael Murphy counts almost fifty cases of the Moses-Parnell analogy in the first half of the twentieth century. Murphy, *The Parnell Myth and Irish Politics, 1891–1956* (New York: Peter Land Publishing, 1986), 169n32.

39. Moses, "The Irish Vampire," 72.

40. *London Times*, Oct. 8, 1881. Qtd. in Lyons, "The Parnell Theme in Literature," 71. Two days after the speech, Healey would recast Gladstone's Moses comparison, saying, "Mr. Parnell had stood between the living and the dead when he went to America and brought back money to save the people from famine." *Irish Times*, Oct. 10, 1881, 6.

41. Moses, "The Irish Vampire," 72.

42. Both groups, as Joseph Valente has written, "concentrated British anxiety over racial adulteration" and "split the distinction of being white-skinned specimens of the other in fin de siècle Britain . . . derogated specifically as primitive, premodern, and deeply superstitious." Valente, *Dracula's Crypt: Bram Stoker, Irishness, and the Question of Blood* (Urbana: Univ. of Illinois Press, 2002), 68.

43. Gladstone would later write of both groups as having been unfairly targeted for prejudice. Using the example of the Jews, Gladstone considers how Ireland, like the Jews, is a nation "whose life has been a life of sorrow, [and is not selfish] to be concentrated in thought and feeling on itself." W. E. Gladstone, *Special Aspects of the Irish Question: A Series of Reflections in and since 1886* (London: John Murray, 1892), 73. Given his fraught relationship with Parnell, it is not surprising that Gladstone consequently assigns the role of Irish Moses to Daniel O'Connell: "By the force of his own personality he led Ireland to Saint Stephen's, almost as much as Moses led the children of Israel to Mount Sinai" (264). But "the sight of his promised land was not given to his longing eyes" (302). See also Valente, *Dracula's Crypt*, 68.

44. Michael Ragussis, *Figures of Conversion: "The Jewish Question" and English National Identity* (Durham, NC: Duke Univ. Press, 1995), 236.

45. The 1904 Limerick pogrom would polarize Irish nationalists on the question of actual—versus metaphoric—Jews who lived among them. See chapter 1 for a discussion of the pogrom and debates on Irish anti-Semitism, including Michael Davitt's support of Irish Jews. Interestingly, Parnell's mother, born Delia Tudor, apparently once described herself as a Jew. Bernard Shillman notes, "she is reported to have told the correspondent of the Daily Telegraph that 'my son is descended from the line of a tribe of Judah, from the Jews who took refuge in Spain.'" Shillman, *Short History of the Jews in Ireland*, 114.

46. See chapter 1.

47. Griffith, *Resurrection of Hungary*, 16. Qtd. in Gibson, *Joyce's Revenge*, 120.

48. Qtd. in Brown, *Politics of Irish Literature*, 345. See also Jules Abels, *The Parnell Tragedy* (New York: Macmillan Co., 1966), 368; and F. S. L. Lyons, *The Fall of Parnell* (London: Routledge and Kegan Paul, 1960), 272–74.

49. Gibson, *Joyce's Revenge*, 5.

50. Barry O'Brien, *Life of Charles Stewart Parnell*, 367. O'Brien establishes a rhetoric that few modern scholars have ignored; for example, Lyons's biography of Parnell introduces one chapter, "The View from Pisgah," with an epigraph from Deuteronomy 34:1–4, and other contemporary historians and literary critics—too many to mention here—not only comment on the trope, but employ it themselves in a similar manner.

51. Joyce, *Critical Writings*, 225.

52. *United Ireland*, Oct. 17, 1891.

53. Lyons, "Parnell Theme in Literature," 71.

54. *United Ireland*, Oct. 10, 1891. Qtd. in Richard Ellmann, *Yeats: the Man and the Masks* (London: MacMillan, 1948), 100.

55. Brown, *Politics of Irish Literature*, 376.

56. Sam Alexander, "Mourn—and Then Onward!" Yale Univ. Modernism Lab, accessed Aug. 6, 2010, http://modernism.research.yale.edu/wiki/index.php/Mourn--_and_then_Onward!

57. W. B. Yeats, ed., *Samhain* (1901–8; repr., London: Frank Cass and Co., 1970), 9. The Irish Literary Theatre, precursor to the Abbey Theatre, was formed in 1897 by Yeats, Lady Gregory, George Moore, and Edward Martyn.

58. Yeats, "The Academic Class and the Agrarian Revolution," in *Uncollected Prose*, vol. 2, ed. John P. Frayne and Colton Johnson (New York: Columbia Univ. Press, 1976), 150, 152.

59. Ibid., 152. Qtd. in Adrian Frazier, *Behind the Scenes: Yeats, Horniman, and the Struggle for the Abbey Theatre* (Berkeley: Univ. of California Press, 1990), 28.

60. Yeats, "Academic Class," 150.

61. Yeats, *Collected Poems*, 345.

62. Although it has been nearly three decades since James Pethica showed the extent of the play's collaborative nature, many critics still refer to the work as exclusively Yeats's. For this reason, I follow the practice set by McDiarmid and Waters in their edition of Gregory's *Selected Writings*, registering Gregory's authorship by referring to the play as *Kathleen ni Houlihan*, Kathleen being Gregory's preferred spelling. See James Pethica, "'Our Kathleen': Yeats's Collaboration with Lady Gregory in the Writing of *Cathleen ni Houlihan*," in *Yeats Annual 6*, ed. Warwick Gould (London: Macmillan, 1988), 3–31.

63. Gregory to Wilfred Scawen Blunt, Nov. 22, 1900, Berg Collection, New York Public Library. Qtd. in Judith Hill, *Lady Gregory: An Irish Life* (Gloucestershire, UK: Sutton Publishing, 2005), 149.

64. Howarth, *Irish Writers*, 4–5.

65. Kelly, "Parnell in Irish Literature," 242. For a discussion of Nietzsche's sacrificial leader as an influence on Yeats, see Michael Valdez Moses, "The Rebirth of Tragedy: Yeats, Nietzsche, the Irish National Theatre, and the Anti-Modern Cult of Cuchulain," *Modernism/Modernity* 11, no. 4 (2004): 561–79.

66. For additional discussion of Freud's book, see the introduction.

67. Sigmund Freud, *Moses and Monotheism*, trans. Katherine Jones (New York: Vintage Books, 1939), 58.

68. Ibid., 9.

69. Marjorie Howes historicizes this gendering in *Yeats's Nations: Gender, Class, and Irishness* (Cambridge, UK: Cambridge Univ. Press, 1996), 20–28.

70. Cathy Caruth, *Unclaimed Experience: Trauma, Narrative, and History* (Baltimore, MD: Johns Hopkins Univ. Press, 1986), 13.

71. Augusta Gregory, *Our Irish Theatre: A Chapter of Autobiography by Lady Gregory*, Coole Edition (New York: Oxford Univ. Press, 1972), 59.

72. Michael Steinmann, "Yeats's Parnell: Sources of His Myth," *Éire-Ireland* 18, no. 1 (Spring 1983): 51.

73. Joyce, *Critical Writings*, 228.

74. See Joseph Valente, *The Myth of Manliness in Irish National Culture, 1880–1922* (Urbana: Univ. of Illinois Press, 2011), 73–93.

75. Gregory, *Our Irish Theatre*, 29; Judith Hill notes that the phrase "became a well-used maxim for her." Hill, *Lady Gregory*, 144.

76. Augusta Gregory, *Seventy Years: Being the Autobiography of Lady Gregory*, Coole Edition, ed. Colin Smythe (New York: Oxford Univ. Press, 1974), 4.

77. Augusta Gregory, *Selected Writings*, ed. Lucy McDiarmid and Maureen Waters (New York: Penguin, 1995), xiii–xiv.

78. Ann Saddlemyer, *In Defense of Lady Gregory* (Dublin: Dolmen, 1966), 18.

79. *Freeman's Journal*, May 13, 1921. Qtd. in Saddlemyer, *In Defense of Lady Gregory*, 23.

80. Gregory, *Selected Writings*, 142. Yet as a young girl, Gregory went through a brief, highly religious phase of "peace with God" during which "the ballads, and poems and patriotic songs had become as ashes; His word, the Bible was her only book." Gregory, *Seventy Years*, 14.

81. Howarth, *Irish Writers 1880–1940*, 93.

82. Qtd. in Gregory, *Seventy Years*, 403.

83. Ibid., 13–15. Many of these ballads, no doubt, were eventually pasted into Gregory's scrapbook of broadsheet and slip ballads, currently in the Rare Books Room of the Princeton Univ. Library.

84. This often-quoted line is from Denis Johnston's play *The Moon in the Yellow River*. See Johnston, *Selected Plays of Denis Johnston*, ed. Joseph Ronsley (Washington DC: Catholic Univ. of America Press, 1983), 150.

85. These alternative titles are found on a holograph draft (July 10–15, 1919) in the Berg Collection of the New York Public Library.

86. Moore had in fact rewritten the play based on an earlier version, *The Tale of a Town*, by Edward Martyn. See Hill, *Lady Gregory*, 210.

87. George Moore, *Selected Plays of George Moore and Edward Martyn* (Gerrards Cross, UK: Colin Smythe, 1995), 76. This sounds not unlike Yeats's letter to his beloved Maud Gonne when she was about to convert to Catholicism and marry the rebel John MacBride (later executed for his part in the Easter Rising): "You possess your influence in Ireland very largely because you came to the people from above. You represent a superior class, a class whose people are more independent, have a more beautiful life, a more refined life." Qtd. in Conor Cruise O'Brien, *Ancestral Voices: Religion and Nationalism in Ireland* (Dublin: Poolbeg, 1994), 71.

88. Moore, *Selected Plays*, 100.

89. Hill, *Lady Gregory*, 144.

90. Gregory, *Our Irish Theatre*, 10.

91. Brown, *Politics of Irish Literature*, 380.

92. Levitas, *Theatre of Nation*, 191.

93. Lady Dunsany recorded the apparent borrowing of his theme in a diary entry: "He read it to her a year ago and she loved it and wrote to me some days later mentioning that 'the play of slaves and kings is much in my mind'. It was, for, leaving her harmless, characteristic and sometimes really funny Irish comedies, she suddenly wrote *The Deliverer* with an Oriental background, slaves, an overseer and even ending in the last act with a remark about 'the King's cats'—Eddie's ending with 'the King's dog'." Jan. 27, 1911, private collection. Qtd in Foster, *W. B. Yeats: A Life*, 1:609n10.

94. Lord Dunsany, *Five Plays* (Boston: Little, Brown, and Co., 1917), 72. Thomas Mann described a similar idea in his 1944 novella *The Tables of the Law*. "What once had been a reason to mistrust and reject [Moses], that is, his mixed blood and that he had one foot in Egyptian life, was now transformed into a source of trust and lent him authority." See Mann, *The Tables of the Law*, trans. Marion Faber and Stephen Lehmann (Philadelphia: Paul Dry Books, 2010), 25.

95. Cruise O'Brien notes that the typical charge against Parnell by his former supporters, and Healy in particular, was that "being a Protestant, he could not share the moral values of the Irish people, or understand how fiercely they resented any offense against chastity." Cruise O'Brien, *Ancestral Voices*, 29.

96. *Lady Gregory's Diaries, 1892–1902*, vol. 1, ed. James Pethica (Gerrards Cross, UK: C. Smythe, 1996), 252. Qtd. in Hill, *Lady Gregory*, 106.

97. Kelly, "Parnell in Irish Literature," 263. Benilde Montgomery similarly notes, "Lady Gregory rewrites scripture so that the Irish are revealed as self-afflicting agents of their own destruction." Benilde Montgomery, "The Presence of Parnell in Three Plays by Lady Gregory," in *Irish Renaissance Annual 3*, ed. Dennis Jackson (Newark: Univ. of Delaware Press, 1982), 109.

98. Lyons, *Ireland since the Famine*, 221.

99. Lyons notes that the overlap between GAA members and Fenians was considerable, and police who reported on the GAA "were perfectly right in recognizing the potentially revolutionary spirit that permeated this outwardly innocent association." Ibid. In her 1924 monologue-play *The Old Woman Remembers*, Gregory would again use hurling in a political metaphor that retrospectively invests it with an anticolonial politics even before the GAA: "Tone and Lord Edward struck the ball— / My grief such hurlers had to die / And leave the goal to the Gall!" Gregory, *Collected Plays*, 2:358.

100. Joseph Valente brilliantly explicates the GAA demonstration at Parnell's funeral, particularly in his reading of the black crepe that draped the marchers' camáns (hurley sticks). He writes, "the drapings not only figured the camáns as

firearms, they served to ritually muzzle the rifles they evoked. In allegorical terms, the covers both acted as an emblematic shield for an especially ballistic expression of revolutionary desire and simultaneously signified a desire to place a shield, a 'safety,' on the revolutionary ballistics themselves" (*Myth of Manliness*, 69). This cloaking or veiling, as Valente describes it, perhaps also serves as a figure for *The Deliverer* itself in its political complexities.

101. For more on the gendering of Irish nationalism, see C. L. Innes, *Woman and Nation in Irish Literature and Society, 1880–1935* (Athens: Univ. of Georgia Press, 1993); Harris, *Gender and Modern Irish Drama*; Howes, *Yeats's Nations*; and most recently, Valente, *Myth of Manliness.*

102. Joseph Valente, "The Myth of Sovereignty: Gender in the Literature of Irish Nationalism," *ELH* 61 (1994): 189.

103. James Brennan, "Types of Irishmen. I.—The Imperialist," *Irish Freedom*, Aug. 15, 1911. Qtd. in Harris, *Gender and Modern Irish Drama*, 130.

104. Ibid., 67.

105. For a discussion of how much Captain O'Shea knew, see Roy Foster's essay "Love, Politics and Textual Corruption: Mrs. O'Shea's Parnell," in *High and Low Moderns: Literature and Culture, 1889–1939*, ed. Maria DiBattista and Lucy McDiarmid (New York: Oxford Univ. Press, 1996), 197–211.

106. Vindicating misunderstood Anglo-Irish nationalists was a particular interest of Yeats's, and he produced a similarly galvanizing effect in his poem "The Ghost of Roger Casement." See Lucy McDiarmid, *The Irish Art of Controversy* (Ithaca, NY: Cornell Univ. Press, 2005), 189–93.

107. Yeats, *Collected Poems*, 490.

108. McDiarmid, *Irish Art of Controversy*, 189.

109. For Gregory's affair with Blunt, see Lucy McDiarmid, "The Demotic Lady Gregory," in DiBattista and McDiarmid, *High and Low Moderns*, 212–34; "Lady Gregory, Wilfrid Blunt, and London Table Talk," *Irish University Review* 34, no. 1 (Spring/Summer 2004): 67–80; and McDiarmid, *Poets and the Peacock Dinner: The Literary History of a Meal* (Oxford, UK: Oxford Univ. Press, 2014), chaps. 3 and 4.

110. *Irish Times*, Jan. 13, 1911.

111. Qtd. in Brown, *Politics of Irish Literature*, 379.

112. Joseph Holloway, *The Diaries of Joseph Holloway, 1895–1944* [microform], part one, reel 16, National Library of Ireland, 63.

113. Ibid., 66–67.

114. Ibid., 68.

115. *The Deliverer* also seemed to provide the literary community with an occasion to attack Lady Gregory's abilities as a dramatist generally, her management of the Abbey Theatre, and the fact that she happened to be a woman. In the midst of

his journal entry on *The Deliverer*, Holloway digresses: "The fact of the matter is that Lady Gregory long since played out as a dramatist and she should be told so at the earliest convenience as her later-work is keeping back the dramatic movement in Ireland in a serious way. Everyone feels that this is so, but the Press don't like to say it out plainly for fear it might seem like an attack on the Abbey, which we all would be sorry to injure in any way" (68). He bemoans her "colossal egotism for her own work to the exclusion of that of all others," and notes that "as the [Daily] Express man in a chat after the performance said to me —There should not be a woman at the head of affairs in the theatre, there was too much of Lady Gregory's stuff produced altogether." It is worth noting too that the play has not fared much better with contemporary scholars, who give it little attention. Malcolm Brown's assessment that "the little play happened to be devoid of literary force and so it sank into oblivion, message and all" (*Politics of Irish Literature*, 380) is a typical reading of *The Deliverer* as a crude polemic.

116. Brown, *Politics of Irish Literature*, 379.

117. Here also the cats are described as "a class in themselves," and when one is shot by a storekeeper, "it went into a sort of a heap, and when he came near, it spoke, and found it was some person, and it said it had to walk its seven acres." Gregory, *Visions and Beliefs in the West of Ireland, Collected and Arranged by Lady Gregory: with Two Essays and Notes by W. B. Yeats*, Coole Edition (New York: Oxford Univ. Press, 1970), 290.

118. Ibid.

119. For a discussion of the cats as the Liberal Party, see Kelly, "Parnell in Irish Literature," 262.

120. Brown, *Politics of Irish Literature*, 378.

121. Holloway, *Diaries of Joseph Holloway*, 82.

122. Ibid.

123. Ibid.

124. Gregory, *Our Irish Theatre*, 266.

125. Possibly Matthew Michael O'Hara, who, having written a book about Parnell, would have been fully aware of the analogy. See his *Chief and Tribute: Parnell and Davitt* (Dublin: Maunsel, 1919), vi.

126. *Evening Telegraph*, Jan. 13, 1911.

127. William Stanley Braithwaite of the *New York Times* would have had the advantage of the printed text, suggesting that perhaps it was the production itself that made the play confusing. See Braithwaite, "Lady Gregory's Plays," *New York Times*, Apr. 14, 1912.

128. *Irish Times*, Jan. 17, 1911.

129. *Irish Times*, Jan. 19, 1911.

130. Levitas, *Theatre of Nation*, 190.

131. *Freeman's Journal*, Feb. 5, 1907. Qtd. in Levitas, *Theatre of Nation*, 133.

132. Qtd. in Peter Costello, *The Heart Grown Brutal: The Irish Revolution in Literature, from Parnell to the Death of Yeats, 1891–1939* (Dublin: Gill and Macmillan, 1977), 27.

133. Gregory, *Selected Writings*, 309.

134. Holloway, *Diaries of Joseph Holloway*, 82.

135. Yeats, *Collected Poems*, 279.

3. Anti-Exodus

1. Declan Kiberd, *Inventing Ireland* (Cambridge, MA: Harvard Univ. Press, 1995), 211.

2. Alan Titley, "The Brass Tacks of the Situation," in *Letters from the New Island: 16 on 16: Irish Writers on the Easter Rising*, ed. Dermot Bolger (Dublin: Raven Arts Press, 1988), 27.

3. See, for example, Mark McCarthy's *Ireland's 1916 Rising: Explorations of History-Making, Commemoration & Heritage in Modern Times* (Surrey, UK: Ashgate, 2012). McCarthy discusses the religious elements of the Rising and 1916 as "Holy War" in chapter 3, 103–9. See also the essays in *The Life and After-Life of PH Pearse / Padraic Mac Piarais: Saol agus Oidhreacht*, ed. Roisín Higgins and Regina Uí Chollatáin (Dublin: Irish Academic Press, 2009).

4. As Peter Costello writes, "the Rising began on Easter Monday so that in future Ireland would be unable to celebrate the Resurrection of Christ without remembering the Insurrection of Ireland. The Risen God became the Risen People." *The Heart Grown Brutal: The Irish Revolution in Literature, from Parnell to the Death of Yeats, 1891–1939* (Dublin: Gill and Macmillan, 1977), 76–77.

5. Yeats, *Collected Poems*, 181.

6. Qtd. in Ruth Dudley Edwards, *Patrick Pearse: The Triumph of Failure* (London: Victor Gollancz, 1977), 168.

7. Ibid., 199.

8. Holloway, *Diaries of Joseph Holloway*, Jan. 5, 1899. Qtd. in Edwards, *Patrick Pearse*, 28.

9. J. J. Lee, "Patrick Pearse," in *Dictionary of Irish Biography*, ed. James McGuire and James Quinn (Cambridge, UK: Cambridge Univ. Press, 2009), accessed July 31, 2014, http://dib.cambridge.org.

10. Arthur Aughey, "What Is Living and What Is Dead in the Ideal of 1916," in *Revising the Rising*, ed. Máirín Ní Dhonnchadha and Theo Dorgan (Derry: Field Day, 1991), 73.

11. For discussions of some of these tensions and instabilities, see Harris, *Gender and Modern Irish Drama* (123–66); and Valente, "The Mother of all Sovereignty," chap. 3 in *Myth of Manliness*, 94–139. My own forthcoming work on Pearse

and images of breast-feeding explores complexities in how Pearse figures the female (and male) nursing body.

12. William Irwin Thompson, *The Imagination of an Insurrection: Dublin, Easter 1916* (New York: Oxford Univ. Press, 1967), 67.

13. Pádraic Pearse, "From a Hermitage," in *Collected Works of Pádraic H. Pearse: Political Writings and Speeches* (Dublin: Phoenix, 1924), 144. I suspect that this passage is responding to Yeats's extended exchange with John Eglinton on the meaning of national drama (although there were many other public conversations on similar topics during the period that were important, if not, as Pearse points out, practical for revolution). Ben Levitas provides a useful discussion of the Yeats-Eglinton debate, which originally took place in the *Daily Express* and was republished as *Literary Ideals in Ireland.* See Levitas, *Theatre of Nation*, 39–41.

14. Pádraic Pearse, "Why We Want Recruits," in *Collected Works: Political Writings and Speeches*, 120–21.

15. Seamus Deane, *Celtic Revivals: Essays in Modern Irish Literature, 1880–1980* (Winston-Salem, NC: Wake Forest Univ. Press, 1987), 64.

16. Sarah Cole, *At the Violet Hour: Modernism and Violence in England and Ireland* (Oxford, UK: Oxford Univ. Press, 2012), 144.

17. Qtd. in Matthew Kelly, "The End of Parnellism and the Ideological Dilemmas of Sinn Féin," in *Ireland in Transition, 1867–1921*, ed. D. George Boyce (London: Routledge, 2004), 144.

18. Ibid.

19. For a discussion of Moran, see chapter 2.

20. Pádraic Pearse, editorial in the *Gaelic American*, Mar. 7, 1914. Qtd. in Edwards, *Patrick Pearse*, 188.

21. Desmond Ryan, *A Man Called Pearse* (Dublin: Maunsel, 1919), 19–20.

22. "Irish or Infidelity, Which?" *Leader*, Jan. 9, 1909, 496–97.

23. An tAthair Cathaoir Ó Braonaia, *Béarla Sacsan agus an Creideamh nÉirinn* (The English Language and the Faith in Ireland) (Dublin: M. H. MacGuill agus a Mhac, 1913), 15–16. Qtd. in Philip O'Leary, *The Prose Literature of the Gaelic Revival, 1881–1921: Ideology and Innovation* (University Park: Pennsylvania State Univ. Press, 1994), 20.

24. An tAthair Peadar Ua Laoghaire, "Sgéal Íóib agus Sgéal na hEireann" (The Story of Job and the Story of Ireland) *An Síoladoir* (The Sower) 1, no. 5 (July 1921): 1–2. Qtd. in O'Leary, *Prose Literature of the Gaelic Revival*, 24.

25. Tom Garvin, *Nationalist Revolutionaries in Ireland, 1858–1928* (Oxford, UK: Clarendon Press, 1987), 84.

26. Pádraic Pearse, "The Coming Revolution," *Collected Works: Political Writings and Speeches*, 91.

27. Garvin, *Nationalist Revolutionaries in Ireland*, 85.

28. Lyons, *Ireland since the Famine*, 228.

29. D. P. Moran, *Leader*, Apr. 27, 1901. Qtd. in Boyce, *Nationalism in Ireland*, 243.

30. Ibid., 276.

31. See, for example, Joost Augusteijn, *Patrick Pearse: The Making of a Revolutionary* (Basingstoke, UK: Palgrave Macmillan, 2010).

32. Rather than trying to determine whether the Rising was truly Catholic or not, I am interested in how Pearse used religious language in his rhetorical strategies for creating a liberation narrative for Ireland. Debates about the extent of the Rising's Catholicism remain polemical. Did Pearse genuinely advocate the Proclamation's inclusiveness, or was it merely "pluralist window-dressing" to distract from a "strain of mystic Catholicism identifying the Irish soul as Catholic and Gaelic," as Roy Foster puts it (*Modern Ireland, 1600–1972*, 497)? To view the Rising as specifically Catholic in this way functions, Seamus Deane has argued, to impugn both the Rising and Catholicism as sources of future violence in Ireland, a (Revisionist) move that, Deane objects, "downplays the oppression the Rising sought to overthrow and upgrades the oppression the Rising itself inaugurated in the name of freedom." Unless the question of the Rising's Catholicism is made more specific, it will remain intractable and not very useful, for the language of the Rising is indeed alternately Catholic and ecumenical. See Seamus Deane, "Wherever Green Is Read," in *Revising the Rising*, ed. Máirín Ní Dhonnchadha and Theo Dorgan (Derry: Field Day, 1991), 91, 100; and Seamus Deane, *Celtic Revivals: Essays in Modern Irish Literature, 1880–1980* (Winston-Salem, NC): Wake Forest Univ. Press, 1987), 63.

33. Ibid., 311.

34. Pádraic Pearse, *Collected Works: Political Writings and Speeches*, 241.

35. Pearse's late poem "The Rebel" insists, "And because I am of the people, I understand the people. / I am sorrowful with their sorrow, I am hungry with their desire." Pádraic Pearse, *Collected Works: Political Writings and Speeches*, 338.

36. Pádraic Pearse, *Collected Works of Pádraic H. Pearse: Plays, Stories, Poems* (Dublin: Phoenix, 1917), 67. As these lines begin to suggest, a number of Pearse's texts contain moments that sexualize young boys. Susan Harris offers a productive treatment of Pearse's contested sexuality, which had previously received simplistic and prejudiced attention. In her reading, "Pearse painfully transformed his forbidden desires into a passionate devotion to the ideal of Irish freedom." Harris, *Gender and Modern irish Drama*, 144.

37. Ita O'Shea, "The Irish Messiah—A Vision," *Irish Review*, Jan. 1914. Qtd. in Garvin, *Nationalist Revolutionaries*, 76.

38. Joyce, *Critical Writings*, 162

39. Pádraic Pearse, letter to the editor of *An Claidheamh Soluis*, May 20, 1899. Qtd. in O'Leary, *Prose Literature of the Gaelic Revival*, 281.

40. Pádraic Pearse, "Some Thoughts," in *An Claidheamh Soluis*, Feb. 10, 1906. Qtd. in O'Leary, *Prose Literature of the Gaelic Revival*, 336. Exemplifying Pearse's persisting hostility is his ironical comment on the occasion of congratulating the directors of the Abbey for standing up to English censors and going on with the production of Shaw's play *The Shewing-Up of Blanco Posnet.* Using an analogy with the Israelites, Pearse writes, "we take no more interest in the literary fate of Mr. George Bernard Shaw than an orthodox Hebrew of the House of Judah may be imagined to have taken in the fate of an erring member of one of the mislaid Tribes. So far as the Gael is concerned, Mr. George Bernard Shaw belongs 'to the legion of the lost ones, to the cohort of the damned.'" Pádraic Pearse, "An English Censorship in Ireland," in *An Claidheamh Soluis*, Aug. 28, 1909. Qtd. in O'Leary, *Prose Literature of the Gaelic Revival*, 341. It is possible that in figuring Shaw as a "member of one of the mislaid Tribes" Pearse is associating the playwright with the imperialist British Israelites of the recent Tara controversy described in chapter 1. For a discussion of the controversy surrounding Shaw's play, see Lucy McDiarmid's chapter "The Shewing-Up of Dublin Castle" in McDiarmid, *Irish Art of Controversy.*

41. Pádraic Pearse, "The Passing of Anglo-Irish Drama," review of *Kathleen ni Houlihan* in *An Claidheamh Soluis*, Feb. 9, 1907. Qtd. in Edwards, *Patrick Pearse*, 103. For a more substantial reading of Pearse's review and his response to the *Playboy*, see Raymond J. Porter, "Language and Literature in Revival Ireland: The Views of P. H. Pearse," in *Modern Irish Literature: Essays in Honor of William York Tindall*, ed. Raymond J. Porter and James D. Brophy (New York: Iona College Press, 1972), 210–12.

42. Joseph Holloway, *Joseph Holloway's Abbey Theatre: A Selection from His Unpublished Journal, Impressions of a Dublin Playgoer*, ed. Robert Hogan (Carbondale: Southern Illinois Univ. Press, 1967), 151.

43. Qtd. in O'Leary, *Prose Literature of the Gaelic Revival*, 333.

44. Gregory, *Selected Writings*, 309.

45. Ibid., 308.

46. Ibid., 306.

47. Ibid., 311.

48. See Valente, "The Mother of All Sovereignty," chap. 3 in *Myth of Manliness*, 94–139.

49. Cole, *At the Violet Hour*, 150.

50. Qtd. in George Watson, *Irish Identity and the Literary Revival: Synge, Yeats, Joyce, and O'Casey* (Washington, DC: Catholic Univ. of America Press, 1994), 39.

51. Yeats, *Collected Poems*, 345.

52. Qtd. in Mary Colum, *Life and the Dream* (Garden City, NY: Doubleday, 1947), 139.

53. Qtd. in Kiberd, *Inventing Ireland*, 200.

54. Cruise O'Brien, *God's Land*, 40.

55. Francis Shaw, "The Canon of Irish History: A Challenge," *Studies* 61, no. 242 (1972): 122.

56. Kiberd, *Inventing Ireland*, 211.

57. Ibid.

58. Pádraic Pearse, *Collected Works: Political Writings and Speeches*, 151, 155–56.

59. Declan Kiberd, "Patrick Pearse: Irish Modernist," in *The Life and After-Life of PH Pearse / Padraic Mac Piarais: Saol agus Oidhreacht*, ed. Roisín Higgins and Regina Uí Chollatáin (Dublin: Irish Academic Press, 2009), 67.

60. For a discussion of typology, see chap. 1.

61. Neil R. Davison, *James Joyce, "Ulysses," and the Construction of Jewish Identity* (Cambridge, UK: Cambridge Univ. Press, 1996), 43.

62. Ian Paisley writes, "we step . . . from the shadows of Old Testament typology to the blazing sunshine of New Testament theology." Deane, *Field Day Anthology of Irish Writing*, 3:898.

63. Kathleen Biddick, *The Typological Imaginary: Circumcision, Technology, History* (Philadelphia: Univ. of Pennsylvania Press, 2003), 1.

64. Frye, *Great Code*, 85. Frye continues, "Naturally, being the indicated and obvious way of reading the Bible, and scholars being what they are, typology is a neglected subject, even in theology, and it is neglected elsewhere because it is assumed to be bound up with a doctrinaire adherence to Christianity" (80).

65. George Moore—a Catholic convert to Protestantism—has his character the Irish Father O'Grady in the novel *The Lake* say, "Biblical criticism is not a Catholic characteristic." Moore, *The Lake* (Gerrards Cross, UK: Colin Smythe, 1980), 80.

66. W. E. Addis, "The Truth and the Falsehood of M. Renan's Lectures," *Dublin Review* 87 (1880): 337. Qtd. in Edward A. Hagan, "The Aryan Myth: A Nineteenth-Century Anglo-Irish Will to Power," in *Ideology and Ireland in the Nineteenth Century*, ed. Tadhg Foley and Sean Ryder (Dublin: Four Courts Press, 1980), 202. Addis sees Protestants, instead, as those who are promoting nationalism: "Protestantism has always exhibited itself as a national religion; or to put it more accurately, the different religions which have been known under the common name of Protestant, have always been national" (202).

67. Father Francis Shaw writes, "the equation of the patriot with Christ is in conflict with the whole Christian tradition, and, indeed, with the explicit teaching of Christ." Shaw, "The Canon of Irish History," 123.

68. Pádraic Pearse, "From a Hermitage," 150–51 (my emphasis).

69. Kiberd, *Inventing Ireland*, 207.

70. Edna Longley, *The Living Stream: Literature and Revisionism in Ireland* (Newcastle upon Tyne, UK: Bloodaxe Books, 1994), 73.

71. Ibid., 74.

72. Pádraic Pearse, "Mionn," in *An Barr Buadh*, Apr. 5, 1912. Qtd. in Edwards, *Patrick Pearse*, 162–63.

73. Kiberd argues for nonsectarianism, whereas Cruise O'Brien suggests the assimilationist argument. See Cruise O'Brien, *God Land*, 39.

74. Ryan, *Man Called Pearse*, 85.

75. Pádraic Pearse, *Collected Works: Plays, Stories, Poems*, 337.

76. Ibid., 339.

77. Ibid.

78. Frye, *Great Code*, 91.

79. Deane, *Celtic Revivals*, 70.

80. Howes, *Yeats's Nations*, 49.

81. Kiberd, *Inventing Ireland*, 228. See also Augusteijn, *Patrick Pearse*, 291–93.

82. Pádraic Pearse, *Collected Works: Political Writings and Speeches*, 91.

83. Ibid., 96–97.

84. Ibid., 98–99.

85. See, for example, the polarized essays in Bolger's edited collection *Letters from the New Island: 16 on 16.*

86. On cleansing and sanctifying, Harris writes, "It is in the hopes of resolving . . . two linked problems—how to preserve Ireland's integrity as a nation, and how to persuade moderate nationalists to embrace physical force—that the rhetoric of sacrifice is refined into the form associated with Padraig Pearse; and it is because these problems were so intractable that cleansing and sanctifying became such important functions." Harris, *Gender and Modern Irish Drama*, 126.

87. Deane, *Field Day Anthology of Irish Writing*, 2:307.

88. Pádraic Pearse, *Collected Works: Political Writings and Speeches*, 372.

89. Ibid., 156.

90. Ibid.

91. Costello, *Heart Grown Brutal*, 76.

92. Valente, *Myth of Manliness*, 159. Valente here compellingly argues that, in transforming the violent and excessive Cuchulain into an (English) model of manly restraint, "Cuchulain is precisely a vehicle in Pearse's writing for establishing aboriginal Irish chivalry in a Christological mode, thereby linking Pagan and Catholic Ireland" (158).

93. Edwards, *Patrick Pearse*, 140.

94. Desmond Ryan, *The Story of a Success* (Dublin: Maunsel, 1918). Qtd. in Mary Trotter, *Ireland's National Theaters: Political Performance and the Origins of the Irish Dramatic Movement* (Syracuse, NY: Syracuse Univ. Press, 2001), 138.

95. Edwards, *Patrick Pearse*, 141. It is worth noting that, as Christopher Clausen points out, Pearse was also "quite generous about comparing other revolutionaries

with Christ." Christopher Clausen, "Padraic Pearse: The Revolutionary as Artist," *Shaw Review* 19 (1976): 90.

96. Elaine Sisson, *Pearse's Patriots: The Cult of Boyhood at St. Enda's* (Cork: Cork Univ. Press, 2005), 41.

97. Nicholas Grene, *The Politics of Irish Drama: Plays in Context from Boucicault to Friel* (Cambridge, UK: Cambridge Univ. Press, 1999), 136.

98. David Cairns and Shaun Richards, *Writing Ireland: Colonialism, Nationalism, and Culture, Cultural Politics* (Manchester, UK: Manchester Univ. Press, 1988), 110.

99. Sisson, *Pearse's Patriots*, 40.

100. Ibid., 44–45.

101. Pádraic Pearse, *Collected Works: Plays, Stories, Poems*, 17.

102. Ibid., 43.

103. Mary Brigid Pearse, ed., *The Home-Life of Pádraic Pearse as Told by Himself, His Family and Friends* (Dublin: Browne and Nolan, 1934), 108.

104. Robert Welch, *The Abbey Theatre, 1899–1999: Form and Pressure* (Oxford, UK: Oxford Univ. Press, 1999), 76. More recently, however, this theory has been questioned.

105. Pádraic Pearse, *The Letters of P. H. Pearse*, ed. Séamas Ó Buachalla (Atlantic Highlands, NJ: Humanities Press, 1980), 377.

106. Ibid., 380.

107. Ibid., 383.

108. *Irish Review*, 1915, 47.

109. Mary Brigid Pearse, *Home-Life of Pádraic Pearse*, 34.

110. Cairns and Richards, *Writing Ireland*, 109.

111. Ibid., 113.

112. John Newsinger, "'I Bring Not Peace but a Sword': The Religious Motif in the Irish War of Independence," *Journal of Contemporary History* 13, no. 3 (1978): 617.

113. Charles Dalton, *With the Dublin Brigade* (London: Peter Davies, 1929), 41. Qtd. in Newsinger, "'I Bring Not Peace but a Sword,'" 618.

114. Moirin Chavasse, *Terence MacSwiney* (Dublin: Clonmore Reynolds, 1961), 132–33. Qtd. in Newsinger, "'I Bring Not Peace but a Sword,'" 622.

115. Pádraic Pearse, *Collected Works: Political Writings and Speeches*, 255.

116. Ibid., 157–58. In Pearse's story "The Mother," the connection between Jesus, Mary, and Ireland is assumed to be self-evident by one character, who asks, "Doesn't the world know that the glorious Virgin goes round the townlands every Christmas Eve, herself and her child?" Pádraic Pearse, *Collected Works: Plays, Stories, Peoms*, 129.

117. Gregory, *Collected Plays*, 3:395. Further references to the play appear parenthetically in the text.

118. Gregory also wrote of Brigit's connection to Christ and Mary in *A Book of Saints and Wonders* (1906).

119. *Irish Times*, Apr. 16, 1924.

120. William Butler Yeats, "Three Irish Poets," *Uncollected Prose*, ed. John P. Frayne (New York: Columbia Univ. Press, 1970–76), 70.

121. McDiarmid, "Demotic Lady Gregory," 226.

122. Lucy McDiarmid and Maureen Waters, introduction to *Lady Gregory: Selected Writings*, xxxi.

123. *Freeman's Journal*, Apr. 16, 1924.

124. See Gregory's collection of Irish broadside ballads and slip ballads (3 volumes) in the Rare Books Division, Department of Rare Books and Special Collections, Princeton Univ. Library.

125. Gregory, *Seventy Years*, 545.

126. For example, *Brigit* seems to me far more explicitly about Parnell than Gregory's *Grania*, which is treated by Benilde Montgomery in her essay "The Presence of Parnell in Three Plays by Lady Gregory."

127. Gregory, *Collected Plays*, 2:268.

128. Ibid., *Collected Plays*, 2:277.

129. Francis Shaw, "The Canon of Irish History," 123.

130. Pádraic Pearse, *Letters*, 377.

131. The poem is also the source for the third woman's meditation on Mary's sadness, "Her darling to be taken from her. . . . And he young, that I thought his keeners would not yet be born." Gregory, *Collected Plays*, 3:337. In the "Keening of Mary," Christ himself speaks these lines.

132. Augusta Gregory, *Lady Gregory's Journals*, Coole Edition, vol. 1, ed. Daniel J. Murphy (Gerrards Cross, UK: Colin Smythe, 1978–87), 477, 523.

133. Gregory, *Journals*, 524.

134. *Freeman's Journal*, Apr. 16, 1924.

135. Gregory, *Journals*, 482.

136. Ibid.

137. Ibid., 619.

138. While Gregory disliked the play, she was tireless in supporting Synge throughout the controversy.

139. Pádraic Pearse, *Collected Works: Political Writings and Speeches*, 145.

140. Gregory, *Seventy Years*, 538.

141. Lennox Robinson, *The Lost Leader* (Dublin: T. Kiersey, 1918), 54.

142. Ibid., 55.

143. Seamus O'Kelly, *The Parnellite* (Naas, IRL: Leinster Leader, 1919), 76.

144. Ibid.

145. On Yeats's Cuchulain plays, see Valente, *Myth of Manliness*, especially 169–78. In Yeats's poetry too, he would move from the restrained celebration of "Easter 1916" to what Elizabeth Cullingford has argued is a veiled criticism of Pearse in "Meditations in Time of Civil War," written amid the violence of the 1920s. Cullingford argues that an obscure allusion to Jacques Molay is a cipher for Pearse in "How Jacques Molay Got Up the Tower: Yeats and the Irish Civil War," *ELH* 50, no. 4 (1983): 775.

146. When asked how he arrived at the central incident of his story, "the meeting between Christ and Paul in an Essene monastery," Moore claimed, opaquely, that "to answer this question fully I should have to write out the story of my life since I came to live in Ireland." *The Apostle: A Drama in Three Acts* (Dublin: Maunsel, 1911), 2.

147. Moore, *Apostle*, 32. Apparently it was John Eglinton who described the book to Moore. See Eglinton, *Irish Literary Portraits*, 96. Eglinton's own extensive use of biblical themes is discussed in chapter 4.

148. Desmond Shawe-Taylor, "The Achievement of George Moore," in *The Life of George Moore, by Joseph Hone; With an Account of His Last Years by His Cook and Housekeeper, Clara Warville* (London: V. Gollancz, 1936), 465.

149. Presumably one of those "clever theories" Gregory's correspondent Huntington notes above.

150. George Moore, *Apostle*, 99.

151. George Moore, *The Brook Kerith: A Syrian Story* (New York: Macmillan, 1917), x.

152. George Moore, *Apostle*, 99–100.

153. Joyce, *Critical Writngs*, 243.

154. Ibid.

155. George Moore, *Brook Kerith*, 480.

156. Ibid., vii–viii.

4. A Pisgah Sight of Palestine from Dear Dirty Dublin

1. See chapter 1 for a detailed discussion of the cantata (and Griffith's rejection of it). On Palmieri, see Ellmann, *James Joyce*, 151.

2. Joyce, *Selected Letters*, 90, 89.

3. Joyce may have taken this image from Maria Edgeworth, who wrote in 1834, "it is impossible to draw Ireland as she now is in a book of fiction—realities are too strong, party passions too violent to bear to see, or care to look at their faces in the looking-glass. The people would only break the glass, and curse the fool who held the mirror up to nature—distorted nature, in a fever." Edgeworth, *The Life and*

Letters of Maria Edgeworth, vol. 2, ed. Augustus J. C. Hare (Boston: Houghton Mifflin, 1895), 550. I am indebted to Natasha Tessone for this reference. Citations for *Ulysses* will appear parenthetically in the text.

4. Joyce, *Selected Letters*, 88.

5. Qtd. in Jacques Mercanton, "The Hours of James Joyce," in *Portraits of the Artist in Exile*, ed. Williard Potts (London: Harvest HBJ Book, 1986), 208.

6. See Marilyn Reizbaum, *James Joyce's Judaic Other* (Stanford, CA: Stanford Univ. Press, 1999), 39–45.

7. In 1994 Enda Duffy published *The Subaltern "Ulysses"* (Minneapolis: Univ. of Minnesota Press, 1994), in which he proposes to establish *Ulysses* "as *the* text of Ireland's independence," revealing it as a novel preoccupied with the anticolonial struggles of oppressed communities (1). Equally important are two studies published the following year: Vincent Cheng's *Joyce, Race and Empire* (Cambridge, UK: Cambridge Univ. Press, 1995), in which Cheng examines the politicized Joyce who "undertook a systematic critique of the repressiveness of both English imperialism and certain forms of Irish Nationalist consciousness" (289); and Emer Nolan's *James Joyce and Nationalism* (New York: Routledge, 1995), which argues for bringing Joyce even further into the nationalist camp. Nolan writes, "the cliché of Joyce's 'ambivalence' towards Ireland suggests mere confusion or ambiguity: we have overlooked the determinate nature of this response" (xiii).

8. In *Joyce's Revenge*, Andrew Gibson has argued that a gap in the critical tradition between Jewish- and Irish-focused scholarship has created the "reluctance to think Jews and Irish together" (42). His chapter on Bloom and Jews (42–59) is exemplary in bridging such a gap, but other valuable work exists as well. See, for example, Cheng's *Joyce, Race, and Empire*; Amardeep Singh's "A Pisgah Sight of Ireland: Religious Embodiment and Colonialism in *Ulysses*," *Semeia* 88 (2001): 129–47; and Marilyn Reizbaum's "Urban Legends," *Éire-Ireland* 45, nos. 1–2 (Spring/Summer 2010): 242–65. For a reading of how Bloom's Jewishness and Irishness are inflected by discourses of manliness, see Valente's *Myth of Manliness*, especially 231–36. Most of the work on Exodus has been done by scholars working on Joyce and Jews, and of particular note are Reizbaum's *James Joyce's Judaic Other*; Neil R. Davison, *James Joyce, "Ulysses," and the Construction of Jewish Identity* (Cambridge, UK: Cambridge Univ. Press, 1996); and Ira Nadel, *Joyce and the Jews: Culture and Texts* (London: MacMillan, 1989). These three studies investigate how Jewishness in *Ulysses* provides, as Reizbaum writes, "a structure, a 'concept,' a complex of ideas in the novel" (4). Stephen Sicari's *Joyce's Modernist Allegory: "Ulysses" and the History of the Novel* (Columbia: Univ. of South Carolina Press, 2001) and Virginia Moseley's *Joyce and the Bible* (De Kalb: Northern Illinois Univ. Press, 1967) consider biblical tropes (including Exodus) mainly in the context of typological arguments about Christian/New Testament elements of *Ulysses*. There are also several shorter essays

that survey the Moses theme in *Ulysses* to varying extents, including M. David Bell, "The Search for Agendath Netaim: Some Progress but No Solution," *James Joyce Quarterly* 12, no. 3 (Spring 1975): 251–58; Irene Orgel Briskin, "Some New Light on 'The Parable of the Plums,'" *James Joyce Quarterly* 3, no. 4 (Summer 1966): 236–51; Francis Bulhof, "Agendath Again," *James Joyce Quarterly* 7, no. 4 (Summer 1970): 326–31; Roderick Davis, "The Fourfold Moses in *Ulysses*," *James Joyce Quarterly* 7, no. 2 (Winter 1970): 120–31; David Weir, "Sophomore Plum(p)s for Old Man Moses," *James Joyce Quarterly* 28, no. 3 (Spring 1991): 657–62.

9. Deane, *Celtic Revivals*, 104.

10. Ibid.

11. Nolan, *Catholic Emancipations*, 179; Davison, *James Joyce, "Ulysses," and the Construction of Jewish Identity*, 232.

12. Walzer, *Exodus and Revolution*, 36.

13. Canon P. A. Sheehan, *The Graves at Kimorna: A Story of '67* (New York: D. D. Longmans, Green and Co., 1915), 230. Qtd. in James H. Murphy, *Catholic Fiction and Social Reality in Ireland, 1873–1922* (Westport, CT: Greenwood Press, 1997), 122.

14. *Irish Review*, 1911, 420.

15. Ibid., 418.

16. Seán Ó Faoláin, *De Valera* (Harmondsworth, UK: Penguin, 1939), 180. Qtd. in Michael Mays, *Nation States: The Culture of Irish Nationalism* (Plymouth, UK: Lexington Books, 2007), 99.

17. Michael Collins, "Advance and Use Our Liberties," in *A Path to Freedom* (Cork: Mercier Press, 1996), 25.

18. For English settlers, of course, the allusion worked in the opposite way: the fleshpots were the stuff of native Irish culture. Of Richard Dawson, brother of Joshua (a prominent English planter of the early eighteenth century), James Anthony Froude writes, "the fleshpots of Egypt and the whiskey tumblers of Cork brought him early to his end, and he died two years after in great misery." Froude, *The English in Ireland in the Eighteenth Century*, vol. 1 (New York: Charles Scribner's Sons, 1888), 284.

19. John Eglinton, *Two Essays on the Remnant* (Dublin: Whaley, 1894), 36.

20. Eglinton, *Two Essays on the Remnant*, 41.

21. Joyce, *Selected Letters*, 144. This mockery is most notoriously evident in the limerick Joyce sent to his brother Stanislaus: "There once was a Celtic librarian / Whose essays were voted Spencerian / His name is Magee / But it seems that to me / He's a flavour that's more Presbyterian." Qtd. in Ellmann, *James Joyce*, 118. Bonnie K. Scott, in her essay "John Eglinton: A Model for Joyce's Individualism," gives evidence of the extent to which Joyce refers to Eglinton in *Ulysses* (*James Joyce Quarterly* 12, no. 4 [Summer 1975]: 347–57).

22. Scott, "John Eglinton," 347. This is not to say that Eglinton was cosmopolitan or egalitarian on all matters; his almost comically reactionary sexism is most blatant in *Two Essays on the Remnant* (see, especially, 18–20).

23. Qtd. in Scott, "John Eglinton," 347.

24. Joyce, *Selected Letters*, 111. Joyce's aversion to Irish Ireland insularity is also evident in his Trieste lecture of 1907, "Ireland, Island of Saints and Sages," where he asks, "what race, or what language . . . can boast of being pure today? And no race has less right to utter such a boast than the race now living in Ireland." *Critical Writings*, 165–66.

25. From the headnote on Eglinton in *Irish Literature*, vol. 6, ed. Justin McCarthy (Philadelphia: J. D. Morris and Co., 1904), 2292.

26. Eglinton, *Two Essays on the Remnant*, 31–32.

27. "The epochs of Aeschylus and Shakespeare make us feel their pre-eminence. In an epoch like those is, no doubt, the true life of a literature; there is the promised land, towards which criticism can only beckon. That promised land it will not be ours to enter, and we shall die in the wilderness: but to have desired to enter it, to have saluted it from afar, is already, perhaps, the best distinction among contemporaries; it will certainly be the best title to esteem with posterity." Matthew Arnold, *The Function of Criticism at the Present Time* (London: Macmillan and Co., 1865), 86.

28. For a discussion of Parnell as Moses, see chapter 2.

29. Joyce, *Critical Writings*, 225.

30. Eglinton, *Two Essays on the Remnant*, 35.

31. Nadel, *Joyce and the Jews*, 26. Nadel notes that Joyce's biographer Herbert Gorman took this view, describing Joyce as "the literary Moses who would lead the post-war procession into the Promised Land." Gorman, *James Joyce* (New York: Rinehart, 1948), 269. Nadel further points out that Joyce read Gorman's manuscript carefully, and "apparently did not object to this designation" (254).

32. Yeats, *Later Articles and Reviews*, 56.

33. Ibid., 57.

34. See Howes's chapter "When the Mob Becomes a People," in *Yeats's Nations*, 66–101.

35. John Eglinton, "The Chosen People at Work," in *Some Essays and Passages by John Eglinton*, ed. W. B. Yeats (Dundrum, IRL: Dun Emer Press, 1905), contents page. Eglinton's caveat reads in full: "The writer of the following pages would like to say that he has had no hand in the selection, which Mr. Yeats has done him the honour to make for the Dun Emer Press Series, and in particular, that if consulted he would hardly have approved of the inclusion of the last essay, written over twelve years ago, in which a metaphor is pressed to the point of being recommended as a gospel." See also Yeats, *Letters*, Vol. 4, 1026.

36. John Eglinton, "A Neglected Monument of Irish Prose," in *Bards and Saints* (Dublin: Maunsel, 1906), 14.

37. Eglinton, *Two Essays on the Remnant*, 48.

38. Lloyd, *Anomalous States*, 114. Lloyd argues that *Ulysses* enacts an aesthetic of adulteration, and like Bakhtin, he opposes the novel to a necessarily monologic epic. Yet perhaps *Ulysses*, modeling the Bible, integrates hybridity into a (modern) version of the epic form—a possibility that cannot be adequately addressed here, however. Although we take different paths, I reach a similar conclusion to that of Len Platt, who writes, "the authenticity of *Ulysses* as an Irish book" is "underwritten by the fact that *Ulysses* is blatant in its own cultural contamination." Platt, *Joyce and the Anglo-Irish: A Study of Joyce and the Literary Revival* (Amsterdam: Rodopi, 1998), 178.

39. Israel Zangwill, *Chosen Peoples: the Hebraic Ideal versus the Teutonic*, with a foreword by the Right Hon. Herbert Samuel and an afterword by Israel Abrahams (London: G. Allen and Unwin, 1918), 63.

40. Eglinton, "Heroic Literature," in *Pebbles from a Brook*, 25.

41. Eglinton, "Irish Books," in *Anglo-Irish Essays*, 87–88.

42. Ellmann, *James Joyce*, 530.

43. Eglinton, "Optimism and Pessimism," in *Pebbles from a Brook*, 115.

44. For a discussion of Joyce's relationships with Zionists in Trieste, see John McCourt, *The Years of Bloom: James Joyce in Trieste, 1904–1920* (Madison: Univ. of Wisconsin Press, 2000), especially 233–36. See also Neil Davison's essay, "'Still an Idea Behind It': Trieste, Jewishness, and Zionism in *Ulysses*," *James Joyce Quarterly* 38, nos. 3–4 (Spring/Summer 2001): 373–94.

45. Theodor Herzl, *The Jewish State*, trans. Sylvie D'Avigdor (New York: Dover, 1988), 135.

46. Ibid. However, this passage can also be read as a sign of a particularly colonial cosmopolitanism, for there are also "English hotels in Egypt" (but hardly the reverse). The issue of Zionism's colonialism is perhaps suggested in the Agendath Netaim advertisement, although Joyce does not appear to have commented on the debate directly.

47. Harry Sacher, "A Century of Jewish History," in *Zionism and the Jewish Future*, ed. Harry Sacher (London: John Murray, 1916), 41.

48. Ibid., 55.

49. Ibid., 58.

50. Nachum Sokolow, "The New Jew," in Sacher, *Zionism and the Jewish Future*, 220. *Zionism and the Jewish Future* also contains introductory remarks by Chaim Weizman that, as Davison notes in quoting them, "must have pleased Joyce": "When the aim of Zionism is accomplished, Palestine will be the home of the Jewish people, not because it will contain all the Jews in the world, but because it will be the only

place in the world where the Jews are the masters of their own destiny . . . Palestine will be the country in which Jews are to be found, just as Ireland is the country in which Irishman [*sic*] are to be found, though there are more Irishmen outside of Ireland than in it." Weizman, "Introduction: Zionism and the Jewish Problem," in *Zionism and the Jewish Future*, 8. Joyce, however, was also apparently bemused by the Zionist project, telling Ottocaro Weiss in 1915, "that's all very well, but believe me, a warship with a captain called Kanalgitter and his aide named Captain Afterduft would be the funniest thing the old Mediterranean has ever seen." Qtd. in Ellmann, *James Joyce*, 396; and in Nadel, *Joyce and the Jews*, 72.

51. Peter Yorke, "The Turning of the Tide," in *An Claidheamh Soluis*, Sept. 16, 1899. Qtd. in O'Leary, *Prose Literature of the Gaelic Revival*, 20.

52. Jacqueline Rose, *The Question of Zion* (Princeton, NJ: Princeton Univ. Press, 2005), 123.

53. M. Gaster, "Judaism—A National Religion," in Sacher, *Zionism and the Jewish Future*, 97; Sacher, "A Century of Jewish History," 57; Leon Simon, "The Hebrew Revival," in Sacher, *Zionism and the Jewish Future*, 109.

54. Douglas Hyde, "The Necessity for De-Anglicising Ireland," 140.

55. Ellmann, *James Joyce*, 91.

56. See, for example, William Irwin Thompson, who has suggested that the speech (inspired, he says, by Eglinton's analogizing of Jews and Irish in the *Daily Express*) "put the messianism of the elect into the mind of every Irishman in the street." Thompson, *Imagination of an Insurrection*, 50.

57. *Freeman's Journal*, Oct. 25, 1901.

58. The poem was originally published in *United Ireland*, Oct. 10, 1891. Qtd. in Ellmann, *Yeats: The Man and the Masks*, 100. See chapter 2.

59. The recording was made in 1924. For an illuminating discussion of its production and textual authority, see Damien Keane, "Quotation Marks, the Gramophone Record, and the Language of the Outlaw," *Texas Studies in Literature and Language* 51, no. 4 (Winter 2009): 400–415. See also Eric D. Smith, "How a Great Daily Organ Is Turned Out: 'Aeolus,' *Techne*, and the Recording of *Ulysses*," *James Joyce Quarterly* 41 (Spring 2004): 455–68; and Sebastian Knowles, "Apres Mot, Le Deluge," review of *James Joyce: The Complete Recordings; Music from the Work of James Joyce*, *James Joyce Literary Supplement* 18 (Autumn 2004): 23.

60. *Freeman's Journal*, Oct. 25, 1901.

61. An tAthair Peadar Ua Laoghaire, "Sgéal lóib agus Sgéal na hEireann." Qtd. in O'Leary, *Prose Literature of the Gaelic Revival*, 20.

62. Eglinton, "A Neglected Monument of Irish Prose," in Eglinton, *Bards and Saints*, 12.

63. Matt 15:24: "[Jesus] answered, 'I was sent only to the lost sheep of the house of Israel.'"

64. Joyce's subversion of the language issue is, however, only one of the ironies he exposes in the Taylor passage—others have been well documented already. Elizabeth Cullingford has noted "the protean slipperiness of the analogical method," and what she terms a "sliding political signifier": "The paradox by which Egypt can stand either for the British oppressor (the high priest) or the victim of British oppression (the fellahin)." Cullingford, *Ireland's Others*, 142. The latter refers to the colonial status of Egypt, as noted by MacHugh: "The masters of the Mediterranean are fellaheen today" (*U* 138). Vincent Cheng describes a related irony, in that "even as [the nationalists] repeatedly invoke the Judaic/Irish analogy, they continue to mistreat and derogate the actual Jewish 'other' in their midst." Cheng, *Joyce, Race, and Empire*, 191.

65. Qtd. in Davison, "'Still an Idea Behind It,'" 387.

66. Joyce, *Selected Letters*, 125. As Marilyn Reizbaum notes, Joyce further rejects the language movement in "Circe" when he parodies Griffith's "Resurrection of Hungary," in which Franz Joseph speaks in the national language, Hungarian—but Bloom speaks in Hebrew: decidedly not Ireland's national language. Reizbaum, *James Joyce's Judaic Other*, 44.

67. The pamphlet, entitled "The Language of the Outlaw," has a complex history, and Casement's authorship of it has rarely been noted by Joyceans, although the text itself is frequently quoted. See my note "The Language of the Outlaw: A Clarification," *James Joyce Quarterly* 44, no. 4 (Summer 2007): 807–12.

68. Roger Casement, "Language of the Outlaw," 4.

69. Joyce, *Critical Writings*, 166.

70. Joyce, *A Portrait of the Artist as a Young Man* (New York: Penguin Books, 1993), 205.

71. Bender, "The Language of the Outlaw," 811n10.

72. Morton P. Levitt, "The Family of Bloom," in *New Light on Joyce from the Dublin Symposium*, ed. Fritz Senn (Bloomington: Univ. of Indiana Press, 1972), 151.

73. Ibid.

74. "The Lord went in front of them in a pillar of cloud by day, to lead them along the way, and in a pillar of fire by night. . . . Neither the pillar of cloud by day nor the pillar of fire by night left its place in front of the people" (Exodus 13:21–22). Irene Orgel Briskin notes, "The Nelson monument, previously referred to as a column in accordance with the newspaper language of the 'Aeolus' episode, becomes a pillar as the women approach it, recalling the pillar of cloud in Exodus." Briskin, "Some New Light," 248.

75. Singh, "Pisgah Sight of Ireland," 145.

76. Sicari, *Joyce's Modernist Allegory*, 76.

77. Michael Begnal's suggestion that the parable is in fact a dirty joke, with Nelson's statue as "onehandled" instead of "onehanded" "since the hand would be

used as a handle or dildo for [the women's] ultimate satisfaction," is not inconsistent with my argument here (although he also writes off other possible readings). Begnal, "Stephen's Terrible Parable," 356. David Weir reads the sex in the parable as fellatio.

78. Willard Potts, *Joyce and the Two Irelands* (Austin: Univ. of Texas Press, 2001), 37.

79. Moran's philosophy is outlined most fully in his book of that name, *The Philosophy of Irish Ireland* (1905). See also Susan Harris's *Gender and Modern Irish Drama* and P. J. Mathews's *Revival: The Abbey Theatre, Sinn Féin, the Gaelic League and the Co-operative Movement* for more on the ideology of Irish Ireland and its practical and cultural effects.

80. Alan Roughley offers a Derridean reading of the sexual signification of fleshpots, but as I have argued, that association is already inherent in their biblical associations. See Roughley, *Reading Derrida Reading Joyce* (Gainesville: Univ. Press of Florida, 1999), 98–100.

81. Several scholars have suggested the ways in which Exodus-related symbols link Stephen and Bloom through, as Francis Bulhof calls it, "the transpersonal principle." Bulhof, "Agendath Again," 331. The cloud that both see as the pillar of cloud, for example, or, as Daniel Mark Fogel points out, how the "bowl of bitter waters" Stephen associates with his mother can also link with the salt water at (Bloom's) Passover Seder. See Fogel, "Symbol and Context in *Ulysses*: Joyce's 'Bowl of Bitter Waters' and Passover," *ELH* 46, no. 4 (Winter 1979): 710–21.

82. David Weir points out that Boylan drinks sloe (plum) gin before going to see Molly.

83. Hugh Kenner (along with many others since) notes of the Moses of Michelangelo, "the horns it wears embody a mistranslation of Exodus, 34:29, by St Jerome, who misread a verb meaning that the face of Moses shone and apparently did not think it odd for the face of the lawgiver to be horned." Kenner, *Ulysses* (London: G. Allen and Unwin, 1980), 138. This in opposition to the correct version that Bloom will embody in Ithaca, "with the light of inspiration shining in his countenance" (*U* 628–29). See also Reizbaum, *James Joyce's Judaic Other*, 95.

84. Don Gifford with Robert J. Seidman, *"Ulysses" Annotated: Notes for James Joyce's "Ulysses,"* 2nd ed. (Berkeley: Univ. of California Press, 1988), 418. Len Platt offers a helpful reading of how "Let Erin Remember," on its own, "perfectly embodies the contradictions that faced cultural nationalists." Platt, *Joyce and the Anglo-Irish*, 59.

85. Gregory, *Selected Writings*, 308. Kathleen earlier in the play tells Bridget that what put her wandering was "Too many strangers in the house" (306). Another meaning of the passage points to the tradition that a woman's adultery brought the English colonizer to Ireland: Joyce remarked on this in his notes to the play *Exiles*, and Deasy captures the idea in his lines to Stephen in "Nestor": "A faithless wife

first brought the strangers to our shore here. . . . A woman too brought Parnell low" (*U* 34).

86. Reizbaum, *James Joyce's Judaic Other*, 39.

87. Reizbaum further notes that Griffith, in an article on the pogrom in his paper, "goes on to attack the Jews for being united against the Transvaal Republic and therefore in league with the English." Reizbaum, *James Joyce's Judaic Other*, 39. For more on the 1904 Limerick incident, see chapter 1, as well as Reizbaum, Nadel, and Gibson, for more extensive discussions. Joyce, however, makes the English Haines and "Britisher" Deasy the first purveyors of anti-Semitism in *Ulysses.*

88. For a detailed reading of how this claim circulated, see chapter 1.

89. Pearse, *Collected Works: Political Writings and Speeches*, 170. In "Circe," Old Gummy Granny (read Kathleen ni Houlihan) gives Stephen the very Pearsian message: "at 8.35 a.m. you will be in heaven and Ireland will be free" (*U* 557).

90. See Joseph Valente, "Stephen's 'Allwombing Tomb': Mourning, Paternity, and the Incorporation of the Mother in *Ulysses*," *Joyce Studies Annual* 2012, no. 1 (2012): 5–28.

91. Joyce, *Selected Letters*, 88.

92. Walzer, *Exodus and Revolution*, 52.

93. Nahum N. Glatzer, ed., *The Passover Haggadah* (New York: Schocken Books, 1953), 119.

94. Nolan, *James Joyce and Nationalism*, 83.

95. For another take on this, see Bryan Cheyette's related argument that Bloom's Jewishness is unstable so as to disrupt "cultural certainties surrounding Jewish assimilation or Irish national and Catholic religious superiority." Cheyette, "'Jewgreek is greekjew': The Disturbing Ambivalence of Joyce's Semitic Discourse in *Ulysses*," in *Joyce Studies Annual* 1992, ed. Thomas F. Staley (Austin: Univ. of Texas Press, 1992), 34.

96. Joyce would have read about Jewish communities rejecting members who failed to keep from the fleshpots. The play *Ahasverus* by Herman Heijermans, which Joyce had in his Trieste library, was set in the pogroms of Russia in 1890; the parents claim their son would have been better off murdered than baptized in order to save his life from the Cossacks. Joyce may also have noticed this passage in his copy of *Zionism and the Jewish Future*: "A Jew who changes his faith is torn up by the roots. There is no longer any connection between him and other Jews. He has practically died." Gaster, "Judaism—A National Religion," 91.

97. It has been suggested by several scholars that Joyce mis-transliterates the word "Agendath" (from Agendath Netaim, or "a company of planters," which would more correctly be rendered, in English, "Agudath," in order to link the word with Stephen's Agenbit of Inwit. Gifford, *Ulysses Annotated*, 74. Both Agendath and

Agenbite evoke the vexed bonds of religious/national identity. See, especially, Francis Bulhof's "Agendath Again," 33.

98. Gifford, *"Ulysses" Annotated*, 74.

99. Ibid., 470.

100. Tindall, "Mosaic Bloom," 6.

101. The "milk and honey" quotation, in particular, has led many critics to this reading; along with Tindall, see Daniel Mark Fogel, "Symbol and Context in *Ulysses*," 720.

102. Gifford, *"Ulysses" Annotated*, 602.

103. Not only in Gregory's play, but likewise in Seamus O'Kelly's play *The Parnellite*, the Irish ingrates stone their deliverer. The theme emerges from Exodus 17:4, in which Moses is threatened with being stoned by his people. Len Platt, in *Joyce and the Anglo-Irish*, includes an appendix on the connection between *The Deliverer* and "Circe," and suggests, convincingly, that Joyce recycles her passages of "choral adoration" and "choral reversal" (234–35). I am at odds, however, with Platt's dismissal of *The Deliverer* as "a mess of triteness that is inadvertently hilarious" (234), a statement that replicates most contemporary assessments of the play. For an extended discussion of the play and its reception, see chapter 2.

104. Joyce, *Critical Writings*, 228.

105. Valente, *Myth of Manliness*, 232.

106. Gibson, *Joyce's Revenge*, 170.

107. Susan Handelman describes the resistance to traditional Judaism as representative of Jewishness itself (reading the work of Kabbalist Gershom Scholem): "In interpreting 'heretical' as truly a 'normative' part of Jewish history, Scholem's 'antinomianism' is here a *return to* tradition. And we can say that so also the 'heretical' impulses of Freud, Derrida, and [Harold] Bloom, are likewise a dialectical return to Jewish tradition. . . . The paradox is, via heresy to return to tradition." Handelman, *Slayers of Moses*, 199.

5. A Bloomsday Seder

1. Philip F. Herring, ed., *Joyce's "Ulysses" Notesheets in the British Museum* (Charlottesville: Univ. of Virginia Press, 1972), 82, 53. Qtd. in Neil R. Davison, *James Joyce, "Ulysses," and the Construction of Jewish Identity* (Cambridge, UK: Cambridge Univ. Press, 1996), 204; Joyce, *Selected Letters*, 271.

2. Yerushalmi, *Freud's Moses*, 15.

3. Glatzer, *Passover Haggadah*, 27.

4. Yerushalmi describes biblical candor as "the most singular aspect of Jewish tradition from the Bible onward," and he notes the text's "almost maddening refusal to conceal the misdeeds of the Jews" (*Freud's Moses*, 84). The context of this

comment is the author's gentle chiding of Freud for his suggestion that all trauma must be relegated to the unconscious (or the subtextual).

5. Zornberg, *Particulars of Rapture*, 197.

6. Qtd. in Anderson, *Imagined Communities*, 6.

7. For two differing analyses of how, as David Henshke writes, "Moses is withdrawn from the founding narrative of his history and that of the people of Israel," see Henshke, "'The Lord Brought Us Forth from Egypt': On the Absence of Moses in the Passover Haggadah," *AJS Review* 31, no. 1 (2007): 61–73, and David Arnow, "The Passover Haggadah: Moses and the Human Role in Redemption," *Judaism* 55, nos. 3–4 (Fall 2006): 4–28.

8. Jan Assmann, *Religion and Cultural Memory*, trans. Rodney Livingstone (Stanford, CA: Stanford Univ. Press, 2006), 51.

9. Yerushalmi, *Haggadah and History: A Panorama in Facsimile of Five Centuries of the Printed Haggadah from the Collections of Harvard University and the Jewish Theological Seminary of America* (Philadelphia: Jewish Publication Society, 2005), 44; Glatzer, *Passover Haggadah*, 59.

10. Neil Gillman, "Theologically Speaking," in *My People's Passover Haggadah*, vol. 2, ed. Lawrence A. Hoffman and David Arnow (Woodstock, VT: Jewish Lights Publishing), 74. Gillman also corrects the traditional translation and expands on its universality: "the text does not say that 'every Jew' must see him—or herself as having come out of Egypt, but rather 'every one' or 'every individual.' The Hebrew word is *adam*, which is, first, gender neutral and, second, means simply a person, a human being. The liberation from Egypt has universal significance that extends way beyond Jewish history" (79).

11. Produced in 1864, the Trieste Haggadah was the most important pictorial Haggadah of the nineteenth century; see Yershalmi, *Haggadah and History*, 47; it is likely enough that Joyce would have encountered it in one of his Jewish friends' homes.

12. Qtd. in Reizbaum, *James Joyce's Judaic Other*, 24.

13. Michael Davitt, *Within the Pale: The True Story of Anti-Semitic Persecutions in Russia* (London: A. S. Barnes and Co., 1903).

14. *Irish Times*, June 10, 1904, 4. On the Limerick incident, see also Dermot Keough and Andrew McCarthy, *Limerick Boycott 1904: Anti-Semitism in Ireland* (Cork: Mercier Press, 2005); and Cormac Ó'Gráda, *Jewish Ireland in the Age of Joyce: A Socioeconomic History* (Princeton, NJ: Princeton Univ. Press, 2006), 191–94.

15. *Irish Times*, Apr. 7, 1906, 2. According to this 1906 article on "The Seder" by Halitvak, in "certain advanced circles in Jewry, where all ancient institutions are interpreted according to modern ideas . . . the Passover is looked upon as the anniversary of Israel's coming into being as an independent people." The author determines that this understanding, however, is accorded only to a few in his Dublin

community, where most Jews "have too great a reverence for the letter of the Law to inquire into its spirit" (2).

16. *Irish Times*, Apr. 22, 1876, 5.

17. Glatzer, *Passover Haggadah*, 25.

18. Daniel R. Schwarz points out the traditional assimilation of new struggles ("the Holocaust, pogroms, the establishment of the State of Israel, persecution of the Jews in Russia") to the telling of the Exodus narrative, and suggests, "Joyce draws upon this elastic and protean tradition to imply that *Ulysses* is to be regarded as the Haggadah of the Irish experience." Schwarz, *Reading Joyce's "Ulysses"* (New York: Palgrave Macmillan, 1987), 120. Ira Nadel describes Bloom's "rescuing the fallen Stephen and leading him out of the darkness into the light" as a further acting-out of the Haggadah's version of Jewish history (*Joyce and the Jews*, 30). A more specific element of Passover ritual in the "Telemachus" episode is detected by Daniel Mark Fogel, who argues that the bowl of bitter waters is linked to the salt water used during the Seder. Elsewhere in the novel other references to Passover are plentiful; those connected with Elijah, whose heralding of the messiah is expected on the night of Passover, are especially frequent.

19. See Barry McCrea, "Family and Form in *Ulysses*," *Field Day Review* 5 (2009): 75–93.

20. *Irish Times*, Apr. 21, 1900, 15. Lipsett also wrote as Halitvak, quoted above.

21. Glatzer, *Passover Haggadah*, 25.

22. Assmann, *Religion and Cultural Memory*, 54. Elaborating, Assmann writes that the biblical book of Deuteronomy in particular articulates an "exceptional situation of a counterfactual memory. It keeps present to the mind a yesterday that conflicts with every today" (53).

23. Amnon Raz-Krakotzkin, "Jewish Memory between Exile and History," *Jewish Quarterly Review* 97, no. 4 (Fall 2007): 533.

24. Reizbaum, *James Joyce's Judaic Other*, 52.

25. Nadel, *Joyce and the Jews*, 10. Yet to say, as Nadel does, that Joyce's "only homeland could be a text" risks marginalizing Joyce's attention to nations, and nationalisms (3).

26. Daniel and Jonathan Boyarin, "Diaspora: Generation and the Ground of Jewish Identity," *Critical Inquiry* 19, no. 4 (Summer 1993): 715, 718.

27. Valente, *Myth of Manliness*, 234.

28. For Bloom, national identities are not jealous: that his nation is Ireland ("I was born here" [*U* 317], he explains) does not undo his Jewishness, as he famously asserts in what follows, "I belong to a race too . . . that is hated and persecuted" (*U* 318).

29. Duffy, "Disappearing Dublin," 37.

30. Said, "Michael Walzer's *Exodus and Revolution*," 86–106. In response to Michael Walzer's 1985 argument that Exodus is about radical revolution, Said

countered with an exposition of "the irreducibly sectarian premises of Exodus" (93), declaring it a narrative of divinely sanctioned settler colonialism and even genocide against the Canaanites. See my introduction for a fuller discussion of the debate.

31. In *Empire* (Cambridge, MA: Harvard Univ. Press, 2000), Michael Hardt and Antonio Negri continually invoke a liberatory "exodus," although, for all of their theological fervor, they mean the word ostensibly emptied of its biblical/religious implications. They imagine "exodus" as a purely subversive force: the destruction of boundaries, a multiplication of ambiguities: "Circulation is a global exodus, or really nomadism; and it is a corporeal exodus, or really miscegenation" (364).

32. David Stern, forward to Joseph Tabory, *JPS Commentary on the Haggadah: Historical Introduction, Translation, and Commentary* (Philadelphia: Jewish Publication Society, 2008), xiii. Yerushalmi points out that the Haggadah looks not only backward, but forward, "not merely as an evocation from the past, but above all [a] prototype and surety for the ultimate redemption yet to come" (*Haggadah and History*, 15).

33. Morton P Levitt, "The Family of Bloom," in *New Light on Joyce from the Dublin Symposium*, ed. Fritz Senn (Bloomington: Univ. of Indiana Press, 1972), 140.

34. In addition to the incidents in Limerick and Kishineff, Joyce may also have had in mind the widely publicized blood libel claim of the Damascus case of 1840. In its aftermath, in order to dispel the myth, the entire text of the Haggadah was printed in the *London Times.* See Yerushalmi, *Haggadah and History*, 77.

35. As Marilyn Reizbaum has suggested, the ballad is presented as a "set text," set apart by its visual difference, "as though for copying and future use by its readers." See "Urban Legends," *Eire-Ireland* 45, nos. 1–2 (Spring/Sumer 2010): 247. Margot Norris notes that the handwriting is Joyce's own; see Norris, "Stephen Dedalus's Anti-Semitic Ballad: A Sabotaged Climax in Joyce's *Ulysses*," in *De-familiarizing Readings: Essays from the Austin Joyce Conference, European Joyce Studies* 18, ed. Alan W. Friedman and Charles Rossman (Amsterdam: Rodopi, 2009), 67. John Brannigan, in *Race in Modern Irish Literature and Culture* (Edinburgh: Edinburgh Univ. Press, 2010), notes how "Joyce reinforces the vivacity of the song by providing not just its words but its musical score also" (54).

36. Norris, "Stephen Dedalus's Anti-Semitic Ballad," 56, 75.

37. Ibid., 72.

38. Reizbaum, "Urban Legends," 251. Reizbaum further suggests how the phrase "host (victim predestined)" suggests "the transubstantiation of Passover matza in the Last Supper into Christ/wafer, or the blood of the lamb on the Jewish doorpost into the lamb of God" (251).

39. Qtd. in Valente, *Myth of Manliness*, 232.

40. Deane, *Celtic Revivals*, 104.

41. Qtd. in Tindall, "Mosaic Bloom," 4.

42. As Gifford notes, the Babylonian Talmud gives "elaborate instructions" that the citron "was to be not only without physical flaw but perfect in every way, including the legal, moral, and religious conditions under which it was grown" ("*Ulysses" Annotated*, 74).

43. Joyce, *Selected Letters*, 279.

44. Attias and Benbassa, *Israel, the Impossible Land*, 19.

45. Glatzer, *Passover Haggadah*, 7.

Coda

1. Edward Said, *Freud and the Non-European* (London: Verso in association with the Freud Museum London, 2003), 44. Aamir Mufti recognizes a related paradox in Said's development of the concept of secular criticism, noting that "the sources for this governing concept in Said's work turn out to be critical traditions that emerged out of a certain experience of Jewish (and, more specifically, German Jewish) exile," and his critical practice "remain[s] productively tied to . . . marginality and homelessness, whose exemplary form in the West in the nineteenth and early twentieth centuries is provided by the Jews." Mufti, "Critical Secularism: A Reintroduction for Perilous Times," *Boundary 2* 31, no. 2 (2004): 4–5.

2. As Donald Akenson writes of Zionist organizations after the creation of the state of Israel, "No longer did they follow the pillar of cloud by day and the pillar of fire by night; now they supported a geographically defined and geopolitically specific Zion." Akenson, *God's People*, 151.

3. Jonathan Boyarin, "Reading Exodus into History," *New Literary History* 23, no. 3 (Summer 1992): 532.

4. Glaude, *Exodus!*, 4.

Bibliography

"A Priest." "Irish or Infidelity, Which?" *Leader*, Jan. 9, 1909, 496–98.

Abels, Jules. *The Parnell Tragedy*. New York: Macmillan Co., 1966.

Adams, David. *Colonial Odysseys: Empire and Epic in the Modernist Novel*. Ithaca, NY: Cornell Univ. Press, 2003.

Akenson, Donald H. *God's Peoples: Covenant and Land in South Africa, Israel, and Ulster*. Ithaca, NY: Cornell Univ. Press, 1992.

Alexander, Sam. "Mourn—and Then Onward!" *The Modernism Lab at Yale University*. Accessed Aug. 6, 2010. http://modernism.research.yale.edu/wiki/index.php/Mourn--_and_then_Onward!

Anderson, Benedict R. "Exodus." *Critical Inquiry* 20 (Winter 1994): 314–27.

———. *Imagined Communities: Reflections on the Origin and Spread of Nationalism*. Rev. 2nd ed. London: Verso, 1991.

Arnold, Matthew. *The Function of Criticism at the Present Time*. London: Macmillan and Co., 1865.

Arnow, David. "The Passover Haggadah: Moses and the Human Role in Redemption." *Judaism* 55, nos. 3–4 (Fall 2006): 4–28.

Ashton, Thomas L. *Byron's Hebrew Melodies*. Austin: Univ. of Texas Press, 1972.

Assmann, Jan. *Religion and Cultural Memory*. Translated by Rodney Livingstone. Stanford, CA: Stanford Univ. Press, 2006.

Attias, Jean-Christophe, and Esther Benbassa. *Israel, the Impossible Land*. Translated by Susan Emanuel. Stanford, CA: Stanford Univ. Press, 2003.

———. *The Jew and the Other*. Translated by G. M. Goshgarian. Ithaca, NY: Cornell Univ. Press, 2004.

Auerbach, Erich. *Scenes from the Drama of European Literature*. Minneapolis: Univ. of Minnesota Press, 1984.

Aughey, Arthur. "What Is Living and What Is Dead in the Ideal of 1916." In *Revising the Rising*, edited by Máirín Ní Dhonnchadha and Theo Dorgan, 71–90. Derry: Field Day, 1991.

Augusteijn, Joost. *Patrick Pearse: The Making of a Revolutionary.* Basingstoke, UK: Palgrave Macmillan, 2010.

Bar-Yosef, Eitan. *The Holy Land in English Culture, 1799–1917: Palestine and the Question of Orientalism.* Oxford, UK: Oxford Univ. Press, 2005.

Begnal, Michael H. "Stephen's Terrible Parable." *James Joyce Quarterly* 23, no. 3 (Spring 1986): 355–57.

Behan, Brendan, and Alan Simpson. *The Complete Plays.* New York: Grove Press, 1978.

Bell, M. David. "The Search for Agendath Netaim: Some Progress but No Solution." *James Joyce Quarterly* 12, no. 3 (Spring 1975): 251–58.

Bender, Abby. "Irish-Mexican Solidarity and the San Patricio Battalion Flag." *Genre: Forms of Discourse and Culture* 36, no. 3 (Fall/Winter 2003): 271–93.

———. "The Language of the Outlaw: A Clarification." *James Joyce Quarterly* 44, no. 4 (Summer 2007): 807–12.

Berger, Harry. *Situated Utterances: Texts, Bodies, and Cultural Representations.* New York: Fordham Univ. Press, 2005.

Biddick, Kathleen. *The Typological Imaginary: Circumcision, Technology, History.* Philadelphia: Univ. of Pennsylvania Press, 2003.

Boehmer, Elleke. *Empire, the National, and the Postcolonial, 1890–1920: Resistance in Interaction.* Oxford, UK: Oxford Univ. Press, 2002.

Bornstein, George. *The Colors of Zion: Blacks, Jews, and Irish from 1845 to 1945.* Cambridge, MA: Harvard Univ. Press, 2011.

———. *Material Modernism: The Politics of the Page.* Cambridge, UK: Cambridge Univ. Press, 2001.

Boyarin, Daniel, and Jonathan Boyarin. "Diaspora: Generation and the Ground of Jewish Identity." *Critical Inquiry* 19, no. 4 (Summer 1993): 693–725.

Boyarin, Jonathan. "Reading Exodus into History." *New Literary History* 23, no. 3 (Summer 1992): 523–54.

Boyce, David George. *Nationalism in Ireland.* 3rd ed. London: Routledge, 1995.

Bracken, Damian. "The Fall and the Law in Early Ireland." In *Ireland and Europe in the Early Middle Ages*, edited by Próinséas Ní Chatháin and Michael Richter, 147–69. Dublin: Four Courts Press, 2002.

Braithwaite, William Stanley. "Lady Gregory's Plays." *New York Times*, Apr. 14, 1912.

Brannigan, John. *Race in Modern Irish Literature and Culture*. Edinburgh: Edinburgh Univ. Press, 2010.

Brennan, James. "Types of Irishmen. I.—The Imperialist." *Irish Freedom*, Aug. 15, 1911.

Briscoe, Robert, with Alden Hatch. *For the Life of Me*. Boston: Little, Brown, and Co., 1958.

Briskin, Irene Orgel. "Some New Light on 'The Parable of the Plums.'" *James Joyce Quarterly* 3, no. 4 (Summer 1966): 236–51.

Brown, Malcolm. *The Politics of Irish Literature: From Thomas Davis to W. B. Yeats*. Seattle: Univ. of Washington Press, 1973.

Buber, Martin. "On the Bible: Eighteen Studies." In *Exodus*, edited by Harold Bloom. New York: Chelsea House Publishers, 1987.

Bulhof, Francis. "Agendath Again." *James Joyce Quarterly* 7, no. 4 (Summer 1970): 326–31.

Burrowes, Arthur. "Fleshpots and Freedom." *Irish Review* 1 (Nov. 1911): 417–21.

Caball, Marc. "The Gaelic Mind and the Collapse of the Gaelic World: An Appraisal." *Cambridge Medieval Celtic Studies* 25 (Summer 1993): 87–96.

———. *Poets and Politics: Continuity and Reaction in Irish Poetry, 1558–1625*. Cork: Cork Univ. Press in association with Field Day, 1998.

Cairns, David, and Shaun Richards. *Writing Ireland: Colonialism, Nationalism, and Culture*. Manchester, UK: Manchester Univ. Press, 1988.

Canny, Nicholas. *Kingdom and Colony: Ireland in the Atlantic World, 1560–1800*. Baltimore, MD: Johns Hopkins Univ. Press, 1988.

Carew, Mairéad. *Tara and the Ark of the Covenant: A Search for the Ark of the Covenant by British-Israelites on the Hill of Tara (1899–1902)*. Dublin: Royal Irish Academy, 2003.

Carlyle, Thomas, ed. *Oliver Cromwell's Letters and Speeches*. London: Chapman and Hall, 1893.

Caruth, Cathy. *Unclaimed Experience: Trauma, Narrative, and History*. Baltimore, MD: Johns Hopkins Univ. Press, 1986.

Casement, Roger. *The Crime Against Europe: The Writings and Poetry of Roger Casement.* Edited by Herbert O. Mackey. Dublin: C. J. Fallon, 1958.

———. "The Language of the Outlaw." [1904 or 1905]. Box 2, folder 37, Maloney Collection of Irish Historical Papers, Manuscripts and Archives Division, New York Public Library.

Castle, Gregory. *Modernism and the Celtic Revival.* Cambridge, UK: Cambridge Univ. Press, 2001.

Casway, Jerrold. "Gaelic Maccabeanism: The Politics of Reconciliation." In *Political Thought in Seventeenth-Century Ireland: Kingdom or Colony*, edited by Jane Ohlmeyer, 176–90. Cambridge, UK: Cambridge Univ. Press, 2000.

Chavasse, Moirin. *Terence MacSwiney.* Dublin: Clonmore and Reynolds, 1961.

Cheng, Vincent. *Inauthentic: The Anxiety over Culture and Identity.* New Brunswick, NJ: Rutgers Univ. Press, 2004.

———. *Joyce, Race, and Empire.* Cambridge, UK: Cambridge Univ. Press, 1995.

Cheyette, Bryan. "The Boy Singer Goes Global." Review of Aamir Mufti's *Enlightenment in the Colony. Times Literary Supplement*, Mar. 21, 2008.

———. "'Jewgreek is greekjew': The Disturbing Ambivalence of Joyce's Semitic Discourse in *Ulysses.*" In *Joyce Studies Annual 1992*, edited by Thomas F. Staley, 32–56. Austin: Univ. of Texas Press, 1992.

Childers, Erskine B. "The Other Exodus." *Spectator*, May 12, 1961.

Clausen, Christopher. "Padraic Pearse: The Revolutionary as Artist." *Shaw Review* 19 (1976): 83–92.

Clayden, Tom, and Ian McBride, eds. Introduction to *Protestantism and National Identity: Britain and Ireland, c.1650–c.1850.* Cambridge, UK: Cambridge Univ. Press, 1998.

Cleary, Joe. *Literature, Partition and the Nation-State: Culture and Conflict in Ireland, Israel and Palestine.* Cambridge, UK: Cambridge Univ. Press, 2002.

Coffey, John. *Exodus and Liberation: Deliverance Politics from John Calvin to Martin Luther King Jr.* Oxford, UK: Oxford Univ. Press, 2014.

Cole, Sarah. *At the Violet Hour: Modernism and Violence in England and Ireland.* Oxford, UK: Oxford Univ. Press, 2012.

Collins, Michael. "Advance and Use Our Liberties." In *A Path to Freedom.* Cork: Mercier Press, 1996.

Colum, Mary. *Life and the Dream.* Garden City, NY: Doubleday, 1947.

Colum, Padraic, ed. *Anthology of Irish Verse.* New York: Boni and Liveright, 1922.

Costello, Peter. *The Heart Grown Brutal: The Irish Revolution in Literature, from Parnell to the Death of Yeats, 1891–1939.* Dublin: Gill and Macmillan, 1977.

Costello, Peter, and John Wyse Jackson. *John Stanislaus Joyce: The Voluminous Life and Genius of James Joyce's Father.* London: Fourth Estate, 1997.

Croatto, J. Severino. *Exodus: A Hermeneutics of Freedom.* Translated by Salvator Attanasio. Maryknoll, NY: Orbis Books, 1981.

Cullingford, Elizabeth. "How Jacques Molay Got Up the Tower: Yeats and the Irish Civil War." *ELH* 50, no. 4 (1983): 763–89.

———. *Ireland's Others: Ethnicity and Gender in Irish Literature and Popular Culture.* Notre Dame, IN: Univ. of Notre Dame Press in association with Field Day, 2001.

———. "Phoenician Genealogies and Oriental Geographies: Joyce, Language and Race." In *Semicolonial Joyce*, edited by Derek Attridge and Marjorie Howes, 219–39. Cambridge, UK: Cambridge Univ. Press, 2000.

———. "'Thinking of Her . . . as . . . Ireland': Yeats, Pearse and Heaney." *Textual Practice* 4, no. 1 (1990): 1–21.

Cunningham, Bernadette. "Native Culture and Political Change in Ireland, 1580–1640." In *Natives and Newcomers: Essays on the Making of Irish Colonial Society, 1534–1641*, edited by Ciaran Brady and Raymond Gillespie, 148–70. Dublin: Irish Academy Press, 1986.

Dalton, Charles. *With the Dublin Brigade.* London: Davies, 1929.

Davis, Roderick. "The Fourfold Moses in *Ulysses.*" *James Joyce Quarterly* 7, no. 2 (Winter 1970): 120–31.

Davison, Neil R. *James Joyce, "Ulysses," and the Construction of Jewish Identity.* Cambridge, UK: Cambridge Univ. Press, 1996.

———. "'Still an Idea behind It': Trieste, Jewishness, and Zionism in *Ulysses.*" *James Joyce Quarterly* 38, nos. 3–4 (Spring/Summer 2001): 373–94.

Davitt, Michael. *The Fall of Feudalism in Ireland.* London: Harper and Brothers, 1904.

———. "Ireland and the Jews: A Letter to the Editor." *Freeman's Journal*, July 13, 1893.

———. *Within the Pale: The True Story of Anti-Semitic Persecutions in Russia.* London: A. S. Barnes and Co., 1903.

Deane, Seamus. *Celtic Revivals: Essays in Modern Irish Literature, 1880–1980.* Winston-Salem, NC: Wake Forest Univ. Press, 1987.

———, ed. *The Field Day Anthology of Irish Writing.* 3 vols. Derry: Field Day, 1992.

———. "Heroic Styles: The Tradition of an Idea." In *Theorizing Ireland*, edited by Claire Connolly, 14–26. New York: Palgrave Macmillan, 2003.

———. "Wherever Green Is Read." In *Revising the Rising*, edited by Máirín Ní Dhonnchadha and Theo Dorgan, 91–105. Derry: Field Day, 1991.

Diner, Hasia. "The Accidental Irish: Jewish Migration to an Unlikely Place." Paper presented to the Shelby Cullom Davis Center for Historical Studies, Princeton Univ., Princeton, NJ, Apr. 4, 2003.

Douglas, Mary. *Purity and Danger: An Analysis of Concepts of Pollution and Taboo.* New York: Frederick A. Praeger, 1966.

Duffy, Charles Gavan, George Sigerson, and Douglas Hyde. *The Revival of Irish Literature.* London: T. Fisher Unwin, 1894.

Duffy, Enda. "Disappearing Dublin: *Ulysses*, Postcoloniality, and the Politics of Space." In *Semicolonial Joyce*, edited by Derek Attridge and Marjorie Howes, 37–57. Cambridge, UK: Cambridge Univ. Press, 2000.

———. *The Subaltern "Ulysses."* Minneapolis: Univ. of Minnesota Press, 1994.

Dunsany, Lord. *Five Plays.* Boston: Little, Brown, and Co., 1917.

Eccleshall, Robert. "Anglican Political Thought in the Century after the Revolution of 1688." In *Political Thought in Ireland since the Seventeenth Century*, edited by D. George Boyce, Robert Eccleshall, and Vincent Geoghegan, 39–72. London: Routledge, 1993.

Edgeworth, Maria. *The Life and Letters of Maria Edgeworth.* Vol. 2, edited by Augustus J. C. Hare. Boston: Houghton Mifflin, 1895.

Edwards, Ruth Dudley. *Patrick Pearse: The Triumph of Failure.* London: Victor Gollancz, 1977.

Eglinton, John. *Anglo-Irish Essays.* 1918. Reprint. Freeport, NY: Books for Libraries Press, 1968.

———. *Bards and Saints.* Dublin: Maunsel, 1906.

———. *Irish Literary Portraits.* London: Macmillan, 1935.

———. *Literary Ideals in Ireland*, with W. B. Yeats, et al. London: T. Fisher Unwin, 1899.

———. *Pebbles from a Brook*. Kilkenny, IRL: S. O'Grady, 1901.

———. *Two Essays on the Remnant*. Dublin: Whaley, 1894.

Ellmann, Richard. *The Consciousness of Joyce*. London: Faber, 1977.

———. *James Joyce*. Oxford, UK: Oxford Univ. Press, 1959.

———. *Yeats: The Man and the Masks*. London: Macmillan, 1948.

Fanon, Frantz. *The Wretched of the Earth*. New York: Grove Press, 1963.

Feiler, Bruce. *America's Prophet: Moses and the American Story*. New York: HarperCollins, 2009.

Feuer, Lewis. *Ideology and the Ideologists*. New York: Harper and Row, 1975.

Fogel, Daniel Mark. "Symbol and Context in *Ulysses*: Joyce's 'Bowl of Bitter Waters' and Passover." *ELH* 46, no. 4 (Winter 1979): 710–21.

Ford, Alan. "The Protestant Reformation." In *Natives and Newcomers: Essays on the Making of Irish Colonial Society, 1534–1641*, edited by Ciaran Brady and Raymond Gillespie, 50–74. Dublin: Irish Academy Press, 1986.

Foster, Roy. "Love, Politics and Textual Corruption: Mrs. O'Shea's Parnell." In *High and Low Moderns: Literature and Culture, 1889–1939*, edited by Maria DiBattista and Lucy McDiarmid, 197–211. New York: Oxford Univ. Press, 1996.

———. *Modern Ireland, 1600–1972*. London: Allen Lane, 1988.

———. *W. B. Yeats: A Life*. Vol. 2, *The Arch-Poet, 1915–1939*. Oxford, UK: Oxford Univ. Press, 2003.

Foucault, Michel. *The Foucault Reader*. Edited by Paul Rabinow. New York: Pantheon Books, 1984.

Fox, Everett, ed. *The Five Books of Moses: Genesis, Exodus, Leviticus, Numbers, Deuteronomy; a New Translation with Introductions, Commentary, and Notes, The Schocken Bible*. Vol. 1. New York: Schocken Books, 1995.

Frazier, Adrian. *Behind the Scenes: Yeats, Horniman, and the Struggle for the Abbey Theatre*. Berkeley: Univ. of California Press, 1990.

Freeman, Martin, trans. and ed. *The Annals of Connaught (A.D. 1224–1544)*. Dublin: Dublin Institute for Advanced Studies, 1944.

Freud, Sigmund. *Moses and Monotheism*. Translated by Katherine Jones. New York: Vintage Books, 1939.

Froude, James Anthony. *The English in Ireland in the Eighteenth Century*. Vol. 1. New York: Charles Scribner's Sons, 1888.

Frye, Northrop. *The Great Code: The Bible and Literature*. San Diego, CA: Harcourt, 1982.

"Gael." "A Note on Standish O'Grady." *Irish Review* 1 (1911): 215–17.

Garvin, Tom. *Mythical Thinking in Political Life: Reflections on Nationalism and Social Science.* Dublin: Maunsel, 2001.

———. *Nationalist Revolutionaries in Ireland, 1858–1928.* Oxford, UK: Clarendon Press, 1987.

———. "Priests and Patriots: Irish Separatism and Fear of the Modern, 1890–1914." *Irish Historical Studies* 25, no. 97 (May 1986): 67–81.

Gaster, M. "Judaism—A National Religion." In *Zionism and the Jewish Future*, edited by Harry Sacher, 87–98. London: John Murray, 1916.

Gibbons, Luke. *Transformations in Irish Culture.* Cork: Cork Univ. Press in association with Field Day, 1996.

Gibson, Andrew. *Joyce's Revenge: History, Politics, and Aesthetics in "Ulysses."* Oxford, UK: Oxford Univ. Press, 2002.

Gifford, Don, with Robert J. Seidman. *"Ulysses" Annotated: Notes for James Joyce's "Ulysses."* 2nd ed. Berkeley: Univ. of California Press, 1988.

Gillespie, Raymond. "Political Ideas and Their Social Contexts in 17th-Century Ireland." In *Political Thought in Seventeenth-Century Ireland: Kingdom or Colony*, edited by Jane Ohlmeyer, 107–30. Cambridge, UK: Cambridge Univ. Press, 2000.

Gillman, Neil. "Theologically Speaking." In *My People's Passover Haggadah.* Vol. 2, edited by Lawrence A. Hoffman and David Arnow. Woodstock, VT: Jewish Lights Publishing, 2008.

Gilroy, Paul. *The Black Atlantic: Modernity and Double Consciousness.* Cambridge, MA: Harvard Univ. Press, 1995.

Gladstone, W. E. *Special Aspects of the Irish Question: A Series of Reflections in and since 1886.* London: John Murray, 1892.

Glatzer, Nahum N., ed. *The Passover Haggadah.* New York: Schocken Books, 1953.

Glaude, Eddie S. *Exodus! Religion, Race, and Nation in Early Nineteenth-Century Black America.* Chicago: Univ. of Chicago Press, 2000.

Gorman, Herbert. *James Joyce.* New York: Rinehart, 1948.

Gray, Peter. *The Irish Famine.* New York: Harry N. Abrams, 1995.

Gregory, Augusta. *Collected Plays of Lady Gregory.* Coole Edition. Edited by Ann Saddlemyer. Gerrards Cross, UK: Colin Smythe; New York: Oxford Univ. Press, 1970.

———. *Lady Gregory's Journals.* Coole Edition. Edited by Daniel J. Murphy. Gerrards Cross, UK: Colin Smythe, 1978–87.

———. *Our Irish Theatre: A Chapter of Autobiography by Lady Gregory.* Coole Edition. New York: Oxford Univ. Press, 1972.

———. *Selected Writings.* Edited by Lucy McDiarmid and Maureen Waters. New York: Penguin, 1995.

———. *Seventy Years: Being the Autobiography of Lady Gregory.* Coole Edition. Edited by Colin Smythe. New York: Oxford Univ. Press, 1974.

———. *Visions and Beliefs in the West of Ireland, with two essays and notes by W. B. Yeats.* Coole Edition. New York: Oxford Univ. Press, 1970.

Grene, Nicholas. *The Politics of Irish Drama: Plays in Context from Boucicault to Friel.* Cambridge, UK: Cambridge Univ. Press, 1999.

Griffith, Arthur. *The Resurrection of Hungary: A Parallel for Ireland.* Dublin: James Duffy and Co., 1904.

Gutierrez, Gustavo. *A Theology of Liberation: History, Politics, and Salvation.* Maryknoll, NY: Orbis Books, 1973.

Gwynn, Stephen. *The Fair Hills of Ireland.* Dublin: Maunsel, 1906.

———. *Thomas Moore.* London: MacMillan and Co., 1905.

Hagan, Edward A. "The Aryan Myth: A Nineteenth-Century Anglo-Irish Will to Power." In *Ideology and Ireland in the Nineteenth Century,* edited by Tadhg Foley and Sean Ryder, 197–205. Dublin: Four Courts Press, 1998.

Hamilton, George. Application 674, in *Parliamentary Papers, House of Commons and Command, Parts 1–2,* "Public Petitions delivered June 21, containing petitions presented June 11–13, 1845." Accessed July 7, 2009. https://books.google.com.

Hammer, Reuven, trans. and ed. *The Classic Midrash: Tannaitic Commentaries on the Bible.* New York: Paulist Press, 1995.

Handelman, Susan A. *The Slayers of Moses: The Emergence of Rabbinic Interpretation in Modern Literary Theory.* Albany: State Univ. of New York Press, 1982.

Hannay, James Owen. [George Birmingham]. *The Lost Tribes.* New York: Thomas Nelson and Sons, 1915.

Harrington, James. *The Oceana and other works of Iames Harrington, with an account of his life by Iohn Toland.* London: T. Becket and T. Cadell, 1771.

Harris, Susan. *Gender and Modern Irish Drama.* Bloomington: Indiana Univ. Press, 2002.

Hardt, Michael, and Antonio Negri. *Empire.* Cambridge, MA: Harvard Univ. Press, 2000.

Hart, William. *Edward Said and the Religious Effects of Culture.* Cambridge, UK: Cambridge Univ. Press, 2000.

Harte, Frank, ed. *Songs of Dublin.* Cork: Ossian, 1993.

Heijermans, Herman. *Ahasverus; A Play in One Act*, translated by Caroline Heijermans-Houwink and J. J. Houwink. Boston: Walter H. Baker Co., c.1934.

Hennig, John. "The Literary Tradition of Moses in Ireland." In *Traditio: Studies in Ancient and Medieval History, Thought and Religion.* Vol. 7. New York: Fordham Univ. Press, 1949–51.

Henshke, David. "'The Lord Brought Us Forth from Egypt': On the Absence of Moses in the Passover Haggadah." *AJS Review* 31, no. 1 (2007): 61–73.

Herzl, Theodor. *The Jewish State.* Translated by Sylvie D'Avigdor. New York: Dover, 1988.

Hill, Judith. *Lady Gregory: An Irish Life.* Gloucestershire, UK: Sutton Publishing, 2005.

Hine, Edward. *Forty-Seven Identifications of the British Nation with the Lost Ten Tribes of Israel founded upon Five Hundred Scripture Proofs.* London: W. H. Guest and S. W. Partridge and Co., 1874.

Hoffman, Lawrence A., and David Arnow. *My People's Passover Haggadah: Traditional Texts, Modern Commentaries.* Vols. 1 and 2. Woodstock, VT: Jewish Lights Publishing, 2008.

Holloway, Joseph. *The Diaries of Joseph Holloway: From the National Library of Ireland, Dublin, 1895–1944. Manuscripts of the Irish Literary Renaissance*, series 1. Reading: Berkshire Research Publications, 1988. 105 Reels.

———. *Joseph Holloway's Abbey Theatre: A Selection from His Unpublished Journal, Impressions of a Dublin Playgoer*, edited by Robert Hogan. Carbondale: Southern Illinois Univ. Press, 1967.

Hone, Joseph. *The Life of George Moore.* New York: Macmillan, 1936.

Howarth, Herbert. *The Irish Writers, 1880–1940: Literature under Parnell's Star.* London: Rockliff, 1958.

Howes, Marjorie. "'Goodbye Ireland I'm going to Gort': Geography, Scale, and Narrating the Nation." In *Semicolonial Joyce*, edited by Derek Attridge and Marjorie Howes, 58–77. Cambridge, UK: Cambridge Univ. Press, 2000.

———. "Tears and Blood: Lady Wilde and the Emergence of Irish Cultural Nationalism." In *Ideology and Ireland in the Nineteenth Century*, edited by Tadhg Foley and Sean Ryder, 151–72. Dublin: Four Courts Press, 1998.

———. *Yeats's Nations: Gender, Class, and Irishness*. Cambridge, UK: Cambridge Univ. Press, 1996.

Howlett, Thomas Rosling. *Anglo-Israel, The Jewish Problem and Supplement: The Ten Lost Tribes of Israel Found and Identified in the Anglo-Saxon Race*. London: 1892.

Hull, J. *An Exposition upon a part of the Lamentations of Ieremie: lectured at Corke in Ireland*. London: Bernard Alsop, 1618.

Humoriensis, Gulielmus Dubliniensis. *Memoir of the Great Original Zozimus (Michael Moran), the Celebrated Dublin Street Rhymer and Reciter: With His Songs, Sayings, and Recitations*. Dublin: McGlashen and Gill, 1871.

Hyde, Douglas. "The Necessity for De-Anglicising Ireland." In *The Revival of Irish Literature: Addresses by Charles Gavan Duffy, K. C. M. G., Dr. George Sigerson, Dr. Douglas Hyde*. London: T. Fisher Unwin, 1894.

Hyman, Louis. *The Jews of Ireland from Earliest Times to the Year 1910*. Shannon: Irish Univ. Press, 1972.

Innes, C. L. *Woman and Nation in Irish Literature and Society, 1880–1935*. Athens: Univ. of Georgia Press, 1993.

Jabès, Edmond. *The Book of Resemblances II, Intimations, The Desert*. Translated by Rosmarie Waldrop. Hanover: Wesleyan Univ. Press, 1991.

Jameson, Frederic. *The Political Unconscious: Narrative as a Socially Symbolic Act*. Ithaca, NY: Cornell Univ. Press, 1981.

Jeffares, A. Norman, and Peter Van De Camp, eds. *Irish Literature: The Nineteenth Century*. 3 vols. Dublin: Irish Academic Press, 2007.

Jewish Historical Society of England. *Transactions of the Jewish Historical Society of England*. Vol. 4. London: Jewish Historical Society of England, 2009.

Johnston, Denis. *Selected Plays of Denis Johnston*. Edited by Joseph Ronsley. Washington DC: Catholic Univ. of America Press, 1983.

Joyce, James. *The Critical Writings*. Edited by Ellsworth Mason and Richard Ellmann. Ithaca, NY: Cornell Univ. Press, 1989.

———. *Joyce's "Ulysses" Notesheets in the British Museum*. Edited by Philip F. Herring. Charlottesville: Univ. of Virginia Press, 1972.

———. *A Portrait of the Artist as a Young Man*. New York: Penguin Books, 1993.

———. *Selected Letters of James Joyce.* Edited by Richard Ellmann. New York: Viking Press, 1975.

———. *Ulysses.* Facsimile of 1922 first edition. Oxford World's Classics. Edited by Jeri Johnson. Oxford, UK: Oxford Univ. Press, 1993. Reissued 2008.

———. *Ulysses.* Paris: Shakespeare and Co., 1922.

Joyce, Stanislaus. Preface to *As a Man Grows Older*, by Italo Svevo. Translated by Beryl De Zoete. New York: New York Review of Books, 2001.

Katz, David S. *God's Last Words: Reading the English Bible from the Reformation to Fundamentalism.* New Haven: Yale Univ. Press, 2004.

Keane, Damien. "Quotation Marks, the Gramophone Record, and the Language of the Outlaw." *Texas Studies in Literature and Language* 51, no. 4 (Winter 2009): 400–415.

Keating, Geoffrey. *Foras Feasa ar Éirinn.* Translated by John O'Mahony. New York: P. M. Haverty, 1857.

Kearney, Hugh. *Ireland: Contested Ideas of Nationalism and History.* New York: New York Univ. Press, 2007.

Kearney, Richard. "Towards a Postnationalist Archipelago." *Edinburgh Review: New Writing and Critical Thought* 103 (2000): 21–35.

Kedourie, Elie. *Nationalism.* 4th expanded ed. Oxford, UK: Blackwell, 1993.

Kelleher, Margaret, and Philip O'Leary, eds. *The Cambridge History of Irish Literature.* Cambridge, UK: Cambridge Univ. Press, 2006.

Kelly, John. "The End of Parnellism and the Ideological Dilemmas of Sinn Féin." In *Ireland in Transition, 1867–1921*, edited by D. George Boyce and Alan O'Day, 130–78. New York: Routledge, 2004.

———. "The Fall of Parnell and the Rise of Anglo-Irish Literature: An Investigation." *Anglo-Irish Studies* 2 (1976): 1–23.

———. "Parnell in Irish Literature." In *Parnell in Perspective*, edited by D. George Boyce and Alan O'Day, 242–83. New York: Routledge, 1991.

Kelly, Ronan. *Bard of Erin: The Life of Thomas Moore.* Dublin: Penguin Ireland, 2009.

Kenner, Hugh. *Ulysses.* London: G. Allen and Unwin, 1980.

Keogh, Dermot. *Jews in Twentieth-Century Ireland: Refugees, Anti-Semitism and the Holocaust.* Cork: Cork Univ. Press, 1998.

Keough, Dermot, and Andrew McCarthy. *Limerick Boycott 1904: Anti-Semitism in Ireland.* Cork: Mercier Press, 2005.

Kiberd, Declan. *Inventing Ireland.* Cambridge, MA: Harvard Univ. Press, 1995.

———. "Patrick Pearse: Irish Modernist." In *The Life and After-Life of PH Pearse / Padraic Mac Piarais: Saol agus Oidhreacht*, edited by Roisín Higgins and Regina Uí Chollatáin, 65–85. Dublin: Irish Academic Press, 2009.

Kidd, Colin. *British Identities before Nationalism: Ethnicity and Nationhood in the Atlantic World, 1600–1800.* Cambridge, UK: Cambridge Univ. Press, 1999.

———. *The Forging of Races: Race and Scripture in the Protestant Atlantic World, 1600–2000.* New York: Cambridge Univ. Press, 2006.

Killeen, Jarlath. *Gothic Ireland: Horror and the Irish Anglican Imagination in the Long Eighteenth Century.* Dublin: Four Courts Press, 2005.

Kinsella, Thomas, trans., and Seán Ó Tuama, ed. *An Duanaire, 1600–1900: Poems of the Dispossessed.* Mountrath, IRL: Dolmen Press, 1981.

Kirk, J. Andrew. *Liberation Theology: An Evangelical View from the Third World.* Atlanta, GA: John Knox, 1979.

Knowles, Sebastian. "Après Mot, Le Deluge." Review of *James Joyce: The Complete Recordings; Music from the Work of James Joyce. James Joyce Literary Supplement* 18 (Autumn 2004): 23.

Kopper, Edward A. *Lady Isabella Persse Gregory.* Boston: Twayne, 1976.

Korshin, Paul J. *Typologies in England, 1650–1820.* Princeton, NJ: Princeton Univ. Press, 1982.

Krause, David. *The Regeneration of Ireland: Renaissance and Revolution.* Bethesda, MD: Academic Press, 2001.

Laffan, Michael. "Insular Attitudes: The Revisionists and Their Critics." In *Revising the Rising*, edited by Máirín Ní Dhonnchadha and Theo Dorgan, 106–21. Derry: Field Day, 1991.

Lee, J. J. "In Search of Patrick Pearse." In *Revising the Rising*, edited by Máirín Ní Dhonnchadha and Theo Dorgan, 122–38. Derry: Field Day, 1991.

———. *Ireland, 1912–1985: Politics and Society.* Cambridge, UK: Cambridge Univ. Press, 1989.

———. "Patrick Pearse." In *Dictionary of Irish Biography*, edited by James McGuire and James Quinn. Cambridge, UK: Cambridge Univ. Press, 2009. http://dib.cambridge.org.

Leerssen, Joep. *Mere Irish and Fíor-Ghael: Studies in the Idea of Irish Nationality, Its Development and Literary Expression Prior to the Nineteenth Century.* Cork: Cork Univ. Press in association with Field Day, 1996.

———. *Remembrance and Imagination: Patterns in the Historical and Literary Representation of Ireland in the Nineteenth Century.* Cork: Cork Univ. Press in association with Field Day, 1996.

Lennon, Joseph. *Irish Orientalism: A Literary and Intellectual History.* Syracuse, NY: Syracuse Univ. Press, 2004.

Levitas, Ben. *The Theatre of Nation: Irish Drama and Cultural Nationalism, 1890–1916.* Oxford, UK: Clarendon Press, 2002.

———. "Yeats and the Ireland of Synge's Time." Lecture at New York Univ., Glucksman Ireland House. Apr. 1, 2004.

Levitt, Morton P. "The Family of Bloom." In *New Light on Joyce from the Dublin Symposium*, edited by Fritz Senn, 141–48. Bloomington: Univ. of Indiana Press, 1972.

Linebaugh, Peter, and Marcus Rediker. *The Many-Headed Hydra: Sailors, Slaves, Commoners, and the Hidden History of the Revolutionary Atlantic.* Boston: Beacon, 2000.

Lloyd, David. *Anomalous States: Irish Writing and the Post-Colonial Moment.* Dublin: Lilliput Press, 1993.

———. *Ireland after History.* Cork: Cork Univ. Press in association with Field Day, 1999.

Longley, Edna. *The Living Stream: Literature and Revisionism in Ireland.* Newcastle upon Tyne, UK: Bloodaxe Books, 1994.

Lynd, Robert. *Old and New Masters.* Freeport, NY: Books for Libraries Press, 1970.

Lyons, F. S. L. *Charles Stewart Parnell.* New York: Oxford Univ. Press, 1977.

———. *Culture and Anarchy in Ireland, 1890–1939.* Oxford, UK: Clarendon Press, 1979.

———. *The Fall of Parnell.* London: Routledge and Kegan Paul, 1960.

———. *Ireland since the Famine.* London: Weidenfeld and Nicolson, 1971.

———. "The Parnell Theme in Literature." In *Place, Personality and the Irish Writer*, edited by Andrew Carpenter, 69–95. New York: Harper and Row, 1977.

Lyons, J. B. *What Did I Die of?: The Deaths of Parnell, Wilde, Synge, and Other Literary Pathologies.* Dublin: Lilliput Press, 1991.

MacAlister, R. A. Stewart, ed. and trans. *Lebor Gabála Érenn* [The Book of the Taking of Ireland]. Part 2. Dublin: Irish Texts Society, 1939.

MacDonagh, Thomas. *The Exodus: A Sacred Cantata.* Dublin: Doremi and Co., 1904.

MacKenzie, Niall. "'Dougal MacCullony, I am glad to see thee!': Gaelic Etymology, Jacobite Culture, and 'Exodus Politics.'" *Scottish Studies Review* 2, no. 2 (Fall 2001): 29–59.

Mandelbrote, Scott. "The Bible and National Identity in the British Isles, c.1650–c.1750." In *Protestantism and National Identity: Britain and Ireland, c.1650–c.1850*, edited by Tony Claydon, 157–81. Cambridge, UK: Cambridge Univ. Press, 1998.

Manganiello, Dominic. *Joyce's Politics.* London: Routledge, 1980.

Mann, Thomas. *The Tables of the Law*, translated by Marion Faber and Stephen Lehmann. Philadelphia: Paul Dry Books, 2010.

Mathews, P. J. *Revival: The Abbey Theatre, Sinn Féin, the Gaelic League and the Co-operative Movement.* Cork: Cork Univ. Press in association with Field Day, 2003.

Mays, Michael. *Nation States: The Culture of Irish Nationalism.* Plymouth, UK: Lexington Books, 2007.

McBride, Ian. *Scripture Politics: Ulster Presbyterians and Irish Radicalism in the Late Eighteenth Century.* New York: Clarendon Press, 1998.

McBride, Lawrence W. *Images, Icons, and the Irish Nationalist Imagination.* Dublin: Four Courts Press, 1999.

McCone, Kim. *Pagan Past and Christian Present.* Maynooth, IRL: Maynooth Univ. Press, 1990.

McCourt, John. *The Years of Bloom: James Joyce in Trieste, 1904–1920.* Madison: Univ. of Wisconsin Press, 2000.

McCrea, Barry. "Family and Form in *Ulysses.*" *Field Day Review* 5 (2009): 75–93.

McDiarmid, Lucy. "The Demotic Lady Gregory." In *High and Low Moderns: Literature and Culture, 1889–1939*, edited by Maria DiBattista and Lucy McDiarmid, 212–34. Oxford, UK: Oxford Univ. Press, 1996.

———. *The Irish Art of Controversy.* Ithaca, NY: Cornell Univ. Press, 2005.

———. "Lady Gregory, Wilfrid Blunt, and London Table Talk." *Irish University Review* 34, no. 1 (Spring/Summer 2004): 67–80.

———. *Poets and the Peacock Dinner: The Literary History of a Meal.* Oxford, UK: Oxford Univ. Press, 2014.

McDiarmid, Lucy, and Maureen Waters. Introduction to *Lady Gregory: Selected Writings*, edited by Lucy McDiarmid and Maureen Waters. London: Penguin, 1995.

McQuillan, Peter. *Native and Natural: Aspects of the Concepts of 'Right' and 'Freedom' in Irish.* Cork: Cork Univ. Press, 2004.

Meigs, Samantha A. *The Reformations in Ireland: Tradition and Confessionalism, 1400–1690.* New York: St. Martin's Press, 1997.

Mercanton, Jacques. "The Hours of James Joyce." In *Portraits of the Artist in Exile*, edited by Willard Potts. London: Harcourt Brace Jovanovich, 1986.

Miller, Kerby. "Emigration, Capitalism, and Ideology in Post-Famine Ireland." In *Migrations: The Irish at Home and Abroad*, edited by Richard Kearney, 91–108. Dublin: Wolfhound Press, 1990.

Miller, Rory. *Ireland and the Palestine Question.* Dublin: Irish Academic Press, 2005.

Mitchell, Angus. "'An Irish Putomayo': Roger Casement's Humanitarian Relief Campaign among the Connemara Islanders, 1913–14." *Irish Economic and Social History* 31 (2004): 41–60.

———. "John Bull's Other Empire: Roger Casement and the Press, 1898–1916." In *Newspapers and Empire in Ireland and Britain: Reporting the British Empire, c.1857–1921*, edited by Simon J. Potter, 217–33. Dublin: Four Courts Press, 2004.

Montgomery, Benilde. "The Presence of Parnell in Three Plays by Lady Gregory." In *Irish Renaissance Annual III*, edited by Dennis Jackson, 106–23. Newark: Univ. of Delaware Press, 1982.

Moore, George. *The Apostle: A Drama in Three Acts.* Dublin: Maunsel, 1911.

———. *The Brook Kerith: A Syrian Story.* New York: Macmillan, 1917.

———. *Hail and Farewell: Ave, Salve, Vale.* Edited by Richard Allen Cave. Washington, DC: Catholic Univ. of America Press, 1985.

———. *The Lake.* Gerrards Cross, UK: Colin Smythe, 1980.

———. *The Passing of the Essenes, a Drama in Three Acts.* Rev. ed. London: Heinemann, 1931.

———. *Selected Plays of George Moore and Edward Martyn.* Gerrards Cross, UK: Colin Smythe, 1995.

Moore, Thomas. *Moore's Irish Melodies: The Illustrated 1846 Edition.* Reprint. Mineola, NY: Dover Publications, 2000.

———. *Memoirs of Captain Rock, the Celebrated Irish Chieftain, with Some Account of His Ancestors. Written by Himself.* Edited by Emer Nolan. Dublin: Field Day, 2008.

———. *Irish Melodies and Sacred Songs.* New York: Oakley, Mason and Co., 1869.

———. *The Journal of Thomas Moore.* Vol. 1. Edited by Wilfred S. Dowden. Newark: Univ. of Delaware Press, 1983.

Moran, D. P. Editorial in the *Leader*, Apr. 27, 1901.

Moran, Patrick Francis. *Historical Sketch of the Persecutions Suffered by the Catholics of Ireland under the Rule of Cromwell and the Puritans.* Dublin: James Duffy, 1862.

Moseley, Virginia Douglas. *Joyce and the Bible.* De Kalb: Northern Illinois Univ. Press, 1967.

Moses, Michael Valdez. "The Irish Vampire: *Dracula*, Parnell, and the Troubled Dreams of Nationhood." *Journal X: A Journal in Culture and Criticism* 2, no. 1 (Autumn 1997): 67–111.

Mufti, Aamir R. "Critical Secularism: A Reintroduction for Perilous Times." *Boundary 2* 31, no. 2 (2004): 1–9.

Muldoon, Paul. *To Ireland, I.* New York: Oxford Univ. Press, 2000.

Murphy, Andrew. *But the Irish Sea Betwixt Us: Ireland, Colonialism, and Renaissance Literature.* Lexington: Univ. Press of Kentucky, 1999.

Murphy, James H. *Catholic Fiction and Social Reality in Ireland, 1873–1922.* Westport, CT: Greenwood Press, 1997.

Murphy, William Michael. *The Parnell Myth and Irish Politics, 1891–1956.* New York: Peter Land Publishing, 1986.

Nadel, Ira. B. *Joyce and the Jews: Culture and Texts.* London: Macmillan, 1989.

Nelson, Bruce. *Irish Nationalists and the Making of the Irish Race.* Princeton, NJ: Princeton Univ. Press, 2012.

Newsinger, John. "'I Bring Not Peace but a Sword': The Religious Motif in the Irish War of Independence." *Journal of Contemporary History* 13, no. 3 (1978): 609–28.

Ní Catháin, Próinséas, and Michael Richter. *Ireland and Europe in the Early Middle Ages: Texts and Transmission.* Dublin: Four Courts Press, 2002.

Nolan, Emer, ed. *Memoirs of Captain Rock, the Celebrated Irish Chieftain, with Some Account of His Ancestors. Written by Himself.* Dublin: Field Day, 2008.

———. *Catholic Emancipations: Irish Fiction from Thomas Moore to James Joyce*. Syracuse, NY: Syracuse Univ. Press, 2007.

———. *James Joyce and Nationalism*. New York: Routledge, 1995.

Norris, Margot. "Stephen Dedalus's Anti-Semitic Ballad: A Sabotaged Climax in Joyce's *Ulysses*." In *De-familiarizing Readings: Essays from the Austin Joyce Conference*, edited by Alan W. Friedman and Charles Rossman, 65–86. European Joyce Studies 18. Amsterdam: Rodopi, 2009.

Norstedt, Johann A. *Thomas MacDonagh: A Critical Biography*. Charlottesville: Univ. Press of Virginia, 1980.

Ó Baoill, Dónall. "A Poem on the Downfall of the Gaoidhil." *Wars and Conflict: The Plantation of Ulster*. Accessed Aug. 4, 2014. http://www.bbc.co.uk/history/british/plantation/bardic/poem08.shtml.

Ó Braonaia, An tAthair Cathaoir. *Béarla Sacsan agus an Creideamh nÉirinn* [The English Language and the Faith in Ireland]. Dublin: M. H. MacGuill agus a Mhac, 1913.

O'Brien, Conor Cruise. *Ancestral Voices: Religion and Nationalism in Ireland*. Dublin: Poolbeg, 1994.

———. *God Land: Reflections on Religion and Nationalism*. Cambridge, MA: Harvard Univ. Press, 1988.

———. *Parnell and His Party, 1880–90*. Oxford, UK: Clarendon Press, 1968.

O'Brien, R. Barry. *The Life of Charles Stewart Parnell, Part 1*. New York: Harper and Brothers, 1898.

O'Brien, William. *The Parnell of Real Life*. London: T. F. Unwin, 1926.

Ó Buachalla, Breandán. "James our True King: The Ideology of Irish Royalism in the Seventeenth Century." In *Political Thought in Ireland since the Seventeenth Century*, edited by D. George Boyce, Robert Eccleshall, and Vincent Geoghegan, 7–35. London: Routledge, 1993.

———. "Poetry and Politics in Early Modern Ireland." *Eighteenth-Century Ireland* 7 (1992): 149–75.

Ó Cléirigh, Lughaidh. *The Life of Aodh Ruadh Ó Domhnaill: Transcribed from the Book of Lughaidh Ó Cléirigh*, edited by Paul Walsh. Dublin: Irish Texts Society, 1957.

Ó Cléirigh, Séamus. *Casement and the Irish Language: Culture and History*. Baile Átha Cliath [Dublin]: Clódhanna Teoranta, 1977.

O'Conor, Charles. *Dissertations on the Ancient History of Ireland*. Dublin: 1753.

Ó Faoláin, Seán. *De Valera*. Harmondsworth, UK: Penguin, 1939.

Ó Gráda, Cormac. *Jewish Ireland in the Age of Joyce: A Socioeconomic History*. Princeton, NJ: Princeton Univ. Press, 2006.

———. "Lost in Little Jerusalem: Leopold Bloom and Irish Jewry." *Journal of Modern Literature* 27, no. 4 (Summer 2004): 17–26.

O'Grady, Standish. *The Story of Ireland*. London: Methuen and Co., 1894.

Ó hAnnracháin, Tadhg. "'Though Hereticks and Poilitician Should Misinterpret Their Goode Zeale': Political Ideology and Catholicism in Early Modern Ireland." In *Political Thought in Seventeenth-Century Ireland: Kingdom or Colony*, edited by Jane Ohlmeyer, 155–75. Cambridge, UK: Cambridge Univ. Press, 2000.

O'Hara, M. M. *Chief and Tribune: Parnell and Davitt*. Dublin: Maunsel, 1919.

O'Hart, John. *Irish Pedigrees; Or, the Origin and Stem of the Irish Nation*. 5th ed. Vol. 1. Dublin: James Duffy and Co., 1892.

O'Hegarty, P. S. *A Bibliography of Roger Casement*. Dublin: Alex, Thom, 1949.

Ó hÓgáin, Dáithí. *The Hero in Irish Folk History*. Dublin: Gill and Macmillan, 1985.

O'Kelly, Seamas. *The Parnellite*. Naas, IRL: Leinster Leader, 1919.

O'Leary, Philip. *The Prose Literature of the Gaelic Revival, 1881–1921: Ideology and Innovation*. University Park: Pennsylvania State Univ. Press, 1994.

O'Neill, George. "The Inauguration of the Irish Literary Theatre." *New Ireland Review* 11, no. 4 (June 1899): 249.

O'Shea, Ita. "The Irish Messiah—A Vision." *Irish Review* (Jan. 1914): 553–55.

Ostriker, Alicia Suskin. *The Nakedness of the Fathers: Biblical Visions and Revisions*. New Brunswick, NJ: Rutgers Univ. Press, 1994.

Pardes, Ilana. *The Biography of Ancient Israel: National Narratives in the Bible*. Berkeley: Univ. of California Press, 2000.

Parnell, Fanny. "Michael Davitt." *Pilot* 43 (Dec. 19, 1880): 1.

Pearse, Mary Brigid, ed. *The Home-Life of Padraig Pearse as Told by Himself, His Family and Friends*. Dublin: Browne and Nolan, 1934.

Pearse, Pádraic (Patrick) H. *Collected Works of Pádraic H. Pearse: Plays, Stories, Poems*. Dublin: Phoenix, 1917.

———. *Collected Works of Pádraic H. Pearse: Political Writings and Speeches*. Dublin: Phoenix, 1924.

———. Editorial in *Gaelic American*, Mar. 7, 1914.

———. "An English Censorship in Ireland." *An Claidheamh Soluis*, Aug. 28, 1909.

———. *The Letters of P. H. Pearse.* Edited by Séamas Ó Buachalla. Atlantic Highlands, NJ: Humanities Press, 1980.

———. Letter to the editor of *An Claidheamh Soluis*, May 20, 1899.

———. "Mionn." *An Barr Buadh*, Apr. 5, 1912.

———. Review of *The Playboy of the Western World. An Claidheamh Soluis*, Feb. 9, 1907.

———. Review of *Kathleen ni Houlihan. An Claidheamh Soluis*, July 10, 1905.

———. "Some Thoughts." *An Claidheamh Soluis*, Feb. 10, 1906.

Pethica, James. "'Our Kathleen': Yeats's Collaboration with Lady Gregory in the Writing of *Cathleen ni Houlihan*." In *Yeats Annual 6*, edited by Warwick Gould, 3–31. London: Macmillan, 1988.

Petty, William. *Collected Works of William Petty.* Edited by T. Hutchinson. New York: Routledge, 1998

Platt, Len. *Joyce and the Anglo-Irish: A Study of Joyce and the Literary Revival.* Amsterdam: Rodopi, 1998.

Porter, Raymond J. "Language and Literature in Revival Ireland: The Views of P. H. Pearse." In *Modern Irish Literature: Essays in Honor of William York Tindall*, edited by Raymond J. Porter and James D. Brophy, 195–214. New York: Iona College Press, 1972.

Potts, Willard. *Joyce and the Two Irelands.* Austin: Univ. of Texas Press, 2001.

———, ed. *Portraits of the Artist in Exile: Recollections of James Joyce by Europeans.* New York: Harcourt, 1986.

Quigley, John. "The History of the Irish Bible." *Irish Church Quarterly* 10, no. 37 (Jan. 1917): 49–69.

Quinn, Antoinette. "Introduction to Lady Wilde." In *The Field Day Anthology of Irish Literature.* Vol. 5, edited by Angela Bourke. New York: New York Univ. Press, 2002.

Ra'ad, Basem L. "Primal Scenes of Globalization: Legacies of Canaan and Etruria." *PMLA* 116, no. 1 (Jan. 2001): 89–110.

Raboteau, Albert J. "African-Americans, Exodus, and the American Israel." In *African-American Christianity*, edited by Paul E. Johnson, 1–17. Berkeley: Univ. of California Press, 1994.

Ragussis, Michael. *Figures of Conversion: "The Jewish Question" and English National Identity.* Durham, NC: Duke Univ. Press, 1995.

Raz-Krakotzkin, Amnon. "Jewish Memory between Exile and History." *Jewish Quarterly Review* 97, no. 4 (Fall 2007): 530–43.

Reilly, Eileen. "'The Very Best Kind of Fiction': James Owen Hannay ('George A. Birmingham') and the Gaelic League." In *Encountering Ireland: Poetry, Politics and Prose since 1880*, edited by Alan Marshall and Neil Sammells, 49–58. London: Sulis Press, 1998.

Reizbaum, Marilyn. *James Joyce's Judaic Other.* Stanford, CA: Stanford Univ. Press, 1999.

———. "The Minor Work of James Joyce." *James Joyce Quarterly* 30, no. 2 (Winter 1993): 177–89.

———. "Urban Legends." *Éire-Ireland* 45, nos. 1–2 (Spring/Summer 2010): 242–65.

Regan, Stephen, ed. *Irish Writing: An Anthology of Irish Literature in English, 1789–1939.* Oxford, UK: Oxford Univ. Press, 2004.

Renan, Ernest. *The Poetry of the Celtic Races, and Other Studies by Ernest Renan.* Translated by William G. Hutchison. Port Washington, NY: Kennikat Press, 1896.

Richardson, Hilary. "Biblical Imagery and the Heavenly Jerusalem in the *Book of Armagh* and the *Book of Kells.*" In *Ireland and Europe in the Early Middle Ages*, edited by Próinséas Ní Chatháin and Michael Richter, 205–14. Dublin: Four Courts Press, 2002.

Robinson, Lennox. *The Lost Leader.* Dublin: T. Kiersey, 1918.

Rogers, Edward. *Some Account of the Life and Opinions of a Fifth-Monarchy Man.* London: N.p., 1867.

Rogers, John. *Ohel or Beth-Shemesh: A Tabernacle for the Sun.* London: N.p., 1653.

Rose, Jacqueline. *The Last Resistance.* London: Verso, 2007.

———. *The Question of Zion.* Princeton, NJ: Princeton Univ. Press, 2005.

———. "Response to Edward Said." In *Freud and the Non-European*, by Edward Said, 65–79. London: Verso, in association with the Freud Museum, London, 2003.

Roughley, Alan. *Reading Derrida Reading Joyce.* Gainesville: Univ. Press of Florida, 1999.

Ryan, Desmond. *The Man Called Pearse.* Dublin: Maunsel, 1919.

———. *The Story of a Success.* Dublin: Maunsel, 1918.

Sacher, Harry. "A Century of Jewish History." In *Zionism and the Jewish Future*, edited by Harry Sacher, 12–58. London: John Murray, 1916.

———, ed. *Zionism and the Jewish Future.* London: John Murray, 1916.

Saddlemyer, Ann. *In Defense of Lady Gregory.* Dublin: Dolmen, 1966.

Said, Edward. *Freud and the Non-European.* London: Verso, in association with the Freud Museum, London, 2003.

———. "Michael Walzer's *Exodus and Revolution*: A Canaanite Reading." *Grand Street* 5, no. 2 (Winter 1986): 86–106.

———. "Reflections on Ireland and Postcolonialism" (afterword). In *Ireland and Postcolonial Theory*, edited by Clare Carroll and Patricia King, 177–85. Cork: Cork Univ. Press, 2003.

———. "Reply to Michael Walzer." *Grand Street* 5, no. 4 (Summer 1986): 252–59.

Sammells, Neil. "Yeats, Exile and Childhood." In *Irish Writing: Exile and Subversion*, edited by Paul Hyland and Neil Sammells. London: Macmillan, 1991.

Schneidau, Herbert N. *Sacred Discontent: The Bible and Western Tradition.* Berkeley: Univ. of California Press, 1976.

Schreiber, Maeera. "The End of Exile: Jewish Identity and Its Diasporic Poetics." *PMLA* 113, no. 2 (Mar. 1998): 273–87.

Schwarz, Daniel. *Reading Joyce's "Ulysses."* New York: Palgrave Macmillan, 1987.

Scott, Bonnie K. "John Eglinton: A Model for Joyce's Individualism." *James Joyce Quarterly* 12, no. 4 (Summer 1975): 347–57.

Seymour, John D. *The Puritans in Ireland, 1647–1661.* Oxford, UK: Clarendon Press, 1921.

Shaw, Francis. "The Canon of Irish History: A Challenge." *Studies* 61, no. 242 (1972): 113–52.

Shaw, George Bernard. *The Drama Observed.* Edited by Bernard F. Dukore. University Park: Pennsylvania State Univ. Press, 1993.

———. *Selected Plays.* Vol. 2. New York: Dodd, Mead, 1949.

Shawe-Taylor, Desmond. "The Achievement of George Moore." In *The Life of George Moore, by Joseph Hone; with an Account of His Last Years by His Cook and Housekeeper, Clara Warville*, 465–92. London: V. Gollancz, 1936.

Sheehan, P. A. *The Graves at Kimorna: A Story of '67.* New York: D. D. Longmans, Green and Co., 1915.

Sheehy-Skeffington, F. *Michael Davitt: Revolutionary, Agitator, and Labour Leader.* London: T. Fisher Unwin, 1908.

Shillman, Bernard. *A Short History of the Jews in Ireland*. Dublin: Eason, 1945.

Sicari, Stephen. *Joyce's Modernist Allegory: "Ulysses" and the History of the Novel*. Columbia: Univ. of South Carolina Press, 2001.

Siev, Stanley A. "The Celts and the Hebrews: Sands of Time." Dublin: Irish Jewish Museum; and Shannon: Centre for International Co-operation, 1995.

Sims-Williams, Patrick. Review of Kim McCone, *Pagan Past and Christian Present. Éigse: A Journal of Irish Studies* 29 (1996): 179–96.

Simon, Leon. "The Hebrew Revival." In *Zionism and the Jewish Future*, edited by Harry Sacher, 99–116. London: John Murray, 1916.

Singh, Amardeep. "A Pisgah Sight of Ireland: Religious Embodiment and Colonialism in *Ulysses*." *Semeia* 88 (Fall/Winter 2001): 129–47.

Sisson, Elaine. *Pearse's Patriots: St. Enda's and the Cult of Boyhood*. Cork: Cork Univ. Press, 2004.

Smith, Anthony D. *Chosen Peoples*. Oxford, UK: Oxford Univ. Press, 2003.

Smith, Eric D. "How a Great Daily Organ Is Turned Out: 'Aeolus,' *Techne*, and the Recording of *Ulysses*." *James Joyce Quarterly* 41 (Spring 2004): 455–68.

Sokolow, Nachum. "The New Jew." In *Zionism and the Jewish Future*, edited by Harry Sacher, 214–34. London: John Murray, 1916.

Spenser, Edmund. *A View of the State of Ireland*, edited by Andrew Hadfield and Willy Maley. Oxford, UK: Blackwell, 1997.

Steele, Karen. *Women, Press, and Politics during the Irish Revival*. Syracuse, NY: Syracuse Univ. Press, 2007.

Steffens, Lincoln. *Moses in Red: The Revolt of Israel as a Typical Revolution*. Philadelphia: Dorrance and Co., 1926.

Steinman, Michael. "Yeats's Parnell: Sources of His Myth." *Éire-Ireland* 18, no. 1 (Spring 1983): 46–60.

Stern, David M. Foreword to *JPS Commentary on the Haggadah: Historical Introduction, Translation, and Commentary*, edited by Joseph Tabory. Philadelphia: Jewish Publication Society, 2008.

Sugirtharajah. R. S. *Postcolonial Criticism and Biblical Interpretation*. Oxford, UK: Oxford Univ. Press, 2002.

Sullivan, A. M. *The Story of Ireland: A Narrative of Irish History, from the Earliest Ages to the Present Time*. Dublin: A. M. Sullivan, 1867.

Sundquist, Eric J. *Strangers in the Land: Blacks, Jews, Post-Holocaust America*. Cambridge, MA: Belknap, 2005.

Swift, Jonathan. *A Short View of the State of Ireland.* Dublin: N.p., 1727.

"Tara Watch." Accessed Apr. 21, 2010. http://www.tarawatch.org/.

Taylor, W. C., and William Sampson. *History of Ireland, from the Anglo-Norman Invasion Till the Union of the Country with Great Britain.* New York: Bradley, 1833.

Temple, John. *The Irish Rebellion.* 1646. Reprint. London: R. Wilks, 1812.

Tindall, William York. "Mosaic Bloom." *Mosaic: A Journal for the Interdisciplinary Study of Literature* 6 (Fall 1972): 3–9.

Titley, Alan. "The Brass Tacks of the Situation." In *Letters from the New Island: 16 on 16. Irish Writers on the Easter Rising*, edited by Dermot Bolger. Dublin: Raven Arts Press, 1988.

Thompson, William Irwin. *The Imagination of an Insurrection: Dublin, Easter 1916.* New York: Harper and Row, 1972.

Tone, Theobald Wolfe. *The Writings of Theobald Wolfe Tone, 1763–98: America, France and Bantry Bay, August 1795 to December 1796.* Vol. 2. Oxford, UK: Oxford Univ. Press, 2001.

Trotter, Mary. *Ireland's National Theaters: Political Performance and the Origins of the Irish Dramatic Movement.* Syracuse, NY: Syracuse Univ. Press, 2001.

Ua Leoghaire, An tAthair Peadar. "Sgéal lóib agus Sgéal na hEireann." [The Story of Job and the Story of Ireland]. *An Síoladoir* [The Sower] 1, no. 5 (July 1921): 1–2.

Vail, Jeffery W. *The Literary Relationship of Lord Byron and Thomas Moore.* Baltimore, MD: Johns Hopkins Univ. Press, 2000.

Valente, Joseph. *Dracula's Crypt: Bram Stoker, Irishness, and the Question of Blood.* Urbana: Univ. of Illinois Press, 2002.

———. *James Joyce and the Problem of Justice: Negotiating Sexual and Colonial Difference.* Cambridge, UK: Cambridge Univ. Press, 1995.

———. "The Manliness of Parnell." *Éire-Ireland* 41, nos. 1–2 (Spring/Summer 2006): 64–119.

———. *The Myth of Manliness in Irish National Culture, 1880–1922.* Urbana: Univ. of Illinois Press, 2011.

———. "The Myth of Sovereignty: Gender in the Literature of Irish Nationalism." *ELH* 61 (1994): 189–210.

———. "Stephen's 'Allwombing Tomb': Mourning, Paternity, and the Incorporation of the Mother in *Ulysses*." *Joyce Studies Annual*, no. 1 (2012): 5–28.

Walzer, Michael. *Exodus and Revolution*. New York: Basic Books, 1985.

———. "Letter to the Editor." *Grand Street* 5, no. 4 (Summer 1986): 246–52.

Watson, George. *Irish Identity and the Literary Revival: Synge, Yeats, Joyce, and O'Casey*. Washington, DC: Catholic Univ. of America Press, 1994.

Way, L. A letter in *Jewish Expositor and Friend of Israel*. London: B. R. Goakman, 1820.

Weir, David. "Sophmore Plum(p)s for Old Man Moses." *James Joyce Quarterly* 28, no. 3 (Spring 1991): 657–62.

Weizman, Chaim. "Introduction: Zionism and the Jewish Problem." In *Zionism and the Jewish Future*, edited by Harry Sacher, 1–11. London: John Murray, 1916.

Welch, Robert. *The Abbey Theatre, 1899–1999: Form and Pressure*. Oxford, UK: Oxford Univ. Press, 1999.

Weygandt, Cornelius. *Irish Plays and Playwrights*. London: Constable and Co., 1913.

Whately, Richard. "The Jews: A Lecture Delivered by Richard Whately, D.D., Archbishop of Dublin, Before the Dublin YMCA." In Tracts 1861.39, box 2 of the Haliday Collection, Royal Irish Academy, [1861].

Whelan, Irene. *The Bible War in Ireland: The "Second Reformation" and the Polarization of Protestant-Catholic Relations, 1800–1840*. Madison: Univ. of Wisconsin Press, 2005.

Whelan, Kevin. "The Green Atlantic: Radical Reciprocities between Ireland and America in the Long Eighteenth Century." In *A New Imperial History: Culture, Identity, Modernity, 1660–1840*, edited by Kathleen Wilson, 216–38. Cambridge, UK: Cambridge Univ. Press, 2003.

Wilde, Jane. *Ancient Legends, Mystic Charms, and Superstitions of Ireland: to which is appended a chapter "On the Ancient Races of Ireland" by the late Sir William Wilde*. Vol. 2. Boston: Ticknor and Co., 1887.

———. *Poems*. 2nd ed. Glasgow: Cameron and Ferguson, c.1871.

Wright, John. *Ireland the Restorer of Israel under the Protection of Louis Napoleon, addressed to the catholic hierarchy and population of Ireland: an appendix to a project for constructing railways in Algeria*. London: Myers, 1853.

Wright, Melanie J. *Moses in America: The Cultural Uses of Biblical Narrative*. Oxford, UK: Oxford Univ. Press, 2003.

Yeats, William Butler. *Autobiographies. The Collected Works of W. B. Yeats*. Vol. 3, edited by William H. O'Donnell and Douglas N. Archibald. New York: Scribner, 1999.

———. *The Celtic Twilight*. Gerrards Cross, UK: Colin Smythe, 1981.

———. *The Collected Letters of W. B. Yeats*. Vol. 3, edited by John Kelly and Ronald Schuchard. Oxford, UK: Clarendon Press, 1994.

———. *The Collected Poems of W. B. Yeats*. rev. 2nd ed., edited by Richard J. Finneran. New York: Scribner Paperback Poetry, 1996.

———. *Essays and Introductions*. New York: Macmillan, 1961.

———. *Later Articles and Reviews: Uncollected Articles, Reviews, and Radio Broadcasts Written after 1900*. Edited by John P. Frayne and Madeleine Marchaterre. New York: Scribner, 2004.

———. *The Letters of W. B. Yeats*. Edited by Allan Wade. New York: Macmillan, 1955.

———. *Prefaces and Introductions*. Edited by William H. O'Donnell. Basingstoke, UK: Macmillan, 1988.

———, ed. *Samhain*. Oct. 1901–Nov. 1908, reprinted in one volume. London: Frank Cass and Co., 1970.

———. *Uncollected Prose*. Edited by John P. Frayne and Colton Johnson. New York: Columbia Univ. Press, 1970–76.

Yerushalmi, Yosef Hayim. *Freud's Moses: Judaism Terminable and Interminable*. New Haven: Yale Univ. Press, 1991.

———. *Haggadah and History: A Panorama in Facsimile of Five Centuries of the Printed Haggadah from the Collections of Harvard University and the Jewish Theological Seminary of America*. Philadelphia: Jewish Publication Society, 2005.

———. *Zakhor: Jewish History and Jewish Memory*. Seattle: Univ. of Washington Press, 1982.

Yodaiken, Leslie. "The Song of Young Zion in Erin." *Young Zionist*, [n.d.]: 10–11. Folder 39, ms. 33,506, Leslie Daiken Collection, National Library of Ireland.

Yorke, Peter. "The Turning of the Tide / Lecture by Rev. P. C. Yorke, San Francisco." *An Claidheamh Soluis*, Sept. 16, 1899.

Zangwill, Israel. *Chosen Peoples: The Hebraic Ideal Versus the Teutonic, with a foreword by the Right Hon. Herbert Samuel and an afterword by Israel Abrahams*. London: G. Allen and Unwin, 1918.

Zornberg, Avivah Gottlieb. *The Particulars of Rapture: Reflections on Exodus*. New York: Doubleday, 2001.

Index

ABBY BENDER teaches literature at Glucksman Ireland House, New York University. She received her PhD in English from Princeton University.